The Country Journal Book of Vegetable Gardening

THE COUNTRY JOURNAL BOOK OF

VEGETABLE GARDENING

by Nancy Bubel

Country Journal Publishing Company, Inc.
Brattleboro, Vermont   1983

Picture credits:
Title and month-name pages, Peter J. Morter, from *The Self-Sufficient Gardener,*
© 1978 by Dorling Kindersley, Ltd.
Pages 16 through 19, Eric Thomas
Pages 69 through 71, Elayne Sears

Library of Congress Cataloging in Publication Data
Bubel, Nancy.
    The Country Journal book of vegetable gardening.
    Includes index.
    1. Vegetable gardening.   I. Title.
SB321.B895   1983   635   82-22202
ISBN 0-918678-03-X (pbk.)

Manufactured in the United States of America
First Edition
10 9 8 7 6 5 4 3 2 1

For my brother, Milton Reay Wilkes, Jr., in memory of our New England childhood.

Also by Nancy Bubel:

Vegetables Money Can't Buy

Working Wood   (*with Michael Bubel*)

The Seed-Starter's Handbook

The Adventurous Gardener

Root Cellaring   (*with Michael Bubel*)

Contents

Introduction

A garden . . . any garden . . . is always in process, never finished. It is, in a way, an ongoing experiment. Since 1975 I have been writing a monthly column for Blair & Ketchum's COUNTRY JOURNAL. My aim has been to help each reader find the growing process more interesting, more understandable, more satisfying. In this book I have brought those columns up to date, revising and enlarging upon some of them and arranging them in monthly order to be more accessible and useful to the gardener.

All of us who garden have experimental gardens, if we watch what's going on there and learn from it. So it has seemed worthwhile to share with the reader old garden lore, present experiences, new discoveries, and concerns for the future. There's more than one way to do things in the garden. Readers have been generous in sharing their own gardening adventures, conclusions, and problems. Indeed, their insights and often well-informed comments have helped to shape the column. We learn from each other all the time.

These days I write from a south-facing hill farm, overlooking the three garden patches that I can't seem to condense sensibly to two —or, even more rationally, to one. We call the place Patchwork Farm, and it is so much what we have always wanted—a hill, fields, some water, lots of woods, trails to climb and bluebirds to watch—that we are content.

But I haven't always been a country gardener. I grew up in cities and after marriage my first garden, in Philadelphia, was followed by other backyard patches in small towns in Indiana, Wisconsin, and central Pennsylvania. Though I've been gardening for twenty-five years, there's always something new to learn, and I still love reading about gardening, talking about gardening, and visiting other people's gardens.

Home vegetable gardening is a way to put the very best and freshest produce on your table, while saving money and getting some mild but regular exercise. More than that, though, it offers a chance to see, to feel, to hear, to smell the life that surrounds and supports us. The eye of the gardener sees the velvety furrowed inside of the squash flower; insects that look like iridescent sequins; just-born pea pods with their blossoms still clinging; the delicate tendril of a vine; the satiny purple sheen that is particular to an eggplant. Hoeing in the morning light, we hear the early birds; the rattle of dry cornstalks summons all our feelings about fall; and when the earth is thirsty, the sound of rain is a source of special delight. As we handle growing things, we feel relationships, continuity. Seeds are tiny round globes, wispy threads, dust motes, thin flakes, grains of corn, wizened peas and, as we plant them, knowing that—despite appearances—they're alive, we sometimes remember to be awed by their potential. Soon they are tentative, hopeful, tender seedlings, and—after a few weeks in the soil, sun, and rain—chunky carrots, ponderous cabbage heads, fistfuls of slender snap beans, corn just right to sink your teeth into. And smells—freshly-turned earth, the mint by the back door, the air after a summer shower, pungent tomato foliage, leaf mold, fresh garlic and onion tops snipped over soup—all belong in a special way to the gardener.

There are weeds and bugs, hail and hungry rabbits, plant diseases and unexplained crop failures out there too, of course. Our gardens aren't always as exclusive as we might wish. You'll find in this collection of columns something of what might be called Garden Clinic: attention to What Went Wrong, as well as to the Joy of Gardening.

I'm especially grateful to COUNTRY JOURNAL editor Richard Ketchum for his kind guidance in directing and defining the Vegetable Garden column. And to my family, for their willingness to try new turnips and tomatoes, squash and lettuce . . . year after year.

JANUARY

Earning a Green Thumb

You've probably complimented a neighbor or friend on having a green thumb. Perhaps you've received such compliments yourself. If you have a green thumb, your seeds sprout, cuttings root, transplants take, trees bear fruit, and eggplants appear when they're supposed to.

There are some who discover when quite young that they enjoy seeing plants respond to their care, but such people are probably exceptional. Most of us who muddle our way into gardening earn our green thumbs gradually. While the gift for growing things can be innate, I believe it is more often earned and learned. If you want to raise plants successfully, you can. Start with something special, something that arouses your enthusiasm; a beautiful or odd or especially delicious growing thing. Perhaps a plot of super sweet corn, a tiny herb patch, or a neat salad garden by the back step. As much as possible, grow your plants from seeds so that you'll be in on the process from the beginning.

"A green thumb is a dirty thumb," maintains herb expert Adelma Grenier Simmons. Surely it's true that not many hard-bitten gardeners are fingernail-proud. Plants need to be tended, and that involves digging, mixing compost, weeding, driving stakes, squashing insects. People who get results in the garden have their hands in it; and their direct involvement doesn't stop with setting out plants, but continues all season long. You learn, for example, to transplant successfully by *doing* it—over and over again, until your hands learn skill and assurance.

In *The Food-Lover's Garden*, (Alfred A. Knopf, 1970) Angelo Pellegrini writes: "A green thumb is a disciplined, diligent, working thumb." Discipline—willingness to do what must be done, knowing when to stop. Most vegetables need to be thinned, and that takes discipline. In spring, it's discipline that helps us to wait until the soil dries sufficiently to work. Green thumbs don't dig in soggy ground! Discipline keeps us picking cucumbers so they'll continue to bear, and sends us out on a cold still evening to cover the new tomato plants before we bank the fire for the night.

Green thumbs grow on busy hands, but they have their roots in alert heads. Most of the outstanding gardeners I know are observant. They look, they compare, they make notes, they see differences, they pause while weeding to absorb what's around them. Observant gardeners put clues together and come up with conclusions. "Those peas I didn't weed did better than the weeded ones. I'll bet it's because they have shallow, easily disturbed roots that like to keep cool." "Potatoes did so well under mulch last year that I'll never grow them any other way again, as long as I can find enough mulch." "Those first early blossoms on the zucchini are male; now I see that it's normal for the female blossoms to appear a week later and I won't worry when the first flowers don't bear fruit."

Successful gardeners have learned, too, about the basic needs of their garden plants:

NUTRIENTS Corn, cabbage, and lettuce, for example, need soil high in nitrogen; root crops require a good supply of potash; peppers and sweet potatoes produce best in soil not overly supplied with nitrogen. Attention to particular plant requirements pays off in good yields.

MOISTURE Water gives life, but it can kill plants too, if drainage is poor. Humus-rich soil retains water and also provides tiny air spaces to promote good root growth. Plants in small containers should be watered thoroughly and frequently and allowed to drain well. If garden plants need water, soak the soil deeply at weekly intervals, not daily.

LIGHT Garden vegetable plants do best in full sun, but seedlings raised indoors must be gradually exposed to outdoor light.

PROTECTION Tending plants, even hovering over them at times, can make the difference between a false start and an early crop. Shielding transplants from frost and wind, and protecting plants from insects are not always convenient, but the results are almost always worthwhile.

My own description of a green-thumbed gardener can be summed up in two words: *serious* and *joyful*. There is evidence—abundantly cited in *The Secret Life of Plants* by Peter Tompkins and Christopher Bird (Harper & Row, 1973)—that plants respond physically, in ways that can be measured, to thoughts and attitudes of persons tending them. Gardeners who talk to plants give them a healthy dose of the carbon dioxide they need, but there seems to be more to it than that. The mental energy you direct at your plants may influence the way they grow. Your interest and enthusiasm matter more than you might suspect.

Cultivated plants need our care, but in a larger sense we are indebted to the plant kingdom for our life on this planet. As Tompkins and Bird put it, "Without green plants we would neither breathe nor eat." To have a green thumb is to participate, in some small way, in this marvelous system.

6

Houseplants from the Kitchen Shelf

Some of our favorite food plants can be encouraged to grow into interesting and attractive houseplants. In some cases, you can even eat the food and grow indoor greenery from the trimmings. Basic supplies are simple: a knife, trowel, flower pots, potting soil, and roots or seeds eager to grow.

From the Root Cellar
CARROT

In the carrot barrel there are often a few woody-looking carrots with leaf sprouts already started. Collect several of these roots to make a dish garden. Cut off most of the pointed end of each carrot, leaving a two-inch stub at the top where the leaves will sprout. If the carrot is very woody, feed the trimmings to the goats. Sound eating carrots make good dish gardens too. Just cut a bit more off the top than you ordinarily would and cook and eat the rest. Embed several two-inch-long carrot tops in a container of small pebbles, cut end down, leaving about half an inch of root showing at the top. Fill the dish with water up to the top surface of the pebbles. If you have a really enormous carrot—the kind only a home gardener could come by—you might try hollowing out its center, leaving the walls intact, filling the cavity with water and hanging it in a sunny window. (To suspend the carrot, poke it into a wire ring onto which you've tied three strong strings for hanging.) Keep the cavity filled with water and the whole surface of the root will produce a mass of attractive ferny leaves. Carrot gardens last three to five weeks.

BEET

To make a beet garden, you'll need a whole beet, but you can use a runt or one that's already started to sprout. Put the beet in a dish, anchor it with pebbles, leaving about two-thirds of its top surface exposed, and add water up to the pebbles. Beet and carrot sprouts do well in indirect light.

SWEET POTATOES

A sweet potato suspended in a jar of water will sprout attractive vines that continue to grow for as long as a year or more. Select a firm tuber and poke three toothpicks into it, about one-third of the way down from the top of the potato, which is usually somewhat less pointed than the root end. Suspend the root in a jar half-filled with water. The tip should always be in water, but it's not necessary to submerge the whole root. Keep the jar in a warm place until sprouts appear. The vines do well in bright light; they draw strength from the root and need no fertilizer for at least the first six to eight months. After that, a small amount of liquid fertilizer once a month should keep them green.

From the Garden
COMFREY

For an attractive and useful houseplant, divide a garden plant and pot up a rooted, leafy section, or bury a root cutting and watch as it develops into a sturdy specimen. You can use the leaves, which contain the healing agent allantoin, as a poultice or in solution to help heal skin cuts.

TAMPALA Also called Malabar Spinach, this is a warm-weather garden vegetable that produces green leaves on a trailing vine. In the fall you can root cuttings from your vines to winter over indoors, providing a welcome touch of greenery. When spring arrives, you can get an early start on the gardening season by rooting short cuttings from your long indoor vine to plant out in the garden.

Kitchen Discards

CITRUS On the way to the compost pile, rescue a few orange, lemon, or grapefruit seeds to grow indoors. Plant them right away, though; they may not germinate well if they dry out. You'll probably have better luck if you plant the seeds in peat pots, using your usual potting soil mix; then embed the little pots in larger pots when the plant is well established. Citrus trees grow slowly—about twelve inches a year—but the glossy leaves are a pleasing sight. Keep them in a sunny spot and add a dash of limestone to the potting soil when you repot them as they grow. Well-fertilized indoor trees may grow to a height of eight or ten feet over the years.

AVOCADO An Avocado Council ad shows a sprouted avocado pit exclaiming: "So there IS life after salad!" According to *The Don't Throw It, Grow It Book of Houseplants,* by Millicent Selsam and Deborah Peterson (Random House, New York, 1977), pits from the large, shiny-skinned Florida avocados are easier to sprout than those from the smaller fruits from California. Air-dry the pit for a day to crack and shrink the tough, brown skin, then peel it. Either suspend the pit in a jar of water on three toothpicks stuck in its side, as you did the sweet potato, or plant it—leaving about an inch of pit uncovered—in damp potting soil, which should be kept moist. Either way, keep it in a warm place to encourage sprouting. Plant water-rooted pits in potting soil, leaving the top part of the bulb uncovered. They like a constant supply of moisture, but should not be flooded. Bright, indirect light is fine for avocado plants, and regular misting is a good idea. The trees live for years indoors.

Seeds

CHICKPEA Chickpeas, or garbanzos, have delicate foliage that trails attractively over the sides of hanging planters. Plant a small handful of presoaked seeds in potting soil in your hanging pot. Keep the soil moist and warm and hang the airy garden in a warm, sunny place. Never let the soil dry out. Under good conditions, chickpea plants will live for about six months.

PEANUT Peanut plants grow to twenty inches high with leaves that fold into a resting position at night. For pot plants, buy *raw* peanuts, carefully crack off the shells (leaving the red skin on the peanut), and bury several nuts under an inch of soil in a flower pot, thinning later to keep only the strongest plant. The next generation of peanuts is formed when the yellow flower embeds itself in the ground. You might want to plant a few extras so the children can poke around in the soil of some to investigate the developing peanut. Peanut plants need a sunny spot and appreciate a pinch of limestone in the potting soil. They don't transplant well.

If you have access to more exotic seeds from wintertime fruit purchases—mangoes, papayas, dates, and such—you might want to consult *The After-Dinner Gardening Book*, by Richard W. Langer (Collier Books, New York, 1969), or *The Don't Throw It, Grow It Book of Houseplants*, cited above.

Planning Something New

The garden we haven't tended for a month or two becomes once again a place of possibility, even adventure, as the year circles into January. We've recovered from our fall weeding weariness and we're ready to try again. With the land locked under frost and snow, we're free to indulge in those new-year rites of the gardener —dreaming and planning. For, no matter how long we've been gardening, we never reach the point where we've done it all. There's always more, beckoning us ahead into the new season.

What new thing will you try in *your* garden this year? Surely each of us has at least a small wish list of new varieties to grow, even if we do think we're immune to seed-catalogue fever. The garden notes we scrawled on last year's calendar help, too, to focus the direction of this year's garden. We see that we could have started lettuce earlier and kept planting it later. The early zucchini succumbed to bugs, and we wish we'd made a second planting. And once again we planted too much cabbage and not enough peas. Will we ever learn? Sometimes it takes a few years!

The list that follows is a starting point, a memory-jogger, to help you to organize your plans for this year's garden. The idea is not to do it all, but to try what most appeals to you. In fact, when you're experimenting in the garden, it's a good idea to limit the number of trial plantings and new techniques you attempt in any one year. Don't take on more than you can comfortably manage and observe; then you'll be able to keep the best of the old and evaluate the new.

GROW A NEW VEGETABLE

The new sugar snap pea, with an edible pod enclosing full-sized peas, lives up to its billing as an entirely new vegetable. The plant is almost as vigorous as my old favorite sugar pea, Mammoth Melting Sugar, and the bonus of sweet peas that don't need shelling makes this delicious vegetable worth its space, especially since it saves time. Provide strings or fencing for support; this one grows tall. I also grew adzuki beans (for dry beans) for the first time last year and plan to reorder this year, for their high protein content, excellent flavor, and marked resistance to Mexican bean beetles. This time, though, I'll plant a wide row to get an even larger yield from the same space.

GROW DIFFERENT VARIETIES

If you've always grown bush limas, try the marvelously rich-flavored pole limas. (King of the Garden or Christmas lima, Vermont Bean Seed Company.) Stumped for interesting lunches? Grow the stuffing tomato (Burgess) for use with your favorite fillings. For a sweet tomato, the cherry-sized Sweet 100 is excellent and wildly productive. The new kohlrabi variety Grand Duke prolongs kohlrabi harvest because it is slow to turn woody when large. Purple beans sound weird, but they're a staple in our garden because they can be planted earlier than other snap beans. Don't worry; they turn green when cooked. Royalty and Royal Burgundy are both excellent. Open-pollinated corn tends to ripen over a longer span of time than hybrid corn, and you can save your own seed. Good varieties to try include Golden Bantam, Stowell's Evergreen, Country Gentleman.

TRY NEW GROWING METHODS

Perhaps this is the year to set up a small raised bed and cram it with lettuces, chives, parsley, carrots. Or to see how many different vegetables prosper when grown in wide rows. (We like to plant onions, carrots, lettuce, parsnips, and bush peas this way.) Or to save garden seeds, an old gardening art worth practicing again.

To make good use of vertical space, train cucumbers, melons, Malabar spinach or climbing beans on a fence. For propping up your tomatoes, caging is much easier than staking and usually more effective. A cylinder of concrete reinforcing wire in 6-inch mesh works well. Snip off the last two horizontal strands of wire on the bottom of a 5-foot-long piece of mesh, fasten the ends together to form a cylinder, and thrust the wire tines into the ground around the plant to anchor the cage.

Have you tried growing potatoes in mulch? Repeated trials have convinced me this is an excellent method. Potatoes are clean, easy to harvest, and virtually free of bug damage. Simply place the seed potatoes on the surface of the ground, cover with 3 inches of mulch, and keep adding more mulch as the plant tops grow, to a depth of 8 to 12 inches if using hay. I used well-aged wood chips topped by hay and had the best crop ever last year.

MAKE SOMETHING FOR YOUR GARDEN

Kathryn and John Hill, whom we visited while researching our book *Root Cellaring*, put it best: "Each year we find ourselves trying to improve something around our place, besides running the garden." What would add to your gardening pleasure now and in the years to come? How about a cold frame, a grape arbor, a series of three compost-pile enclosures, a root cellar, window boxes, soil sifters, or even a simple, well-made row marker? Now's the time to draw up plans, gather materials, light the workshop stove, and get a good building start on the busy growing season ahead.

NOTE: Vegetables for which sources are not mentioned are widely available.

Planning the Ideal Vegetable Garden

We all know what happens to those plans we draw up for the garden. If they're not blown away in the March wind or crumpled up by mistake to start the morning fire, they're soon smudged beyond legibility when we scrawl on them with muddy fingers as we record our progressive plantings. By then the plans have served their purpose; they have pointed us in the right direction, and they have saved our sanity on more than one frigid January day when all we could do for the garden was to dream about it. Even if you don't follow your plan to the letter, it is worth making —if for no other reason than that you need to know whether the garden patch is large enough to accommodate all the vegetables you want to plant.

The ideal garden that glimmers in our mind's eye this ice-locked January day is the very picture of abundance. Crisp ruffled lettuce gives way to slim green snap beans, while tomatoes redden and squash gradually fills in the corners with its exuberant vines and sturdy fruit. The ideal garden is continuously productive. It starts early and lasts late.

While an absolutely perfect garden—the kind that glows in our heads in midwinter—will probably always lie just beyond reach, small steady improvements, made over a period of years, can transform an ordinary plot into a highly productive one that is a delight all summer. Good gardens are built by a continuing process, one in which we try to remedy the mistakes of the past while looking to the future with new techniques and varieties.

The garden-planning progression for most of us goes something like this: first we order our seeds, then we map out the garden, and finally we figure out our planting timetable. Now, in January, we take the first, heady step: we order seed for what we boldly hope will be our lushest garden ever.

The seed catalogues start to arrive in December, before we are ready for them. We stack them neatly in the study. January brings more—and even those that are printed in black-and-white, even those that lack clever line drawings, tempt us with their description of fresh food, of old favorites and new strains, of classic varieties we've somehow overlooked—all of which could be thriving a few steps from our back door, once we plant the seeds.

Seed-catalogue fever is one of the in-jokes among gardeners. It *is* easy to get carried away, to order three kinds of zucchini for a family of two, more flowers than we have seed flats for, exotic vegetables that are unsuited to our climate. By January, we've forgotten the claim those rows had on us last August. We think, once again, that we can do it all. We watch the icicles grow from the porch roof and add another ten lines to our seed order.

But why not? How many other order forms do you fill out on

which the addition of another item will add only fifty cents or a dollar to your bill? Overdoing the seed order is a harmless enough indulgence, especially when you take into account the cost of an evening out or a trip to the grocery store. Ordering seeds is a matter of practical necessity, it is true, but there's nothing wrong with making pleasure out of it, either. Treat yourself. Buy something pretty or silly, and try some of those unfamiliar flowers and vegetables. If you don't get it all planted this year, most vegetable seeds last at least one year, so you'll have another year to try them. Meanwhile the vision of what the garden could become warms a wind-whipped day spent indoors. I usually order more seeds than I can plant, but I have no regrets. It is good to be well supplied with possibilities if extra space becomes available sooner than planned.

After living with the catalogues for a few evenings, I jot down all the kinds of seed I usually plant, from beans to zucchini. Then I get out my seeds saved from last season and check off from the list all varieties for which I already have seed. That leaves a list of necessities to be filled, usually from six or seven of the thirty or so catalogues I consult. With the basics taken care of, I explore unfamiliar territory, ordering new varieties and perhaps new vegetables and flowers. When choosing between several varieties, I consider their flavor, disease resistance, yield, hardiness, earliness, growing habit (bushy or climbing), and vitamin content. Some qualities are more important for certain vegetables: for example, disease resistance is crucial in cucumbers, at least in my area; earliness is important in lettuce and radishes; growing habit in snap beans. I like to have a sound nucleus of open-pollinated vegetables in my garden, too, so that if I want to I can save seed from them for next year's garden. Although I usually have some radish seeds on hand, I always order more—a lot more. The reason is that I plant radishes not only to eat, but also to protect each hill of cucurbits in my garden from cucumber beetles.

Seed catalogues are generally free of jargon, but there are certain terms you'll need to know as you read them in order to compare vegetable varieties. If you have a brand-new case of seed-catalogue fever, perhaps you'd like to have some of these commonly used terms defined.

HOW LONG CAN SEEDS BE STORED?

Kind of Seed	Number of years seeds can be stored	Average number of seeds per ounce
Asparagus	3	1,400
Lima bean	3	20–70
Snap bean	3	100
Beet	4	2,000
Broccoli	3	8,100
Brussels sprouts	4	8,500
Cabbage	4	7,700
Carrot	3	22,000
Cauliflower	4	8,600
Celeriac	3	50,000
Celery	3	76,000
Chard, Swiss	4	1,500
Chicory	4	20,000
Chinese cabbage	3	7,000
Sweet corn	2	140
Cucumber	5	1,100
Eggplant	4	7,200
Endive	5	17,000
Kale	4	10,000
Kohlrabi	3	9,200
Leek	2	9,900
Lettuce	6	26,000

ALL-AMERICA SELECTION   A vegetable variety chosen in annual competition for its reliable performance in home gardens.

ANNUAL   A plant that lives for only one year or growing season.

BIENNIAL   A plant that blooms, bears seed, and usually dies the year after it is planted.

GYNOECIOUS   Plants that bear mostly female flowers and thus may produce more fruit than plants that have male and female flowers evenly divided (Example: some new varieties of cucumbers).

HYBRID   A plant grown from seed obtained by cross-fertilizing two different plant varieties.

PERENNIAL   A plant that survives the winter and bears flowers and fruit or

12

seed each year. Some perennials may live as long as thirty years, others from five to fifteen years.

Capable of withstanding disease or insect attack, but not immune from them.

Often unaffected by disease or insect infestation, but more sensitive to these than the resistant plant.

Many corn, legume, and cole family seeds are treated with fungicides to prevent rotting in the ground. You may prefer to use untreated seed; many seed companies will send it to you if you request it on your order.

Planning for a continuously productive garden begins with the seed order. Turnip greens, spinach, leaf lettuce, scallions, and radishes provide the first fresh eating of the season, along with the asparagus in the perennial bed and the wild greens in the fields. If you have seeds on hand for these earliest crops, you'll be prepared to drop them in the row as soon as the soil can be worked. With such an early start, you'll have time to raise another crop in the same row.

It's also wise to look ahead to fall and to buy seed for the hardy fall-bearing crops (Brussels sprouts, cauliflower, broccoli, kale, and such) that you'll set out as seedlings in early summer. Seed orders are usually promptly filled in summer, but if you're like me you won't have time to make out the order. Winter is the time to order for the whole season. If you include a good supply of early quickies and hardy late vegetables, you'll stretch the harvest at both ends, and thus reap more good food from the same amount of ground.

Your choice of vegetables and vegetable varieties can affect the yield of your garden in other ways, too:

Pole beans produce for a longer time than bush beans, although they are slower to start bearing.

A short-cored cabbage like Ruby Ball will give you extra usable leaf in each head.

Short thick carrots like Nantes Half-Long or Royal Chantenay will yield more on heavy soils.

New bush varieties of cucumbers, squash, and pumpkins yield less than the traditional vining kinds, but they may be your best choice if your garden area is limited.

Tall-growing sugar peas like Mammoth Melting Sugar and the new Sugar Snap yield more than dwarf kinds; all it takes are tall stakes, chicken wire, string, or brush to support them.

Spinach doesn't produce a lot for the space it takes, but because it can be planted so early and finishes early, it leaves time for a substantial second crop to be grown in the same space.

Zucchini, at least in our area, is more disease resistant than cucumbers, so it is often easier to produce a bumper crop of zucchini than a bumper crop of cukes. If you've never tried preserving small zucchini by your usual dill pickle recipe, I recommend it. They're good.

RESISTANT

TOLERANT

UNTREATED SEED

HOW LONG CAN SEEDS BE STORED?

Kind of Seed	Number of years seeds can be stored	Average number of seeds per ounce
Muskmelon	5	1,100
New Zealand spinach	3	430
Okra	2	500
Onion	1	8,500
Parsley	1	18,000
Parsnip	1	6,800
Pea	3	50–230
Pepper	2	4,500
Pumpkin	4	200
Radish	4	3,100
Salsify	1	2,000
Spinach	3	2,900
Squash	4	180–380
Tomato	4	10,000
Turnip	4	14,000
Watermelon	4	320

Based on table in "Vegetable Seed Germination," by J. F. Harrington and P. A. Minges, a pamphlet published by the University of California Extension Service.

Vegetables like tomatoes, kale, broccoli, carrots, and cabbage, which produce a sustained harvest for several months, are always a good investment.

In the depths of winter, a sustained harvest of fresh vegetables sounds awfully good. One way to extend that harvest is to order your seeds promptly, so you'll have them on hand when the snow melts and the rick, dark soil beckons.

Plotting and Planting the Garden

The Ideal Site

The ideal site for a vegetable garden receives day-long sun. It has friable, humus-rich soil that drains well; it slopes slightly to the south and is protected from chilling winds. This perfect plot lies close to the kitchen door, but far from competing tree roots, and it was never contaminated—either sprayed with chemical pesticides or used as a dump for sewage sludge containing toxic metals.

Most of us start with something less than that ideal and must work to improve it. Soil can be enriched, drainage improved, windbreaks planted or built, even trees cut down, if need be. If shade from other buildings limits your garden's sun to less than eight hours a day, you might consider other approaches: planting vegetables in containers set in spots that receive more sun, concentrating a small intensive bed in the sunniest place and planting lettuce, or renting a plot in a community garden. Soil treated with sludge that contains residues of heavy metals should not be used to grow food for many years. Soil contaminated by pesticides or herbicides, a more likely problem, can be healed by generous additions of humus. The resulting increase in soil microbial life will encourage fast breakdown of noxious chemicals.

Laying Out The Garden

The garden map changes during the winter, as we revise and refine our plan. And the plan is likely to be changed yet again when we begin to plant. In addition to the basics there is so much we want to grow—adzuki beans, okra, broom corn, new melons —that we really need a map to help us get it all in. I save my garden maps from year to year as an aid in planning the current garden.

To make an exact plan, you need to have some idea of what weed-control methods you will use—mulching, hoeing, or rotary tilling. That in turn depends on the resources available to you. Coarse mulch is fine for rows more than eighteen inches apart, but for closer spacing you'll also need a supply of finer mulch. If your garden soil is rich, you can get away with close spacing of plants and rows, but in marginal soil you might be better advised to space rows farther apart and even to alternate them with bands of cover crops to be plowed under for soil improvement.

Rows you intend to till should be spaced about eight inches wider than the tiller's full tine-to-tine measurement. (Technically, six inches is enough, but only if the rows are absolutely straight and you have excellent control of the tiller.)

In determining what size garden to plant, bear in mind that a small plot that is easy to tend is better than a huge garden that requires more time than you have. On pages 16 and 17 we suggest three possibilities. The smallest—a soup-and-salad garden—will perk up the menu for a couple or a family of three from spring through fall. The 25- by 35-foot kitchen garden will keep four to six people in vegetables all season long, with some to freeze and store. The large, full-spectrum garden, 50 by 100 feet, will provide four to six people with a sumptuous variety year-round, with occasional extras for sale or barter.

The conventional garden is laid out in rows, different kinds of plants growing single-file, with paths between each row. Vining vegetables like squash, melons, and cucumbers are usually planted in hills allowing five to eight feet for them to spread, or some vines can be trained to grow up. Perennial vegetables like asparagus, horseradish, and rhubarb should be planted at the edge of the garden or in a separate bed so they won't be dug up when the garden is tilled in the spring. Many vegetables, especially peas, carrots, lettuce, onions, and spinach, do well when planted in wide rows—about twelve inches wide for carrots, up to two feet wide for peas. After one or two initial weedings, the plants tend to shade out weeds and conserve soil moisture. Less growing space is wasted on paths, too.

For crops like radishes, that are planted early and harvested by early summer, I usually use narrowly spaced rows eight to ten inches apart and hoe between them. Then, when tilling up these narrow rows to be replaced by a summer succession crop, I may combine two of them into a single wide row for kale or late lettuce.

One way to make good use of widely spaced rows of midseason vegetables is to plant lettuce, spinach, scallions, or another early crop between the widely spaced rows of rambling vegetables like squash, cucumbers, or tomatoes. The early crop will be eaten by the time the midseason vegetable spreads to take up the row space. Another is to plant bush beans in the same row with pole beans. The low plants bear first, and the climbing ones take over later.

You want to use your garden space efficiently, but ease of cultivation is important, too. If the spaces between rows are too narrow to hoe readily, or the rows are too wide to weed thoroughly, or if there is not enough mulch to suppress weeds for a whole season, then the area may produce less than it would have under more conventional management.

50' X 100'

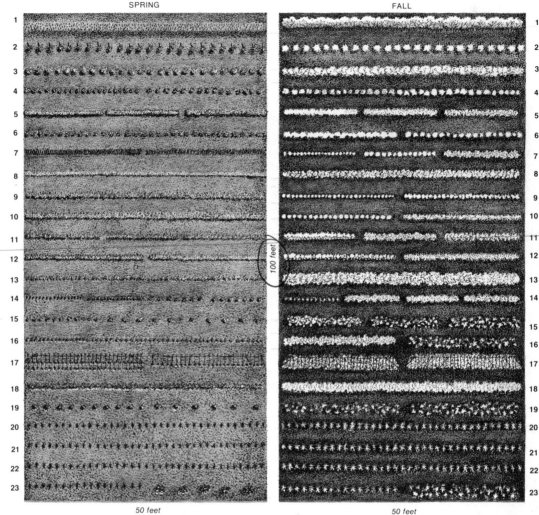

SPRING

FALL

100 feet

50 feet

50 feet

LARGE HOUSEHOLD GARDEN

Spring
1. Asparagus
2. Tomatoes
3. White potatoes
4. Cabbage and broccoli
5. Lettuce, radishes, and spinach
6. Snap beans
7. Onions and garlic
8. Carrots
9. Peas
10. Peas
11. Rutabagas, long-season beets, and Swiss chard
12. Parsnips and salsify
13. Soybeans
14. Leeks, peppers, eggplant, and okra
15. Zucchini, cucumbers, and yellow crookneck squash
16. New Zealand spinach
17. Pole beans and pole limas
18. Sweet potatoes
19. Cantaloupe and watermelons
20. Early corn
21. Early corn
22. Early corn
23. Early corn and pumpkins

Fall
1. Asparagus
2. Tomatoes
3. White potatoes
4. Snap beans
5. Turnips, carrots, and winter radishes
6. Kale and Brussels sprouts
7. Chinese cabbage, cauliflower, and collards
8. Spinach
9. Lettuce and escarole
10. Cabbage and celery
11. Rutabagas, long-season beets, and Swiss chard
12. Parsnips and salsify
13. Soybeans
14. Leeks, peppers, eggplant, and okra
15. Zucchini, cucumbers, and yellow crookneck squash
16. New Zealand spinach, winter squash
17. Pole beans and pole limas
18. Sweet potatoes
19. Cantaloupe and watermelons
20. Midseason or late corn
21. Midseason or late corn
22. Midseason or late corn
23. Pumpkins and midseason or late corn

16

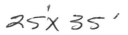

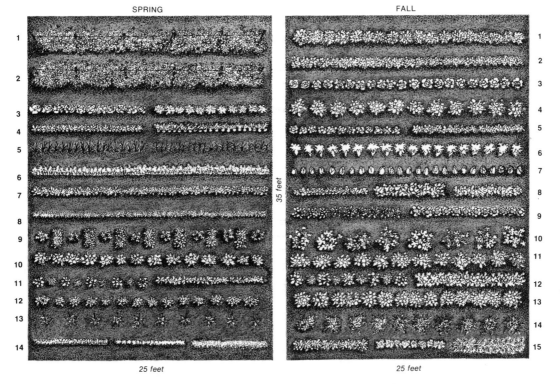

SPRING

FALL

1 2 3 4 5 6 7 8 9 10 11 12 13 14

1 2 3 4 5 6 7 8 9 10 11 12 13 14 15

35 feet

25 feet

25 feet

MEDIUM-SIZED KITCHEN GARDEN

Spring
1. Peas
2. Peas
3. Head lettuce and romaine
4. Turnips and kohlrabi
5. Onions and garlic
6. Carrots
7. Spinach
8. Beets
9. Zucchini, yellow crookneck squash, and bush cucumber (radishes interplanted)
10. Snap beans
11. Peppers (hot and sweet) and Swiss chard
12. Soybeans
13. Tomatoes
14. Radishes, leaf lettuce, and dill

Fall
1. Kale
2. Turnips
3. Cabbage
4. Snap beans
5. Lettuce and radishes
6. Brussels sprouts
7. Chinese cabbage
8. Beets, rutabagas, and winter radishes
9. Broccoli and cauliflower
10. Zucchini, yellow crookneck squash, and bush cucumber (radishes interplanted)
11. Snap beans
12. Peppers (hot and sweet) and Swiss chard
13. Soybeans
14. Tomatoes
15. Radishes, leaf lettuce, and dill

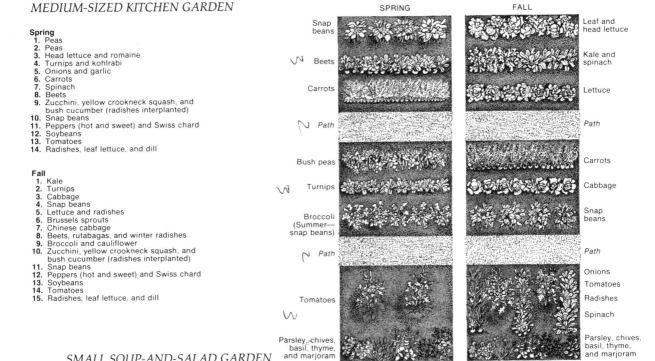

SPRING   FALL

Snap beans — Leaf and head lettuce

Beets — Kale and spinach

Carrots — Lettuce

Path — Path

Bush peas — Carrots

Turnips — Cabbage

Broccoli (Summer—snap beans) — Snap beans

Path — Path

Onions
Tomatoes
Radishes
Spinach

Tomatoes

Parsley, chives, basil, thyme, and marjoram — Parsley, chives, basil, thyme, and marjoram

SMALL SOUP-AND-SALAD GARDEN

DEEP DOUBLE DIGGING

1 Spread a layer of
finished compost over
the area to be dug.

Rotating Crops

Intensive raised beds are increasingly popular because they make efficient use of space and preserve good, rich soil. Permanent paths keep foot traffic out of the growing area, so soil remains loose and well aerated and all soil improvements benefit the productive ground. As an alternative to a large garden, you might find that you can grow almost as much in a smaller area planted in beds rather than rows. Vegetables are planted close together in solid blocks in raised beds, and they tend to crowd and shade out weeds. Because the soil is easy to work and the growing area usually fairly small, not much equipment is needed for raised-bed gardening; just a shovel and fork, possibly a hoe. Deep double-digging when laying out the beds is hard work, but it's probably worth the trouble, because plant roots grow best when soil contains some air spaces. Beds may be any convenient length or shape, but should not be wider than three feet unless you have unusually long arms. It's not necessary to enclose a raised bed, but some gardeners do—using boards or bricks, but not railroad ties (they are soaked with creosote, which is no friend of living things). Allow at least a one-foot walkway between beds.

In square-foot plots, a variation of the intensive bed described by Mel Bartholomew in his recent book *Square Foot Gardening,* one-foot squares replace the usual garden rows. Garden beds consist of four-by-four-foot blocks, containing sixteen one-foot squares, each planted to a single kind of vegetable. This method has special appeal for gardeners who are short of space and time; harvesting and replanting a one-foot square does not loom as a large project. Moreover, Bartholomew saves money on seeds by sowing only a few seeds in each square; this avoids broadcasting of full packets, which results in many wasted plants or—worse—in overcrowding.

Crop rotation is an important consideration for all gardeners. Switching vegetable families around helps to prevent a build-up of diseases and insect infestations that are common to certain groups of related plants. Vegetable plants vary, too, in the amount of different soil nutrients they use up. For example, corn and green, leafy vegetables require a good supply of nitrogen; root vegetables need potash; legumes add nitrogen to the soil; sweet potatoes do well on soil not overly supplied with nitrogen. It makes sense, then, to alternate the type of demand made on a given row, in order to avoid depletion of any one soil nutrient.

Rotation of vegetables is more complicated in the garden than in the farm field, where large areas are usually planted with relatively few crop varieties. Gardeners may grow as many as fifty different kinds of foods, which may be roughly grouped into about seven categories. Moreover, some of the more demanding crops —like corn, tomatoes, and squash—often occupy a relatively large proportion of the garden. If you're good at three-dimensional chess, you'll enjoy planning for vegetable rotations.

2 Make a trench one foot wide and one foot deep. It should extend the width of the garden or bed. Put the soil that is removed at one end of the bed—it will be used to fill the last trench.

3 In good soil, loosen the earth at the bottom of the trench to an additional depth of one foot.

4 In compacted soil, loosen the earth by pushing a spading fork into the bottom of the trench and levering the tines up through the soil.

5 Dig out a second trench of the same dimensions, throwing the soil into the first trench and mixing it well. Continue in this manner until the entire bed has been dug.

Some parts of the garden, where second plantings succeed a fast-maturing early crop, go through two rotations in one growing season. Others, where a single crop occupies the row all year long, will rotate annually. To organize your rotation plan, list the vegetables you grow according to category. I divide my garden's plant population into seven groups:

(1) Legumes (peas, lima beans, soybeans, snap beans, clover);

(2) Green, leafy vegetables, including lettuce, chard, endive, and the cole or brassica group (broccoli, cabbage, kale, cauliflower, Brussels sprouts, collards);

(3) Root vegetables (beets, carrots, turnips, salsify, parsnips, radishes, rutabagas);

(4) Cucurbits (melons, squash, pumpkins, cucumbers);

(5) Onions, garlic, and leeks (sometimes grouped with root crops);

(6) The tomato family (tomatoes, peppers, eggplant, potatoes);

(7) Corn and other grains.

Some serious gardeners add an eighth group: cover crops. Good cover-crop plants include buckwheat, annual rye grass, clover, soybeans, and oats.

In an ideal rotation a single row or bed in your garden would be planted to each of these different groups successively. For example, one row might grow early peas followed by kale for fall and winter this year. Then next year you'd plant parsnips there, with squash the following year, then the year after that, onions—with perhaps a late crop of beans tucked in; and the last year in the rotation the row would be occupied by peppers all season long. The following year would begin the rotation again with a planting of legumes.

When you're juggling different space requirements and maturity dates as well as the characteristics of a plant group, you may not find it possible to follow such a rotation to the letter. Perhaps it will be necessary to plant cabbage and lettuce in succession or to keep your tomato patch in the same spot. In such cases, plan to feed the second crop several doses of compost or manure tea.

Corn takes so much out of the soil that every effort should be made to rotate placement of the corn patch, or at least to alternate corn with a cover crop or legume. Any vegetable with which you have had a disease or insect problem—especially tomatoes, potatoes, the cole crops, and cucurbits—should be rotated. To help prevent further problems, such vegetables should not be planted in the same place more than once every three years.

Some gardeners use the row as the basic rotation unit. Others divide the garden into different sections or beds in which they plant related crops. Some prefer a simpler rotation, alternating the heavy feeders taken as one group (corn, tomatoes, cole crops, cucurbits), with root vegetables, legumes, onions, and possibly a cover crop.

If your main garden is not close to the house, you might want to add a small kitchen garden to the plan. Such a plot need not be large. Even a three- by six-foot space, or a few raised beds, can accommodate the parsley, herbs, onions, and lettuce that the good cook will snip for each meal. Include a row of calendulas or nasturtiums for culinary flowers and bouquets, and single plants of pepper, tomato, kale, and chard for quick additions to a soup, and this small jewel of a plot will be as beautiful as it is useful.

Tilling Methods

Just how are you going to work your plot? Most likely your garden layout will determine the method and tools you use.

Tilling, or breaking up the soil, is done for several reasons: to prepare a seedbed, both in spring and throughout the season when making succession plantings; to control weeds between rows during the growing season; and to turn under green manure crops for soil enrichment.

(1) Shovel, fork, rake, and hoe are kind to the land because they don't press heavily and compact the soil as power equipment tends to do. You use your own power, buy no gas, have few

breakdowns, and get good exercise. Even with the shovel, though, you want to be careful not to work the soil when it is so wet that it breaks into clods. Wait until a ball of soil shatters into crumbs when dropped: then you can dig without ruining the structure of the soil. When preparing a seedbed, you'd first turn over the soil with a fork or spade, then rake the surface to make the soil finer so that seeds can grow more easily. The hoe is useful for opening a narrow trench when planting seeds, and for chopping weeds.

(2) The wheel hoe is, as the name suggests, a hoe attached to a wheel. It is a people-powered tool used to cultivate between rows that have been previously dug, tilled, or plowed. For best results, soil should be cultivated often to keep it loose. The wheel hoe can't penetrate sod or densely weedy soil.

(3) Power rotary tillers can break up sod, turn under weeds and green manure, and prepare a fine seedbed. They are convenient and versatile. Tillers shouldn't be used on wet land, though, or the underlying soil will pack, and the topsoil's texture will be damaged. The tiller works much more gently than the plow. Although it is possible, even with a tiller, to develop a layer of hardpan—hard-packed soil—just below the depth of the tiller's tines, few gardeners experience any practical problems of this nature. Rotary tillers have been responsible for the enlargement and continued productivity of a multitude of back yard gardens.

Whenever soil is broken up and exposed to the air, by whatever means, organic matter is oxidized—used up. Because power tillers pulverize soil more thoroughly and extensively than hoes, they use up the soil's organic matter at a faster rate. That is seldom a problem unless tilling is frequent, but it is a fact the gardener should know. The ability of the rotary tiller to turn under weeds and green manure crops, however, may mean more organic matter can be added to the soil than would be possible working by hand in a large garden.

(4) The tractor is sometimes used to plow up a large plot for spring planting, and perhaps again in the fall to plow down crop residues or to prepare a patch for planting of a cover crop of rye grass. With a corn-cultivator attachment, it may also be used to weed widely spaced rows of young corn or sunflower plants in large plantings. Tractors are heavy, though, and they tend to compact the soil even when it seems dry. Repeated plowing with a moldboard plow also leads to the formation of a layer of hardpan just below plow depth. On any land that is regularly plowed, it's wise to go over the area with a chisel plow every few years to open up deeper channels into the subsoil. That deeper penetration of the soil by the chisel plow's thin blades improves drainage and permits more root growth.

Many gardeners use several different tilling methods over the course of a season. Those who plant a large garden might, for example, plow in early spring and then immediately use a rotary tiller to make a fine seedbed. Then, during the season, they use

CONTAINER GARDENING

For those who have no ground around them, or who want to supplement small beds, the container garden is the logical extension of the intensive bed and the square-foot plot. Simply take that square foot of soil (but make it a cubic foot) and put it in a bucket, tub, or clay pot; then plant a single vegetable in the container, and set it in a sunny spot. You can even put it on wheels—in a child's wagon, for example—to move as the sun moves. Plants in containers need deep soil—at least eight to ten inches, as much as five gallons for a tomato plant; they also need drainage (punch holes in the bottom of buckets or boxes), almost daily watering, and frequent feeding. Large plants like tomatoes must be staked, pruned, and tied.

the tiller for widely spaced rows, and they hoe or mulch between close rows.

A rotary tiller should be adequate to prepare the soil each spring in a medium-sized garden, perhaps followed by mulching or hand cultivation. The medium-sized garden illustrated on page 17 could also be dug by hand, and the small garden would certainly be easy to spade.

Mulch has many of the benefits of tilling. It not only helps control weeds and—eventually—enriches soil; it also reduces soil compaction by absorbing some of the impact of footsteps. In cool climates, where the growing season is short, mulching is not beneficial to all crops (see "Tending the Garden," page 70). Where slugs are a problem, remove or turn under the mulch in the fall, and during the season trap the slugs in saucers containing beer or a solution of baker's yeast and water.

In a small garden, if you don't dig intensive beds, you could put down planks where you're going to walk, both to keep mud off shoes and prevent soil compaction. Planks are not practical for a large garden, but, however you've planned access to your garden, it is always a good idea to mark all projected rows with stakes early in the season, before they're planted, so that you won't be stepping on ground where you intend to plant seeds later. Careful gardeners walk *around* the garden, not across it, to avoid compacting the soil unnecessarily.

Timing

Judicious timing of spring plantings is one of the arts of gardening. Always it is a matter of balance: our eagerness to be working the ground and our hunger for fresh food versus the seed's natural reluctance to sprout before conditions are right for its survival. Seeds need warmth, air, and moisture to germinate. If the soil is too cool, they may rot before they can sprout. If the soil is sodden and lumpy, as it will be if dug too soon, the germinating seeds will not get the air they need.

Even when the air temperature is cold, though, the increasing warmth of the spring sun heats the soil. When the growing bed is well drained and rich in air-holding humus, and especially when it is raised above the surrounding ground, solar heating of the soil is more effective. For early vegetables, a starting bed that receives reflected light and heat from a nearby house or wall will warm up even sooner. Raking away mulch and spreading black plastic on the ground also help to increase the soil temperature.

If the soil texture is loose and porous, the hardy crops we like to plant early—peas, spinach, lettuce, and such—can wait out a cold snap and germinate when conditions are right. Lettuce and spinach will begin to sprout at 32°F, but peas wait till the soil warms to around 40°F. With frost-tender crops, you don't have this kind of leeway. Some, in fact, like cantaloupe and eggplant, will be retarded by temperatures below 50°F (see "Days for Vegetable Seedlings to Emerge at Different Temperatures," page 23).

DAYS FOR VEGETABLE SEEDLINGS TO EMERGE AT DIFFERENT TEMPERATURES

Crop	32°F	41°F	50°F	59°F	68°F	77°F	86°F	95°F	104°F
Asparagus	0*	0	52.8	24	14.6	10.3	11.5	19.3	28.4
Lima bean	—**	—	0	30.5	17.6	6.5	6.7	—	—
Snap bean	0	0	0	16.1	11.4	8.1	6.4	6.2	0
Beet	—	42	16.7	9.7	6.2	5	4.5	4.6	—
Cabbage	—	—	14.6	8.7	5.8	4.5	3.5	—	—
Carrot	0	50.6	17.3	10.1	6.9	6.2	6	8.6	—
Cauliflower	—	—	19.5	9.9	6.2	5.2	4.7	—	—
Celery	0	41	16	12	7	0	0	0	—
Cucumber	0	0	0	13	6.2	4	3.1	3	—
Eggplant	—	—	—	—	13.1	8.1	5.3	—	—
Lettuce	49	14.9	7	3.9	2.6	2.2	2.6	0	0
Muskmelon	—	—	—	—	8.4	4	3.1	—	—
Okra	0	0	0	27.2	17.4	12.5	6.8	6.4	6.7
Onion	135.8	30.6	13.4	7.1	4.6	3.6	3.9	12.5	0
Parsley	—	—	29	17	14	13	12.3	—	—
Parsnip	171.7	56.7	26.6	19.3	13.6	14.9	31.6	0	0
Pea	—	36	13.5	9.4	7.5	6.2	5.9	—	—
Pepper	0	0	0	25	12.5	8.4	7.6	8.8	0
Radish	0	29	11.2	6.3	4.2	3.5	3	—	—
Spinach	62.6	22.5	11.7	6.9	5.7	5.1	6.4	0	0
Sweet Corn	0	0	21.6	12.4	6.9	4	3.7	3.4	0
Tomato	0	0	42.9	13.6	8.2	5.9	5.9	9.2	0
Turnip	0	0	5.2	3	1.9	1.4	1.1	1.2	2.5
Watermelon	—	0	—	—	11.8	4.7	3.5	3	—

* Little or no germination of seeds at these temperatures.
** Vegetable not tested at these temperatures (assume temperatures are too low or high to permit germination).

From: "Vegetable Seed Germination," by J. F. Harrington and P. A. Minges, a pamphlet published by The University of California Agricultural Extension Service, Table 2, page 5.

In a truly complete garden, there are five waves of plant groups, enough to occupy the gardener from February through June. The five groups are: (1) Hardy vegetables to grow as transplants; (2) Hardy vegetables for direct seeding in the garden; (3) Tender vegetables to grow as transplants, started indoors from seed and planted out immediately after the last frost; (4) Tender vegetables to grow from seed in the garden; and (5) Tender vegetables to plant, as seeds or started plants, two to three weeks after the last frost when settled, consistent warm weather has arrived.

The first time you plant a garden, ask your neighbors and the county extension agent about the average dates in your area for the last spring frost and for the first one in fall. After a few seasons, you'll learn about your own piece of ground—which plots warm up early and drain well, which are in frost pockets. Keeping records of planting and harvest dates will give you the information you need to keep pushing those planting dates up as far as you can, to keep beating your own records until you arrive at a safe, comfortable average planting date for each vegetable.

A survey of seed companies reported by Ken and Pat Kraft in *Horticulture* (September 1979) revealed that maturity dates of the same vegetable differ, sometimes widely, from company to company. Moral: Consider the maturity dates listed in catalogues as guidelines, not absolutes. Many factors influence the readiness of the crop: soil quality and type, temperature, wind, latitude, cultural practices, rainfall. Especially in early fall, when days are shorter and nights cool, many vegetables mature more slowly. Yet in a hot summer with ample moisture I've had bush beans and zucchini come in a day or two earlier than the catalogue estimated. The days to maturity are figured from date of direct seeding for vegetables that are sown directly in the garden, like beans and cucumbers, and from the date of transplanting to the garden for vegetables that are commonly started indoors and later planted out as seedlings, like tomatoes and peppers.

Timing can affect your workload, too. If you're putting in a large patch of peas for freezing, you'll want your largest bean plantings to mature after you've dealt with the peas; otherwise you may have trouble picking and processing both crops. It's also a good rule to keep food in the freezer for as short a time as possible. For example, it's much more efficient to freeze broccoli in the fall, closer to the time when you'll need it, than it is to do so in early summer. The same is true of cauliflower, spinach, and other greens. In order to have a flourishing fall crop for late picking, you'll need to plan some midsummer plantings to follow the early spring crops, as suggested on the illustrations of garden layouts.

A good planting plan integrates timing and spacing to keep each row as productive as possible. Planning provides an opportunity to consider what we really want from the garden. Perhaps this is the year to start that long hoped-for asparagus patch, to plow up another strip for soybeans, to reduce a large garden to compact intensive beds, to try growing potatoes in mulch, or to raise more garden fruits. Planning aims at an ideal, and even though that utopian landscape, when we get close to it, may have some crooked rows and bean beetles and weeds and an odd lone sunflower volunteer that we couldn't bear to pull up, our plan helps us to improve the garden gradually, year by year.

What does your garden need? What do you want it to be? Putting your dreams on paper can be the first step toward making them come true.

New Varieties

Like the mythical Janus, for whom this month is named, we gardeners find ourselves facing two ways in January. On the one hand, we are loyal to the old vegetable varieties that have served us well in the past, and we look forward to growing them again. At the same time, we're drawn to the new seed offerings—hoping, perhaps, for a different flavor or color, or a vegetable that will resist disease or cold or answer some other gardening problem.

Our preoccupation with new models for a new year may be peculiarly American, but some recent introductions are imports from Europe, where several have been prized for years. The aromatic *Small-Leaved Basil,* for example, is the choice of many Italian cooks for making pesto sauce. For another authentic touch, you might choose *Finocchio di Montagna,* the wild fennel of Sicily, or *Cicoria Rossa di Treviso,* a tart red chicory found only near Venice. All of these are available from the Epicure Seed Company, which also lists the aromatic, thick-growing *Persil Clivi* (curly parsley) from Belgium and *Romeo,* a new charentais-type melon noted for its ability to retain flavor and quality after picking, from France.

One of the most useful-sounding newcomers is *Kuta,* a squash that can be eaten either raw or cooked while green and later matures into a yellow, hard-shelled winter squash that keeps for weeks. The cylindrical-shaped fruits form fifty days after planting. Kuta could put an end to that old gardening tradition, the summer squash giveaway. It's available from Park Seed Company.

Indian Summer Spinach also sounds good for both ends of the season. It is unusually slow to go to seed, an important quality in spring, and it matures in only thirty-nine days, so it will produce a quick fall crop. You can get it from Johnny's Selected Seeds.

New corn offerings include Park Seed Company's *Butterfruit,* a supersweet corn said to retain its flavor well after picking, and *Calypso* from Johnny's Selected Seeds, a variety bearing large ears of narrow, deep, yellow and white kernels. Both are hybrids.

My favorite cauliflower has been Self-Blanche, which doesn't require tying up the leaves to keep the heads white, because the leaves naturally grow over the heads. The only trouble is that it matures late. Now, Dr. S. Honma of Michigan State University, who developed Self-Blanche, has improved on his own work with two earlier self-blanching cauliflower varieties. *Stovepipe* matures in forty-seven days and has long, upright leaves. *White Empress* takes sixty days to mature, but that's still three weeks faster than Self-Blanche. Both new varieties are available from Johnny's Selected Seeds.

Two new ornamental vegetables are *Goldie,* a gold-colored tomato with 2-inch fruit, and Tequila Sundown, a decorative red pepper. Both are distributed by Park Seed Company.

Several seed companies offer an odd but promising new pea variety. *Novella Dwarf Leafless Pea* has only a few leaves, all concentrated around the stiff central stem. The tendrils—hundreds of them—weave together to support the plants, making this a good choice for intensive gardening. According to the growers, Novella requires only one-third as much space as other pea varieties.

One of the three All-America bronze medal winners for 1981 is a pepper, the sweet yellow hybrid *Gypsy*. (The other two winners are flowers.) Gypsy, while not as thick-fleshed as some later-bearing peppers, is tender and early. Fruits were ready as early as fifty-five days after plants were set out in the test garden.

Seeds for winners of All-America awards are available from most of the larger seed companies. Most of the candidates for the awards each year are submitted by seed companies, although government agencies and private breeders are also eligible. The nominated varieties are grown in twenty-eight trial plots and evaluated in comparison with the established variety they resemble most closely. In selecting winners, judges emphasize taste and texture, high yield, compact growth, and disease resistance. Of the eighty or so new flower and vegetable varieties submitted each year, an average of six to ten are chosen for a gold, silver, or bronze award, depending on the merit of the new variety.

The 1979 gold medal winner was the *Sugar Snap Pea*, touted (justly, I think) as a wholly new vegetable. Having tried Sugar Snap its first year out, I doubled my planting last year. This pea really is super; it's good to eat not only when the edible pod is slim and crisp, but also when it's filled with peas. Shelling is not necessary. If you haven't tried Sugar Snap yet, I recommend it. That one deserves its gold medal.

Another good recent introduction is the 1979 silver medal winner *Grand Duke Kohlrabi*, a vigorous, quick-maturing strain that remains tender longer than other varieties.

Other recently developed vegetables you might want to try include *Triple Treat Seedless Pumpkin* from Burpee Seeds; *Quicksilver* white corn, which matures nearly three weeks earlier than Silver Queen and can be obtained from Harris Seeds; and the *Stuffing Tomato* from Burgess Seed and Plant Company, a hollow tomato that is delicious stuffed with chicken salad or macaroni and cheese.

As you do your armchair seed shopping, think of all those seed packets as tickets to independence from stale produce, sprayed food, grocery bills, and mediocre taste. Happy catalogue browsing!

Some Vegetables Grow Best in the North

As I savor the yearly ritual of ordering seeds—first the quick glance through each catalogue, then the serious study of new varieties, old favorites, and different strains I've been meaning to grow, followed by evenings of deliberation on the relative merits of untried tempters, tried-and-true standbys, bush or vining squash, rambling or climbing beans—all the while taking great pleasure in the process, not wanting to conclude it too soon, I am always struck by the fact that there are so many fine vegetables that perform well in northern gardens.

Take English peas, for example. In some of our warmer states it is difficult, if not impossible, to grow a decent green pea. Spring simply comes on too quickly and too warm, cheating the peas of that period of slow, crisp, cool growth they need in order to produce well. Crowder peas and black-eyed peas are grown as substitutes, but they're not tender little green peas and they never will be. How *could* there be lamb stew without green peas? Or salmon, without peas?

There are ways of coaxing even better and earlier-than-usual peas out of the soil, and ways of making them bear longer, as well.

For earlier peas:

(1) Choose an early-maturing variety like Beagle, Little Marvel, or Frosty.

(2) Prepare your pea rows in the fall by digging or plowing the soil, making a furrow and mulching the row with thick wads of hay or leaves. Then sow the crop in the prepared trench when the first spring thaw hits. Some gardeners even sow the seed in the fall, covering it well. Sometimes it rots, but sometimes it sprouts and when it does, your successful gamble is rewarded with an extra-early crop of peas.

(3) Soak the seed in warm water for a few hours before planting.

(4) Plant on light, well-drained soil if at all possible.

For a longer pea season:

(1) Plant the legumes in bands one or two feet wide. The plants will shade (and therefore cool) each other's roots and discourage weedy competition within the bed.

(2) Once blossoms form on the peas, let weeds grow up around the perimeter of the bed to further shade the roots.

(3) When picking, snap the peas off from the stem rather than pull them. The vines are very easily uprooted.

(4) Keep the peas picked. If the pods become overmature, the plant will stop bearing.

Be glad, too, for cabbages. Cabbage seedlings are among the first to be planted out in spring, and the mature heads are one of the last fall vegetables to succumb to frost. And in between, cabbage leaves in soup, coleslaw, sauerkraut, and boiled dinner sustain us through many a meal. Grow cabbage cool, in rich soil, and you'll have beautiful, crisp, green, extravagant-leaved heads.

What else can you do to cultivate a worthy cabbage patch? Here are some suggestions:

(1) Raise plants indoors, harden them off in a protected outdoor spot for a week, and set them out about one month—no sooner—before the date of your last expected frost.

(2) Sow the seeds sparingly. Overcrowded cabbage seedlings grow into second-rate plants.

(3) Fertilize the growing plants every two or three weeks with manure tea or diluted fish emulsion fertilizer.

(4) Plant some cabbage seed in late spring for a fall crop.

Kale, that robust, leafy, longer-stemmed cousin of cabbage, is a plant perfectly suited to snappy climates. Its flavor is improved by frost and the leaves stand under a covering of snow throughout the winter, ready to be plucked for the soup. In addition, kale is an excellent source of vitamins A, B1, B2, and C, as well as of calcium and other minerals. It is one of the few vegetables available fresh-picked to northern gardeners during the winter months.

Kale fares well when sown right in the garden row; there's no need to start plants indoors. Perhaps the following hints will help you to grow more and better kale:

(1) Plant kale for fall and winter use when you put in the main part of your spring garden. Later plantings may be made, up until about the end of July, but the earlier sowing will yield a large, bushy plant from which you can cut heavily all fall.

(2) Pick the young, tender leaves in preference to the large outer foliage.

(3) Don't feed your kale during the warm summer months when it is growing slowly, but give it a few doses of manure tea when cool days bring the plant back into active growth.

Parsnips reward the patient gardener with long, sweet, tasty roots in late fall. Plant them, along with kale, at the edge of the garden where they won't be uprooted if you plow or rototill in the fall. To cooperate with this fine root crop, you should:

(1) Always use fresh parsnip seed. Although a vigorous plant when full grown, parsnip is a frail beginner; the seed is notoriously low in vitality.

(2) Plant parsnip seed no earlier than two or three weeks before your last expected spring frost, or the seed may rot.

(3) Cover the seed very lightly with just a sprinkling of fine soil. Deeply covered seed sprouts often fail to break the surface of the soil.

(4) Refrain from digging the roots until your garden has been touched at least once, and preferably two or three times, by hard frost. The low temperature changes some of the parsnip's starch to sugar.

Turnips, sown as early in the spring as you can break ground, will put greens on your table as soon as four or five weeks from planting. (Tokyo Cross hybrid from Stokes takes only thirty days.) After the long, closed-in winter, that first bite of garden-fresh food is true spring tonic. Turnips like northern gardens and respond to:

(1) Ordinary garden soil well supplied with organic matter. The best turnips are small; larger specimens often turn strong and fibrous.

(2) A loose, well-dug bed or trench.

(3) Cool, moist weather. To be good, turnips must be grown rapidly, before hot weather strikes.

The rutabaga, that staple of midwestern lumber camps, thrives in the northern climate. In hot latitudes, in fact, the roots will be small and the flesh stringy. Whether the Swedish turnip—as the yellow-fleshed, bulbous-rooted vegetable is sometimes called—is a familiar staple or a new experiment for you, I hope you'll find an idea among the following pointers that will add even more to your enjoyment of this hardy, hearty food.

(1) Sow the seeds somewhat later than your main spring plantings, but not much after mid-June. The plant needs at least ninety days to mature.

(2) Control troublesome flea beetles with diatomaceous earth (marketed as Perma-Guard).

(3) For a change, try mixing two cups of cubed rutabagas into your next pot of baked beans. Or grate and sauté the roots.

(4) Remedy boron deficiency (indicated by soft brown spots in the flesh of the vegetable) by applying a well-balanced compost. If possible, include some cantaloupe leaves, known to accumulate boron, when you mix the compost.

(5) Since the roots protrude from the soil, they are vulnerable to a hard freeze. Either harvest them before black frost, or cover the plants well until you find time to dig them up.

Most gardeners develop a fondness for vegetables that do well for them where they live. We have a saying in our family: "I'm glad you like it, because that's what we've got!" When what you've got is a hardy, nutritious, tasty, dependable food plant like some of the cool-climate lovers outlined above (not to mention lettuce, radishes, endive, potatoes, and other cool growers not discussed here), the gardening season that lies ahead—admittedly around a few corners—should be a good one. And now, back to those catalogues.

SOURCES

PERMA-GUARD
George Park Seed Company
J. Mullin Nursery

EARLY PEAS
Little Marvel
Olds Seed Company
George Park Seed Company
Joseph Harris Company
Stokes Seeds
Beagle
George Park Seed Company
Johnny's Selected Seeds
Frosty
Joseph Harris Company

Economies of Home-Grown Produce

This year, your vegetable garden will be more valuable than ever. Food prices are higher with every market-basket report, and rising costs of transporting foods from distant growers can only lead to further price increases. More ominous yet is the likelihood that irrigated western farms, where much of our produce is grown, will find it increasingly difficult to compete with industry and with residential developments for scarce water, a trend that will push grocery bills even higher.

According to a recent Gallup poll, the average 595-square-foot garden (a plot about 20 by 30 feet) produces $368 worth of vegetables at a cost of $19. The money saved is worth much more than its face value, because it's tax-free extra cash. For a gardener in the 30 per cent tax bracket, $500 saved by growing vegetables is equivalent to the annual return on $12,987 in a savings account at 5½ per cent interest.

So, you're saving money already by growing your own vegetables. What you really want to know is how you can save even more. There are three ways to increase your garden savings: produce more valuable crops, cut costs, and increase productivity.

The vegetable crops that have the highest cash value are those that cost a lot when purchased and those that yield a lot. Last summer, for example, I bought several cantaloupes for a dollar each before my garden melons were ripe. But the garden patch, with an investment of eighty-five cents in seed, produced fifty-nine super cantaloupes. (Cantaloupes do take a good bit of space. I had plenty of room for them, but if your garden space is limited, you should also consider space efficiency in choosing the vegetables with the highest value to you.)

In a recent survey conducted by the National Garden Bureau, thirty-six home garden experts rated garden vegetables by value, considering total yield, average value per pound harvested, and seed-to-harvest time.

Crops have value only if you can use them. For example, if you plant a 30-foot row of leaf lettuce because it looks so neat, but really need only a 15-foot row, the remainder will go to seed before you can use it. But if you had planted half the row to beets, you'd have a storage crop that would keep for winter.

There are many ways to cut costs in the garden. Here are some I've used.

(1) Save seeds from nonhybrid crops. Lettuce and tomatoes are especially easy. If you select seed from your best plants, you may develop an improved strain while you're saving money.

(2) Sell seedling plants or surplus vegetables, or purposely plant a cash crop.

(3) Trade surplus vegetables with friends. If you and a friend

The top ten vegetables, rated on a scale of 1 to 10, are:

Tomatoes (supported to save space)	9.0
Green bunching onions	8.2
Leaf lettuce	7.4
Turnips, for greens and roots	7.4
Summer squash	7.2
Edible podded peas	6.9
Onion bulbs for storage	6.9
Snap beans (pole or runner)	6.8
Beets, for tops and leaves	6.6

On the bottom of the list are some delicious vegetables that take more space than others:

Corn	4.1
Winter squash	3.8
Melons	3.8
Watermelons	3.8
Pumpkins	1.9

both tend to overplant, agree to overplant different crops and then swap.

(4) Mix your own potting soil for starting seedlings. One good formula consists of equal parts of good garden loam, finished compost, and vermiculite.

(5) Compost household wastes for free fertilizer.

(6) Find other sources of free fertilizer in your community. Check the Yellow Pages for local industries with usable natural by-products. Look for horse farms, zoos, circuses, riding stables, and sources of wood chips, seaweed or lakeweed, aged sawdust.

(7) Scythe weeds before they go to seed and use them as mulch instead of buying hay or peat moss.

(8) Buy seeds on sale. Seeds on store racks are often reduced at the end of the season. Most, except for onions and parsnips, will still be good next year if kept cool and dry.

(9) Use insect controls you can make at home, such as the popular garlic/red pepper spray. (In an electric blender, mix four hot peppers, four cloves of garlic, and four cups of water. Let stand for an hour and then strain. Spray garden weekly.)

(10) Cut processing costs by storing root vegetables, cabbage, and other suitable crops in a root cellar or other natural cold-storage area.

To increase productivity, consider doing one or all of the following:

(1) Plant earlier, using hardy vegetables and perhaps developing a sheltered plot or cold frame where you can nurse along early plantings.

(2) Extend your harvest later in the season by making continuous succession planting.

(3) Provide fences, poles, or other support for climbing vegetables so you can plant more in the same space.

(4) Dig up another row or two of garden. You won't notice the small amount of extra work, but the additional crops you can grow will further reduce your food bill.

FEBRUARY

An Armchair Gardener Looks Ahead

If February is here, can spring be far behind? A couple of quick flips of the calendar, surely, will bring spring. But having lived through these intervals between the shortest month and the day of the robin, the seasoned northern gardener knows that the road to spring will detour through blizzards, power failures, freezing rain, slush, and late frosts. The days are lengthening, but winter's back isn't broken yet.

It's not a bad time to be an armchair gardener, though—to gaze at the flames in the fireplace and envision the garden you'll have this year. No peppers are so red, eggplants so satiny, or radishes so crisp and mild as those that will grow in our gardens *this* year.

It just could happen, too. Planning is certainly essential to a good garden, and who can plan in the spring when a hundred things must be done on one perfect afternoon before it rains or freezes again? Don't let the old Puritan conscience nag you. Relaxed planning is a legitimate and useful gardening activity.

Where to begin? How about those seeds you saved from last year's vegetable plantings, those left from your last seed order, or those accepted from your neighbor, who may grow an unusual variety? It might be wise to test them for germination to avoid an early failure if seed isn't viable; last year I lost valuable time when I planted outdated parsnip seed.

To run a germination test on your seeds, count out an even number—no less than twenty, and fifty should be plenty. Spread the seeds evenly on a damp paper towel or old bath towel and cover them with a moist (but not wringing wet) layer of the same material. Keep the whole bunch moist and as near to 70–80 degrees as you can manage. Germination is more rapid in this temperature range than in the cool 50 degrees that may prevail in your back room or summer kitchen. Peek at the seeds each day: if mold begins to form, they need more air. Put a few small wads of crumpled newspaper between the two damp outer layers of toweling to admit a bit more air. Simply raising the cover to check on the seeds usually wafts in the small amount of air that the germinating seeds need.

When the seed has developed a sprout, it qualifies as a germinated seed. Most seeds that are viable will have germinated within three weeks, many sooner than that. When it appears that all possible seeds have sprouted, count them. If twenty seeds sprout out of a total of twenty-five tested, your germination rate is 80 per cent. If your germination test is low, 30 to 50 per cent, your seed can still be used; just plant it thickly. A rate of 5 to 10 per cent means it's time to order from the seed catalogue. For that reason, if you're going to test your seeds for germination, it's wise to do so before completing your seed order.

The seed catalogues are mostly in by now. If you've received only two or three, why not send for a few more? They duplicate each other in many areas, of course, but I don't believe I've ever yet sent for a new seed catalogue that didn't have some new or interesting strain that seemed worth trying.

You have your favorite way of making out a seed order, I'm sure. Our ritual always includes a sizeable list of old dependables —the Buttercrunch lettuce, Cylindra beets, Bell Boy peppers, and Jersey Wakefield cabbage that we know will perform for us. Then we must have a few unusuals—things we grow once in awhile but not every year, like celeriac and collards. Finally, we add on several of the irresistible new varieties—a better-flavored bush squash, an earlier zucchini, a good new bean.

As you make out your order, remember that electric power is costly (in many ways) and canning-jar lids aren't cheap. You might be very glad indeed, next winter, for a supply of vegetables that keep well without processing. Beets, carrots, cabbage, celeriac, horseradish, kale, Jerusalem artichoke, parsnips, potatoes, rutabagas, turnips, onions, winter squash—how many of these good keepers did you grow last year? You'll want tender new beets for early summer meals, but a specially chosen variety like Long Season (available from Harris) is a necessity for best results in storage. You may want to go through your whole list of vegetables in this way, adding to the usual choices you make on the basis of flavor, earliness, or food value, the selection of another variety bred for both eating quality and longevity in storage. What's left in your root cellar right now? The seeds of next winter's good eating are in this winter's careful planning.

Keep a copy of your seed order, too. More people than ever are ordering seeds this year and if your order should get shipped to North Carolina, as one of mine from a reliable seed house did last year, you'll have a check sheet to go by in straightening things out. Another thing you should do is check each order against your list as it comes in. Last year I didn't, and instead of the two pounds of garlic I had ordered, I received only one pound; I didn't open the little ventilated carton to check until it was time to plant, and by then the supply was sold out. We've been short of our own fresh garlic all winter long; the bulbs we must buy are never as juicy. We're tempted to order five pounds this year.

Once you've mailed your seed orders, you can turn your attention to mapping out the garden. If you've saved last year's mudsplotched, much-revised planting plan, you'll have a head start in planning this year's plot. Here are a few important practices to remember in laying out your rows on paper:

(1) Rotate heavy feeders, such as cabbage, with less-demanding crops.

(2) Provide for succession crops—early lettuce followed by late turnips, for example.

(3) Plan for a block of garden space where crops finish early and you can grow a protective, soil-building cover crop.

(4) Point rows north and south to give plants maximum sun.

(5) Plan row spacing according to projected method of cultivation —narrow for hoeing, wider for rototilling.

(6) Keep perennial crops at the edge of the garden or in a separate plot.

(7) If you are enlarging the garden, plant coarse-seeded crops like peas and beans in the rougher soil of recently tilled sod.

Sketch out several different planting plans and choose one that allows you to grow as many different vegetables as possible while caring well for your soil. Then leave plenty of blank space on the paper, for even that final version is sure to be revised somewhat, once you get out in the patch.

February Job List

February can be the longest month. For most gardeners, it is a time of looking ahead—often with some impatience. We long to start planting, but we know we have to be sensible. There are some worthwhile things you can do now, though, to get ready for the spring garden that seems so far away. Even if the ground is buried under two feet of snow, it's worth taking care of the puttering tasks that are often put off—or worse yet, not done at all— when the growing season begins.

Here are a few suggestions from which you might like to choose —perhaps at random—when it seems you must do *something* to hasten the turning of the season.

Prepare Seedling Flats

Is any gardener ever over-supplied with flats? I doubt it. Although many people purchase the long, shallow plastic trays made especially for raising seedlings, there is much to be said for making your own soil containers out of scrap wood. The boxes you knock together may be made in sizes that fit your available light space and seedling requirements, and certainly the price is right.

To make a seedling flat, cut four side pieces of scrap wood approximately 3 inches high and any length—up to 24 inches or so—that you wish. Keep the dimensions of the box no larger than about 12 by 24 inches, or the weight of the soil it holds will make extra bracing necessary. Nail the four sides of the box together to form an open rectangle. Then nail slats of scrap wood across the bottom of the box, leaving ⅛- to ¼-inch cracks between the strips to permit drainage. Flats need not be deep; 2–3 inches of soil is plenty for young seedlings.

Make a Cold Frame of Spare Windows

If you design your frame to match the sash you have available, you'll have a snug-fitting cover for your earliest outdoor plantings in spring. Be sure to provide a hook or other device to secure the windows when they're open. One gust of wind can break a good many hard-to-replace panes. Drawing up plans for a new cold frame while lounging by a warm box stove, with a pile of seed catalogues at your side, is a sure cure for those midwinter doldrums we call "the februaries."

Take Stock of Your Garden Tools

It is exasperating to spend part of a clear April morning looking for the transplanting trowel. Find it now and decide on a convenient place to keep it. Consider treating yourself to an extra trowel or two—perhaps one of the long, thin ones or a large, heavy-duty model.

If your shovel and fork are still plastered with mud from fall tree planting, clean and oil them to prevent rust. Are the handles in good shape? Some gardeners like to paint their handles a bright color so they are less likely to be overlooked outdoors. I must confess I've never really gotten around to doing this, but I *am* tempted to follow a magazine suggestion I read recently and install an old rural mailbox at the edge of the garden to hold the garden gloves, trowel, seeds, garden plan, string, bag of rotenone, and other necessities that always seem to be at the four corners of the farm when I need them.

Cut Poles for Plant Supports

If you own even a small woods, you probably have saplings to be thinned, brush to be trimmed, and firewood to cut. And no doubt you're spending some fine February days doing just that. As you cut and split, think past the immediate need for firewood and set aside the best straight, sound poles to support your next crop of Kentucky Wonders. Trim off the branches, size and stack your poles and stakes, and you'll be a step ahead of schedule come spring.

Spread Wood Ashes

Choose a calm, windless day, or your ashes may go far. The new, efficient box stoves produce far less ash than conventional fireplaces or Franklin stoves. Save every fleck of the residue, and put it to work on your garden. You can spread ashes whether the ground is snow covered or not.

You'll want these to ward off late frost damage to your tender seedlings. Bottomless plastic jugs, berry baskets, half-bushel baskets, and assorted tin cans may be nested for storage. It's too early to keep these devices handy on the porch, but not too soon to start saving them and to take note of what you have and where it's stored.

Mend the grape arbor. Repair the birdhouse. Replace the broken rake handle. Fix the gate latch. Tinker with the faulty sprinkler head. Perhaps no February is ever long enough for the tackling of all these chores, but the completion of any one of them will give you a well-deserved feeling of satisfaction.

It's true, February drags; but spring will come. And when it does and you're hurrying about, trying to accomplish thirty-five tasks in one day, you'll be glad that you got some of those necessary jobs done ahead of time. Happy puttering!

Heirloom Vegetables

Where have they gone . . . the good old varieties of corn and beans, the odd homey vegetables, the old dependables from another day? Who grows cardoon, martynia, or cranberry beans any more? It is still possible to do so, since seed for these and other favorite vegetables of our grandfathers is available. In case you'd like to try some heirloom vegetables in your next garden, here are some candidates to consider.

CARDOON

Cynara cardunculus. This relative of the globe artichoke is a tender herbaceous perennial. In New England gardens, hardened-off seedling plants may be set out at the same time as tomatoes and blanched by tying or banking with earth in the fall. Quality is best after an early fall frost. The plants must be treated as annuals in northern climates, but the blue, thistlelike flower self-sows readily. Set plants one and a half to two feet apart in rows three feet apart. In the deep rich soil it prefers, cardoon may grow to a height of four feet or more. The plant resembles a large clump of celery and is served in much the same way. The stalk may be braised, stewed, cooked in soup, or fried in batter.

MARTYNIA

Proboscidea jussieri. Martynia is an easily cultivated annual that requires the same conditions as the tomato. Sow seeds or set out started plants after danger of frost, allowing two to three square feet for each vigorous, sprawling plant. Martynia has three useful stages. The large flowers, resembling those of the catalpa, are ornamental. The young fruits may be pickled like cucumbers. And the seed pods, which are responsible for the plant's common name, Unicorn Plant, make unusual dried arrangements.

CORN SALAD   *Valerianella olitoria.* Also called Lamb's Lettuce, Corn salad nourished our ancestors for centuries. For a spring crop, sow seed in August either in the coldframe or in a protected spot with a mulch cover. Spring sowing should be as early as possible, since the plant gives out in hot weather. This mild green, useful for both soup and salad, grows six to ten inches high in ordinary garden soil. Thin the plants to stand five to six inches apart.

HAMBURG ROOTED PARSLEY   This plant makes flavorful soup, cooked with corn, milk, and onion. The white, carrot-shaped roots may be sliced and cooked as you would carrots or parsnips. The plain leafy top makes a good soup garnish too. Plant seed as soon as the ground can be worked. Roots may be wintered in the ground under mulch for spring digging.

DRY BEANS   There are many highly localized strains of the baking and cooking bean, often known only as Neighbor Snow's, Aunt Hannah's, or Mrs. Tewkesbury's-up-the-road. Some bean-loving families have kept their own private strain of the bean down through the years.

Favorite traditional named varieties include:

Vermont Cranberry bean Has beans larger than those of other dwarf shell beans.

Trout bean, also called Jacob's Cattle A kidney-shaped, mottled red and white bean that matures early, producing dry beans in two and a half to three months.

Soldier bean A large white bean with a brown "man-at-attention" marking on the edge. It matures somewhat later than the trout bean, but its yield is higher.

French horticultural bean Has red-streaked pods. Despite its name, it is said to have originated in New England.

Maine Yellow Eye A much-beloved baking bean, oval and smaller than most others mentioned here.

Wren's Egg bean An old variety grown for both snap beans and baking beans. A red-speckled tan bean.

All of these beans should be allowed to remain on the plant until almost dry. Harvest them and spread or hang them until pods are brittle, shell them, and treat them to kill weevils by heating them in an oven at 180 degrees for fifteen minutes, leaving beans in the oven for an hour after turning the heat off.

SWEET CORN   The open-pollinated favorites of our ancestors are still worth growing, and there is some evidence that they are higher in protein than overbred hybrid varieties. You can save your own seed, too, provided you keep other kinds of corn at least two hundred feet away from your seed crop.

Golden Bantam A family favorite since 1902.

Black Mexican An extra-hardy legacy from the Indians. The kernels change from white, in the edible stage, to bluish-black when mature.

Country Gentleman At least one hundred years old and as good as ever. A late, white, sweet corn with kernels arranged irregularly rather than in rows.

Stowell's Evergreen The large ears remain in the milk stage for a

long time before maturing, assuring a long picking season.

Whipple's Early White Has deep, narrow kernels, good yield, and early. Credited to Silas S. Whipple of Norwich, Connecticut.

Flint corn is best for corn meal, dries hard, and can be ground well without gumming up the grinder. Perhaps you'll want some cornbread to go with those baked beans. Allow more time for growing flint corn than for sweet, since the ears must mature on the plant. Named varieties are included in the catalogues of the seedsmen on the accompanying list.

There are more worthy heirloom vegetables for which we haven't space here. We'd be delighted to hear from readers about their own knowledge, experiences, and sources for good old vegetables. When a variety runs out, it may be lost forever. Let's keep our vegetable heritage alive and growing! Guardians of special old seed strains may be interested in the Seed Saver's Exchange, a nonprofit organization of gardeners dedicated to keeping old varieties of vegetables alive in this day of proliferating hybrids and changing seed catalogue fashion. See page 213.

Seed-Patenting Legislation

When you open those hopeful-looking seed packets to begin a new growing season, are you ever struck by the thought that it hasn't always been this way? Only in the last eyeblink of time, considering the long sweep of human history, have seeds come in pretty packets with directions printed on the back.

Wild foods nourished the human race until about 10,000 years ago, when people began to select seeds of especially good wild varieties of grains and fruits and to plant them intentionally. Over the centuries, natural selection and human management have combined to foster the gradual development of thousands of varieties of food plants that are "as genetically distinct as beagles and Great Danes," in the words of Cary Fowler of the Rural Advancement Fund. This genetic diversity ensured that, even in a year of poor growing conditions or heavy insect infestation, some plants would thrive and bear seed. Domesticating our food plants—selecting qualities important to us—has made these plants dependent on us. Few domesticated plants would survive long without intentional replanting, weed control, and cultivation.

In very recent times we've manipulated our seed heritage less gently. Chemical pesticides, which have made it possible to grow less sturdy strains, have also contributed to the evolution of resistant insects. Many of our hybrid seeds are highly inbred, and this narrow genetic base has made some crops even more dependent on human intervention and more vulnerable to disease. For example, the Southern corn blight, which affected only T-cytoplasm corn, wiped out 20 per cent of the corn crop in 1970.

Few American gardeners pay much attention to the maintenance of genetic diversity in their gardens, partly because threats to that diversity are not overt. We can still order a wide variety of seeds and plant our old favorite home-saved strains. (In 1857, though, according to the Graham Center Seed Directory, twenty different kinds of turnips were listed in the Wethersfield Seed Gardener's Almanac. In 1979 the Burpee catalogue listed five varieties, and in 1982 only four. Some companies carry even fewer.)

In Europe, the freedom of home gardeners to grow what they like is being seriously eroded by the enactment of plant-patenting laws that will permit corporations to patent distinct varieties of vegetables, with the result that only highly uniform varieties listed in the European Common Catalogue will be sold. Other varieties, including many tasty, disease-resistant old favorites, will be unavailable from seed companies and it will actually be illegal to grow them where they might cross-pollinate stands of commercial seed stock. Since the only way to keep plant varieties alive is to continue to grow them, varieties not replanted will die out, and there is no way they can ever be recovered.

In recent testimony before a House Agriculture Subcommittee, Cary Fowler quoted Dr. Erna Bennet of the United Nations' Food and Agriculture Organization, who estimates, "By 1991, fully three fourths of all the vegetable varieties grown in Europe will be extinct due to the attempt to enforce plant-patenting laws." Lost forever will be what Lawrence Hills of England's Henry Double-day Research Association calls "the Goyas and Rembrandts of the kitchen garden." The loss of present-day choice and variety is sad; the effect on future generations, who might need seeds with different genetic traits to breed necessary strengths back into their narrow-based wonder plants, could be tragic.

What is happening in Europe could happen here. Recent amendments to the U.S. Plant Variety Protection Act not only expand coverage to include tomatoes, celery, peppers, carrots, cucumbers, and okra, but also smooth the way for the U.S. to join with the European organization that coordinates and promotes plant-patenting laws on an international basis.

The recent scramble by large corporations, especially petro-chemical and drug companies, to purchase seed companies is a portent that bears watching. "Plant-patenting laws," writes Cary Fowler, "offer protection for corporate profits while further narrowing the genetic basis on which agriculture itself depends."

Effective actions that concerned gardeners can take to help preserve our seed heritage include:
(1) Developing seed-saving skills;
(2) Searching out good old vegetable varieties in your neighborhood and family and replanting them to keep the seed available;
(3) Planting some non-hybrid varieties in the vegetable garden;

(4) Supporting and promoting funding for collectic
of our plant genetic resources and for plant preserve
enous plants can be grown and protected.

The truism that vegetables are good for you may
than we have suspected. Everyone knows that v
sources of vitamins, but recent studies have shc
of garden vegetables contribute to our health
well.

Plant cells contain cellulose, an indigestible carbonyurac
grandmothers called it "roughage," and they did more good than
they realized when they urged raw vegetables on their families.
Dr. Denis Burkitt's pioneering work, showing that a high incidence of lower bowel disease is linked to low fiber consumption,
has been followed by other studies indicating that fiber helps to
control high blood cholesterol and to rid the body of toxic metals
and radioactive strontium 90. Citing these studies and others, including his own extensive research, Dr. Benjamin Ershoff of Loma
Linda (California) University School of Medicine has concluded
that dietary fiber assists the body to nullify toxic effects of medi-
cines, food additives, and ingested chemicals.

In the typical American diet of today, fiber has been largely
replaced by fat, sugar, and meat, all of which are not only lacking
in fiber, but are also positively correlated with a high incidence of
intestinal cancer. So, those colorful vegetables on the relish tray—
the crisp carrots, scallions, celery, and radishes—should be much
more than mere appetizers.

According to research conducted at Rutgers University, pectin
from fruits and vegetables is also effective in controlling high
blood cholesterol. And pectin helps to bind heavy metals such as
lead, preventing their absorption into the blood stream. Apples
are an excellent source of pectin, but it is also found in other foods,
including tomatoes, currants, raspberries, and quinces.

Other studies have shown that pumpkins, cabbage, cauliflower,
turnips, and radishes all help to counteract the carcinogenic effect
of nitrosamines found in ham, bacon, and other processed meats.
So, if you're packing a ham sandwich, you'd be wise to tuck in a
few radishes too, and you should serve some raw cauliflower florets with a BLT sandwich, or coleslaw with a plate of cold cuts.

Onions and garlic also help to lower blood cholesterol—a good
reason to include them in salads or sauces when you serve high-

meat or dairy dishes. Garlic has been eaten for 6,000 years, sometimes as much for its medicinal effect as for its pungently appetizing flavor. A large body of folklore attests to its ability to fight infection, promote healing, and aid digestion. More recent research has corroborated some of those ancient claims and even pointed to new therapeutic uses for garlic.

Allicin, a compound formed when garlic cloves are crushed, was found in 1944 to be the agent involved in garlic's antibacterial action. It is especially effective against stubborn infections of Gram-negative bacteria, and it is marketed in Russia as a recognized therapeutic agent. Fujiwara, a Japanese researcher, has demonstrated that garlic helps the body to assimilate vitamin B-1, which is required for normal digestion, proper growth, and proper functioning of the nervous system. Garlic also helps to prevent the formation of atherosclerotic lesions in blood vessels, and it has been shown to reduce high blood pressure to more normal levels. Whether you use it as a treat or a treatment, garlic will do you good.

British researcher Sir Richard Doll says that regular consumption of raw carrots and fresh green vegetables can reduce the risk of cancer by up to 40 per cent. And studies by a University of Idaho biochemist suggest that enzyme inhibitors in potatoes may prevent primary malignant growths from spreading. These and other discoveries related to vegetables and health were reported in *The Avant Gardener*, which also listed the "top twelve" vegetables with especially high vitamin and mineral content. Those vegetables are asparagus, broccoli, Brussels sprouts, carrots, cauliflower, corn, greens, lima beans, peas, red peppers, sweet potatoes, and winter squash.

If a diet rich in vegetables is good for your health, then one rich in homegrown vegetables should be even better. When you grow your own, you can make sure that they are raised in rich soil, are free of toxic sprays, and are picked and eaten when perfectly ripe. In addition, you get another benefit mentioned in every authoritative recipe for longevity: regular, purposeful exercise in the fresh air.

Garden medicine works!

My Favorite Varieties

I've always admired the late Ruth Stout's refusal to be dogmatic in giving gardening advice. "This is what I've done and the results have been good," she would say, "but it's not the only way to do things. Experiment and decide for yourself."

In that spirit, I've listed here the vegetable varieties that appear on my seed list year after year. Although I try new kinds of vegetables too, as I have for the past twenty springs, my annual seed order is planned around these tried-and-true varieties that have grown well and tasted good in Philadelphia, Wisconsin, Indiana, and the hills of central Pennsylvania. Family tastes vary, of course, as do soils and growing conditions. But if you're knee-deep in seed catalogues and wondering where to begin, you might want to check this list of Old Dependables.

BEANS We grow at least three different kinds of snap beans every year. The third one varies, but the first two are always the same: *Royal Burgundy* (or the older variety, *Royalty*), a purple-podded bean with excellent flavor that can be planted early when the soil is cool. (They turn green when cooked.) *Bush Blue Lake*, our second choice, is a beautiful bean—round as a pencil and quite long. Like the purple bean, it is available in both bush and pole form.

BEETS Both of our favorite beets take an unusual form. *Cylindra*, also called *Formanova*, is longer and thinner than the usual beet. It is smooth, dark maroon, and cylindrical—easy to slice into rounds and perfect for pickling. *Long Season* (or its alternate *Lutz's Green Leaf*) doesn't look like much—the mature root is coarse and knobby in appearance, but no matter how large it grows, the flesh is always tender, sweet, and fine textured. It keeps well, too. We plant Cylindra for our early crop and *Long Season* for fall eating and storage.

BROCCOLI *Green Comet* wins hands down. This early hybrid is ready 55 days after plants are set out and produces fine big heads with excellent flavor.

CABBAGE We grow *Early Jersey Wakefield* (also called *Jersey Queen*) for the early crop. The pointed heads are mild and sweet, though not always as solid as the ballhead types. *Savoy Ace* and *Savoy King*, with their crinkled crisp leaves, have good flavor and unusually consistent solidity—excellent for coleslaw and sauerkraut.

CARROTS Stump-rooted *Danvers Half Long* and *Nantes Forto* or *Nantes Tip Top* are dependable in heavy soil and keep well in storage. *Tendersweet* is long, thin, and tapered with a small core and sweet flavor —excellent for fresh use all summer long.

CORN Preferences in sweet corn seem to be highly personal, but I'll go on record here as a devotee of *Butter and Sugar* and *Sweet Sue* in the yellow-white line and *Silver Queen* for its large, extra-sweet white-kerneled ears. *Wonderful* is fine, too—a long-standing corn with a thin ear.

LETTUCE It's fun to try all kinds of lettuce, but if I had to choose just three, they would be these. *Buttercrunch:* the loosely formed head has crisp ribs with good flavor and stands longer in the garden without bolting to seed than other early lettuces. *Kagran:* a loosely bunched butterhead type; its leaves are lighter green than Buttercrunch and it's not quite as crisp, but it lasts a week or two longer in summer heat before it goes to seed. *Ithaca* head lettuce: the solid heads with large ruffly outer leaves make this a good ego builder for the home gardener. Start seedlings indoors.

ONIONS   *Elite* forms a vigorous plant with good-sized bulbs that keep well. *Italian Red Bottle* onions are long and thin with purple skin and excellent sweet flavor, although somewhat less vigorous than other varieties I've grown.

PEAS   Thanks to Ruth Stout, I started planting *Lincoln* peas some years ago and have found none better. For a sugar pea I like *Mammoth Melting Sugar,* far more tender than the dwarf varieties.

PEPPERS   Here it's *Bell Boy* hybrid, a consistent producer of sweet, thick-walled, blocky peppers. *Hungarian Wax* is our choice for a not-too-hot condiment pepper. *Long Red Cayenne* is hot and dries well.

SQUASH   We grow others, but always have blocky green *Buttercup* for top flavor in fall eating and schmoo-shaped *Butternut* for winter keeping. *Vegetable Spaghetti* is prolific, tasty under cheese or tomato sauce, and keeps well, too.

TOMATOES   Tomato choices can be as controversial as corn, though perhaps less emotionally defended. For what it's worth, we always grow the plum-shaped *Roma* for catsup and sauces, *Moira* for amazingly deep red color, *Moreton* and *Supersonic* for main season eating and canning, *Jubilee* or *Sunray* for delicious meaty orange fruit, and *Sweet 100* for incredibly sweet and abundant cherry tomatoes.

Note: Most of the above-mentioned varieties are widely available. Sources for the less common exceptions are noted below.

Nantes Forto and *Tip Top carrots:* Johnny's Selected Seeds

Kagran lettuce: Johnny's Selected Seeds
Ithaca head lettuce: Joseph Harris Seeds
Elite onion: Stokes Seeds Inc.
Italian Red Bottle onion: Nichols Garden Nursery

Moira tomato: Johnny's Selected Seeds
Moreton and Supersonic tomatoes: Harris Seeds
Sweet 100 tomato: Harris Seeds, and Thompson and Morgan
Wonderful sweet corn: Harris Seeds

Hybrid vs. Open-Pollinated Varieties

Current seed catalogues list hybrid varieties in many kinds of vegetables. Since many gardeners find themselves perplexed at seed-ordering time, it may be useful to consider what hybrid seed is, and when it is a good choice.

Hybrid seed is the first-generation result of a cross between two highly inbred parent plants. Plants grown from this seed (the F_1 generation, in botanical terms) often exhibit what botanists call hybrid vigor—marked superiority to both parent plants. Preparation of hybrid seed involves not only hand-pollination and, in some cases, removal of the pollen-bearing parts of the flower to prevent unscheduled fertilization, but also the deliberate inbreeding of the parent plants over the course of several previous generations to intensify their characteristics and purify the strain.

Non-hybrid seed (also called open-pollinated, standard, or regular) on the other hand, may have been isolated to prevent undesirable cross-pollination, but it has not been hand-bred or purposefully crossed. Plants grown from non-hybrid seed will be like the parents unless some random crossing (not likely in commercially grown seed) has taken place. Hybrid plants, though, produce seed that grows into "throwbacks"—plants that display more of the weak or ingrown qualities of their ancestors than the generous endowment of desirable characteristics possessed by their parents.

The genetic manipulation of plants that produces hybrid forms has given us many improved vegetable varieties. Some of these new hybrids yield exceptionally well. Others are early bearing or large or long-standing or flavorful. A few contain extra vitamins or protein. A good many have been bred for insect and/or disease resistance. All these good qualities are appreciated by the home gardener. The uniformity that is often a hallmark of hybrid vegetables is generally of no importance to the backyard grower. It is a valuable trait for the commercial grower, however, as is the simultaneous, rather than gradual, ripening that has been bred into some varieties of hybrid seed sold to large growers who depend on machine harvesting.

Size, flavor, texture, earliness, yield, and disease/insect resistance, then, are the main advantages offered by hybrid seed. Few hybrids can boast superiority in *all* of these categories, of course. Your local growing conditions and family preferences will determine which of these qualities are most important to you. Earliness, for example, may be more valuable to the northern gardener than to one below the Mason-Dixon line who is able to winter-over hardy vegetables. The gardener in a warmer climate, on the other hand, will sometimes have more need for an insect-resistant strain. Apart from the sense of pride to be gained from raising a whopper, large size in vegetables may be less desirable for a couple or small family than steady yield.

Disadvantages of planting hybrids include the higher price of hybrid seed and the fact that it doesn't pay to save seed from this year's hybrid plants to start next year's garden. Seed produced by some hybrid plants is sterile. Even fertile seed, though, will generally grow into plants that are quite ordinary, or—often—markedly inferior to the parent. While it's true that you *might* get something worthwhile from seed produced by a garden-raised hybrid vegetable, the chances are that you won't, and you certainly can't count on the quality of your crop, in any case.

There is good reason for the higher cost of hybrid seed, especially that of tomatoes, eggplant, and other commonly self-pollinating vegetables in which the pollen-bearing portion of the flower must be removed by hand before its pollen is ripe enough to be shed, and pollen from the desired parent variety manually applied to the pollen-receptive parts of the flower. There is, so far, no substitute for the human hand in hybridizing tomatoes.

Although a few hybrid plants have been developed especially for their nutritional qualities, there is some evidence that—especially in the case of corn—the older, open-pollinated varieties are higher in protein. It must be noted, though, that soil quality is also known to affect protein content in some cases, just as it can affect size and flavor.

Another consideration has to do with what might be termed genetic conservation. There is a danger that, in the pursuit of ever more refined and spectacular hybrid varieties, the old dependable native strains of certain vegetables might be allowed to peter out, and the genetic base of commonly planted strains might become precariously narrow. That's not just a theoretical concern. The 1970 epidemic of corn blight affected only T-cytoplasm corn, but that was about 20 per cent of the U.S. crop of field corn, all of which had been developed from plants that shared a relatively narrow (inbred) genetic base.

Choosing between hybrid and open-pollinated seed, then, involves considerations not only of plant performance, food value, and cost, but also the larger question of maintaining basic native varieties of favorite vegetables. Some gardeners plant only open-pollinated seed as a matter of principle. Others (and I am one of this group, while sympathizing fully with the open-pollinated school), plant some selected hybrids for special purposes, but rely mainly on nonhybrid seed. I do gratefully use hybrid seed for my crops of spring broccoli and some, but not all, peppers, cantaloupes, corn, cucumbers, and onions. All my cabbage, carrots, tomatoes, winter squash, eggplant, pumpkins, and cauliflower are raised from non-hybrid seed. In general, I've chosen hybrid seed only when it distinctly outperformed the standard kinds in my garden. And when I find a new open-pollinated variety, like the admirable Black Magic zucchini, that performs as well or better than my old hybrid choice, then I gratefully switch to the open-pollinated seed.

MARCH

Starting Seeds Indoors

The days are longer now, even if a chill wind does blow over the snow heaps that remain in the yard. Winter may, in fact, have the last word with a thick, heavy March snow. No matter. Seeds have been arriving in the mail, and spring can begin indoors with seedlings on the windowsill. It's time to plant pepper, tomato, cabbage, lettuce, and other transplantable vegetables in the house. These head-start seedlings will give you early harvests of varieties often unavailable at your local greenhouse. Equally important, the act of committing seeds to soil and tending new green sprouts helps to cheer away the late winter doldrums and carry us through to the spring the calendar promises.

Start seedlings of cool weather crops like cabbage, lettuce, broccoli, and cauliflower in early to mid-March, tomatoes and eggplant toward the end of the month in most states north of the Mason-Dixon line. Peppers, which grow somewhat more slowly, can be started early in March. Marigolds, snapdragons, calendulas, and other flowering garden-border annuals may be planted indoors any time during the month. It's still too early for heat-loving plants like cucumber, squash, and melons; save those for early May so they'll be sturdy but not too leggy when you set them out in warm settled weather. Celery, leeks, and onions are usually planted in February, but early March is not too late. If you're counting on windowsill light to bring those seedlings along, start a bit on the late side; pale, weak, winter sunlight tends to make seedlings grow straggly in their search for more light.

Begin by rounding up containers. Cut-down milk cartons and derelict cake tins make good homes for seedlings, but the best planters are flats—shallow, open boxes made of scrap wood. Sides should be 2 to 3 inches high, and the slats you nail across the bottom should be spaced ⅛ inch apart so that water can drain.

Line each flat with one or two sheets of newspaper to retain the soil, but don't let the paper protrude above the soil line; it's an effective wick that will quickly dry out the soil.

Now fill each flat with your favorite seed-starting medium. I prefer a mixture of equal parts of vermiculite, perlite, and either milled sphagnum moss or sifted compost. You can also use plain vermiculite or potting soil, especially if you lighten the soil with vermiculite or spread a layer of it on top. But you should not use soil straight from the garden. No matter how good your soil is, it tends to harden when kept inside in small containers.

Next moisten the seed-starting mixture in the flats, scatter the seeds (not too thickly!), and cover them with no more than ¼ inch of a fine soil mixture. Firm this layer gently over the seeds to ensure good contact. Now cover the flats with sheets of damp newspaper or recycled plastic bags and keep them in a warm place. Warmth and moisture promote germination. Each kind of seed has an optimum temperature range for best germination, but it's generally safe to aim for 70–80 degrees.

Time required for germination depends on the temperature and also on the kind of seed. Sprouts are slower to show if it's quite cool. Cabbage family seeds usually sprout within a week. Peppers can take three weeks, tomatoes two. Keep watching the flats for three reasons: (1) you'll want to put the new seedlings under light as soon as possible after they sprout so they don't develop long weak stems; (2) flats occasionally need to be remoistened if kept in a very warm place; (3) mold formation on the soil surface, which can hinder germination, is a sign of insufficient air circulation. Remove the cover for half a day but don't let the seedbed dry out.

Young seedlings need at least fourteen hours of light each day, which can be supplied by window light, fluorescent tube lights, or a greenhouse. You don't need special plantlight tubes to raise non-flowering plants; one warm-white and one cool-white tube on each fluorescent fixture is adequate for seedlings. If you keep your seedlings on a windowsill, be sure to turn them every few days to keep them straight. Left in the same position, they'll lean toward the light.

Garden stores and some seed catalogues carry special plant-light fixtures and stands. The least expensive, most adaptable way to arrange a light environment for your plants is to purchase standard utility fixtures at hardware stores or through mail order from Sears, Ward's, or Penney's. If at all possible, purchase a fixture that will accommodate at least two 4-foot 40-watt bulbs . . . for two reasons:

(1) Plant-light space is like compost; you never have enough.
(2) The extreme ends of the tubes give off less light than the center portion. Short tubes, with proportionately more of their length radiating less intense light, are less efficient.

Plants need light rays from both ends of the spectrum. Red rays stimulate leaf and stem growth, and blue rays regulate enzyme and respiratory processes. The usual cool-white fluorescent bulb emits rays concentrated on the blue end of the spectrum. Warm-white tubes give off more red rays. Most experienced indoor gardeners I've consulted have recommended pairing one cool-white and one warm-white tube. When we started using fluorescent lights, we bought the special wide-spectrum plant-growing tubes, but we are replacing them with the less costly ordinary tubes as they burn out. (Whenever an *expert* advises me to simplify, believe me—I take him seriously.)

Light intensity may be varied by changing the distance between the plant and the light, or by rotating plants from center to end position. In our experience, seedlings grow best when kept as close as possible to the lights, just short of touching, and no more than three inches away. You can either change the position of the fixture by suspending it higher or lower on chains, or boost the plants to a higher position by setting the flats on egg cartons, cans, or other household findings. Allow 15–20 watts of light per square foot of growing space.

Put the seedlings under lights as soon as they germinate. Plants growing under fluorescent lights thrive when given sixteen hours of light a day. Many gardeners cut that to fourteen hours to conserve energy—with continuing good results, especially with nonflowering seedling plants. The plant can make use of light up to about nineteen hours a day, but light, like fertilizer, has its upper limits of effectiveness. While receiving light, plants accumulate carbohydrates synthesized from carbon dioxide and water, but they need a period of darkness to convert these stored compounds into a form they can use to build new tissue. The dark period is vital; don't skip it. Since I habitually let my spring plantings outrun my light space, I have been growing seedlings in rotating twelve-hour shifts under lights that are never turned off. I cover the seedlings when they are not under lights. This far-from-ideal arrangement still gives me good seedlings, but I'll admit I'm looking for an odd corner to set up a fourth fixture.

The high temperatures required for germination aren't necessary for growing seedlings. Most cool-weather plants do well at 55–60 degrees; tomatoes, peppers, and eggplant thrive at 60–70 degrees.

Young seedlings need room to grow and water and food to grow on. Thin young plants to stand two inches apart. Water them when soil begins to dry. (Poke into the soil with your finger or judge by the weight of the container.) Don't let seedlings wilt. Some, like eggplant and cauliflower, will fail to bear well later although they may seem to recover. Feed seedlings weekly with a dilute solution of plant food. I like to use fish emulsion.

Remember, though, that a plant that isn't growing has little need for fertilizer. If a well-fertilized seedling is doing poorly, check for other problems rather than pouring on yet another dose of plant food. A greenish scum (algae) appearing on the pots or soil surface indicates overfeeding and possibly overwatering too. Before you set out plants in the garden, allow them to harden off for a few hours outdoors in a protected spot on warm days, or put them in a cold-frame until all danger of frost is past.

It's a good rule of thumb to transplant all seedlings (except melons, squash, and cucumbers) into a roomier container with richer soil when they have their second true leaves. I use a mixture of

We start our plants in flats (shallow, open boxes made of scrap wood). When they develop their true leaves, we transplant them into larger flats or peat pots. The only plants we seed directly into peat pots are those that do not take kindly to transplanting: cantaloupes, squash, and the like.

No single soil mixture is "right" for growing seedlings; there is a variety of effective combinations to choose from. We tend to use what we have available here, so our mixture is never exactly the same two years in a row. Generally, though, we follow Thalassa Cruso's recommended potting mixture proportions. Equal amounts of each of the following: (1) leaf mold *or* purchased potting soil; (2) shredded sphagnum *or* peat moss (wet before mixing); (3) perlite (expanded volcanic rock) *or* sharp sand. Mix well in a large tub, and firm the potting soil well around each transplanted seedling.

one part compost, one part loamy soil, and one half part each perlite and vermiculite. Transplanting gives you a chance to select the seedlings for root development, vigor, and type. Keep only the best ones. Then help them to maintain steady growth by watering regularly, fertilizing weekly, and giving them plenty of light, until it's time to plant them outside. You can set cabbage, lettuce, broccoli and such out in the garden about three or four weeks before your last expected frost date. Wait until just after your last frost for peppers and tomatoes, and keep the eggplant on the porch for still another week.

Sturdy-stemmed, well-leafed plants . . . deep green, early to flower, with compact branching and well-developed roots . . . that's the ideal to aim for, here at the growing edge of a new gardening season. Plants raised under lights should qualify on most of those counts, provided they are grown in good soil and judiciously fed and watered.

The Cold Frame

"The growing season is never long enough. No matter where they live, gardeners are forever searching for ways to earn another few weeks, another month."
James Underwood Crockett

A cold frame is a simple device that will help you to capture an extra month of growth at each end of the season—an early start in spring, an extension into fall. It can also be used in winter to store vegetables like Brussels sprouts and cauliflower, chill tulips for forcing, and protect half-hardy plants. In the summer, with the sash propped open, the frame can be covered with a short length of snow fencing to shade a bed of lettuce from the hot sun. Cold frames are something like compost: once you start using them, you want more. Happily, they are easy to make, you can use recycled materials, and even a small garden has room for at least one frame.

The classic cold frame is simply a bottomless box with sloping sides, covered by a hinged, transparent lid. Wood is commonly used for the box. Locust, cedar, cypress, Osage orange, and redwood are ideal decay-resistant woods for use in contact with the soil. You should treat pine, oak, and other rot-prone woods with linseed oil or Cuprinol (green) before setting them in the ground. (Toxic wood preservatives like creosote, pentachlorophenol, and mercury compounds should not be used in plant-growing structures.) Cold frames made of stone, brick, concrete block, adobe, or poured concrete are durable and offer the added advantage of heat-retaining mass, but obviously they can't be moved. Excavation for such structures should extend several inches below the frost line so they won't crack when the soil heaves.

Solar cold frames like those designed by the staff of the Rodale Experimental Farm and by Leandre Poisson of Solar Survival make use of double glazing, insulation extending below soil level, and sometimes thermal mass to produce an environment that will encourage the active growth of some cold-weather vegetables even in winter.

There are so many discarded storm windows kicking around that it is rarely necessary to buy new materials to glaze a conventional cold frame. If you can't latch onto an old window or two, you can use a fiberglass panel or a wood frame covered with a sheet of clear polyethylene. Cold frames are usually about 3 feet wide; wider frames are cumbersome to work in, and narrower frames make for crowding. Customary cold-frame length is 6 feet —never less than 4 feet, or the sides shade the bed too much— but much longer frames are fine if there is enough space. The ideal site is a southern exposure on a slight, well-drained slope, and if there's a building on the north side to ward off chill winds, so much the better. The back board of the cold frame is usually 12 to 18 inches high and at least 6 inches higher than the front board. The frame is most effective as a solar device when the sun's rays strike the glass at a 90-degree angle. Many gardeners slant the glass top at 45 degrees to catch early spring sunshine. A steeper 52-degree angle, perhaps more appropriate for a solar cold frame, will capture more energy from the low winter sun.

You can fasten the frame sides together with nails, bolts, hooks, or screws. Reinforce the corners by nailing them to 2-by-2 interior stakes, by using metal corner braces, or by bracing them with exterior 1-by-3s. If you want the frame to be portable, attach handles or assemble it with hooks at each corner and let it sit on top of the ground. But if you want maximum plant protection, sink the frame 8 to 10 inches in the ground and bank hay or earth around it. Attach the windows to the back board with 2 or 3 hinges.

For spring seedlings, ordinary garden soil of good tilth will serve well in the cold frame. Avoid heavy fertilizing of early spring plantings; the sappy growth that results is vulnerable to frost damage. Soil can be richer for fall-grown plants, but avoid feeding them around the time of first frost, or as Anne Moffat warns in her article ''Life After Frost'' [*Horticulture*, September 1978], the plants will ''miss important clues to the hardening process.'' For the same reason, let fall crops experience some chilling before giving them full cold-frame protection.

You'll want to check the cold-frame temperature daily when seasons are changing. Steady sun can cook plants under glass. Vent the frame by propping up the lid when the interior temperature is too high for the plants. Crockett's guidelines are helpful here: hardy plants thrive at 45 to 60 degrees; half-hardy crops prefer 50 to 60 degrees, and tender plants need 60 to 75 degrees. When the outdoor temperature is 60 degrees or more, it's safe to raise the lid all the way. At 40 degrees you can prop it up a few inches. If night temperatures will dip into the 30s, though, it's a good idea to close the sash in midafternoon to retain the soil-stored warmth. (The Solar-Gro, a redwood and acrylic cold frame developed by Garden Way, has a temperature-sensing vent that opens automatically when the interior gets hot.)

Insulating the cold frame from the outside on frigid nights may give you a few extra days of salad harvests. Pile old blankets, door mats, leaf-stuffed bags, or hay over the sash and bank the perimeter of the frame with hay, earth, or leaves. Tacking on an extra layer of glazing, which can be simply a sheet of clear plastic, will increase the greenhouse effect, trapping warmth in the cold frame by blocking conduction and convection to the outside. According to Conrad Heeschen [*The Solar Greenhouse Book*, edited by James McCullagh. Rodale Press, Emmaus, Pennsylvania. 328 pp.], a second layer of glazing can cut conductive heat loss by a good 34 per cent.

Row Spacing

As we begin to lay out the garden rows, at least on paper, the annual dilemma confronts us; how can we, in our planning, allow room for cultivation of the vegetables without wasting great gobs of growing space? If we leave space for the rototiller to pass between each row, we're left with wide-open middles that will not produce any crops. But if, on the other hand, we space all our rows foot-width or so apart, we are committed to hand hoeing and/or mulching for the season. Is there a way to have the best of both worlds? Maybe, maybe not. There *are* a number of workable options open to you, though.

Before we discuss those options, let's first consider some of the factors that influence row spacing.
(1) The nature of the plant. Well-disciplined rows of carrots or beets can be planted closer together than rambling tomatoes—or closer than tall, robust plants like collards or Brussels sprouts.
(2) Fertility of the soil. If you do try to cram a concentration of vegetables into your garden patch, you will need to be generous in enriching the soil with dug-in manures, mulches, and minerals.
(3) The purposes of cultivation. The first is to suppress weeds. According to George Abraham, writing in *The Green Thumb Book of Fruit and Vegetable Gardening*, the average 50- by 50-foot vegetable

garden plot contains about 170 pounds of weed seeds. Weeds, then, will surely take over unless we take action—either to smother the weeds with mulch or to rout them out with the hoe or tiller. One way or another, we must—as Candide advised—cultivate our gardens.

The second purpose is to loosen and aerate the soil. Roots need oxygen, and most plants thrive better in ground that is porous rather than packed.

(4) Use of mulch. Mulch can replace cultivation in many parts of the garden when the growing season is in full swing, but since heat-loving crops such as tomatoes, cantaloupe, and squash, should not be mulched until the soil is thoroughly warm, there is a period of weeks during the early part of the season when the space between these plants must be cultivated. At least, that is the case in our garden. I usually need to rototill twice between our tomato, pepper, squash, soybean, and eggplant rows before piling on the mulch.

(5) Width of tiller or other cultivating tool. The space between rows that will be rototilled should be about 6 to 8 inches wider than the tiller's tine-to-tine measurement. Some front-end tillers can be modified to work narrow rows. To adjust your tiller to fit between rows spaced as close as 8 inches apart, author Gene Logsdon suggests that you remove the outer sets of tines and reverse the position of the inner tines so that their prongs face the center. For rows that are planted a bit farther apart, you can either remove just the outer tines of the rototiller, or reverse them as suggested above for the inner tines, so that the blades point inward.

(6) Vulnerability of roots. When cultivating the soil, whether by hoe, tiller, wheel-hoe, or iron rake, take care not to damage plant roots. Caution is especially necessary in a rainy season when roots remain close to the soil surface.

Now for the options. You need not treat the whole vegetable patch the same, of course. Most likely, you'll want to choose several of the following plans for use in different growing areas:

(1) Wide spaces between the rows, (30 to 40 inches) with cultivation by rototiller.

Easy to work.   ADVANTAGES

Leaves growing room for rambling vegetables.

Sometimes possible to sow cover crop between rows.

Wastes growing space, at least in early spring.   DISADVANTAGE

(2) Widely spaced rows (3 feet or more), with a quick-maturing crop planted between the rows. For example, we planted a row of Contender bush beans last year in the 6-foot space between our young tomato plants and a row of squash hills. By midsummer, the beans had yielded several pickings, and the squash and tomatoes had filled in the space. I mulched right over the beans when they finished bearing, just before the burgeoning squash and tomato vines took over.

Good use of space to gain an extra crop.   ADVANTAGES

Mulching works well if you have a good supply of material.

DISADVANTAGE: Some hand cultivation necessary in early stages.

(3) Widely spaced rows with mulch between them.

ADVANTAGES: Eliminates weeding in midsummer.

Mulch enriches soil, adds humus, cushions vegetables, retains moisture.

DISADVANTAGES: If garden is large, it may be difficult to accumulate enough mulch.

Some cultivation still necessary early in season, for heat-loving crops that should be mulched later.

(4) Drills (single-file rows) spaced 8 to 15 inches apart, with cultivation by hoe or modified front-end tiller, or mulched.

ADVANTAGES: More vegetables can be grown in a given area.

Well-planned companion plantings effective when vegetables grown close together.

DISADVANTAGE: Requires intensive tending—hoeing or careful placement of mulch.

(5) Wide bands of vegetables grown in rows 6 inches to 3 feet wide (depending on the vegetable) with rows separated by a tiller-wide space or by a mulched path.

ADVANTAGES: More efficient use of space than single-file drill.

Easy to harvest vegetables.

Vegetables help to shade out weeds, keep soil moist.

DISADVANTAGES: Easy to plant such areas unevenly.

Careful weeding and thinning necessary at first.

We have been planting 6- to 10-inch-wide bands of carrots, beets, herbs, spinach, garlic, and lettuce, and 2- to 3-foot-wide swaths of peas, with fine results.

(6) Strips of sod or cover crop (rye or clover) the width, or double the width, of your lawnmower—alternated with strips of vegetable garden 3 to 4 feet wide.

ADVANTAGES: Easy to reach vegetables from all sides without compacting soil.

Good possibilities for soil improvement and crop rotation with alternating cover crops.

Easier, quicker to mow grass than to cultivate ground.

Pleasing visual effect when well cared for.

DISADVANTAGES: Requires fairly intensive maintenance.

Grass may encroach on vegetable territory.

To prepare garden in spring, you must either rototill or hand dig. Plowing would be impossible.

This method is probably best used in a small, rather intensive garden.

As you can see, there is something good to be said for each of these methods of row spacing. There is no "right" or "wrong" way—and none of the options I've mentioned is perfect. But if you were to pin me down to selecting the two methods that would most effectively utilize your garden space without adding too greatly to your cultivating chores, I would have to single out the use of wide bands of non-spreading vegetables like carrots, beets, lettuce, and others (in preference to narrow drills of those vegetables) and the planting of quick-maturing crops between two widely spaced rows of later-bearing vegetables.

Next time there's a lull in the wind, I'll be out there measuring the rototiller, pacing off the garden, and evaluating the pile of mulch. You too? May your spring come early, and all your rows grow straight!

Intensive Raised-Bed Gardens

This year I must plant a smaller garden, and that won't be easy. Having steadily expanded the size of our vegetable operation over the past twenty years, I've gotten into the habit of planting three gardens covering about half an acre of land, raising everything from asparagus to zucchini, with several varieties of each. But now, since we have a major building project planned for the summer, I must cut back on my garden area in order to be available to help. The garden size restriction will only be temporary, and I fully expect to go back to hoeing at least two gardens in a year or so when I'm not needed on the construction crew. To be honest, I don't relish the prospect of trimming the garden, but I realize in my more sensible moments that the necessity for doing so might be a very good opportunity for me to see how much I can grow in a limited space. And so I'm trying to approach the cut-back as an experiment, rather than a restriction.

In the course of my reading to discover how other gardeners have handled such space and time limitations, I've come across John Jeavons' book *How to Raise More Vegetables than You Thought Possible on Less Land than You Can Imagine*. Jeavons, a disciple of master gardener Alan Chadwick, who introduced the Biodynamic/French Intensive method of gardening to California in 1966, describes a system of gardening that has its roots in the past, but that offers practical relevance for today and the future. The methods Jeavons advocates are not for everyone. Intensive hand labor, particularly in preparing the bed, is vital to the success of the method. The majority of gardeners, I'd venture to guess, would rather rototill a large plot than hand-dig a small one.

The results of this intensive raised-bed method are impressive. Data gathered over a three-year period of working with test gardens indicate that intensive raised beds can produce four times as much food per acre as conventional, mechanized, chemical-based commercial agriculture, while consuming only one per cent of the energy and half of the water used in commercial operations.

The implications are far-reaching. People who, for lack of land, time, or water must now buy their vegetables, *can* grow them in tiny, lovingly tended plots. In water-poor California, where three fourths of the cropland is irrigated, adoption of this method might make more backyard gardens feasible, even in the face of dropping water tables and municipal water shortages.

Since the method works, it isn't really important what it's called, but the name adopted by its practitioners points up the historical grounding of the Biodynamic/French Intensive philosophy. The French Intensive technique, developed near Paris in the 1890s, depended on the use of 18-inch-deep beds of horse manure. Biodynamic gardening, worked out in the 1920s by philosopher Rudolph Steiner and his followers, brought back the ancient Greek observation that plants grow well in pockets of loose soil left by landslides. Biodynamic principles emphasize the relationship of plants to each other and to their surroundings, leading to heavy reliance on companion planting, composting, and planting by moon sign. In combining these gardening practices, British gardener Alan Chadwick worked out a unified system utilizing small beds of rich, porous, well-aerated soil in which vegetable plants may be set close together in a solid block, rather than in rows. The plants form what Jeavons calls a living mulch, effectively smothering most weeds and maintaining soil moisture.

The backbone of the Biodynamic/French Intensive method is the deep double-digging of the whole plot. That sounds like a prescription for a backache, and it is, indeed, hard work, but Jeavons contends that the well-prepared raised beds require less work throughout the gardening season than those tended by conventional methods. Weeds, for example, are very easily uprooted from the deep, loose soil.

A bed should be no wider than 3 to 5 feet, so that its center can be reached easily from both sides. Jeavons estimates that a 5-by-20-foot plot would require a total of six to twelve hours for initial preparation. Briefly summarized, his description of the soil preparation process goes like this:

(1) First, use a spading fork to loosen the soil to the depth of a foot and then let it rest for a day. If your soil is heavy clay, you may need to soak the soil to soften it for digging. Wait two days after soaking before you dig, so the soil won't be too wet when you work it.

(2) Next, dig in 1 to 3 cubic yards of compost or aged manure for each 100-square-foot garden bed. Let the soil rest for one day if it's heavy clay.

(3) Now, add 8 to 24 cubic feet of compost to the bed and double-dig the entire area. Double-digging is an unfamiliar technique to many American gardeners. It is neither quick nor easy. Thus forewarned, take up your spade (one with a flat blade is best) and dig a one-foot-wide trench, one foot deep, across the bed. Save the dug-up soil in a wheelbarrow to fill in your final trench on the other end of the bed.

Then dig a second trench next to the first one, using the topsoil to fill in the first trench. Proceed in this way across the bed, filling in your last trench with the soil saved from the first. Again, let heavy clay soil settle for a day.

After the first digging, work your way down the trench once more, loosening the hard-packed subsoil as deeply as you can by cutting in and wiggling the shovel. You don't remove soil on this second digging, just loosen it.

(4) Next, sprinkle 2 to 4 pounds of bone meal, 2 to 4 pounds of wood ashes, and 2 to 4 cubic feet of manure over the surface of the bed. Using your digging fork, mix these materials lightly into the top 3 inches of soil. Pat the bed into shape, making 45-degree slopes toward the top surface on each side. In new beds with soil still in need of improvement, you might need to rake up a 2-inch-high ridged edge all around the bed to control runoff. Erosion is more likely to occur if the sides of the bed are at right angles to the soil surface. The incorporation of air and additional organic material should make your bed 4 to 10 inches higher than the surrounding soil.

(5) Finally, plant seeds or seedlings in a solid block clear across the bed, using the usual spacing between plants, with no wide spaces between the rows. (Biodynamically grown seedlings, according to Chadwick's method, are transplanted into better soil each time they are moved.)

Avoid stepping on the bed after it's prepared, for compaction of the soil harms plant roots. If you must set foot in the garden, step on a wide board laid across the soil.

After the first year, recommended yearly preparation of the bed begins at step 3 above and proceeds through step 5.

If you intend to follow the Biodynamic/French Intensive method to the letter, you must forget all you have learned about the advisability of watering gardens deeply but infrequently. Jeavons and his colleagues recommend, instead, a daily light watering, meant to duplicate the effect of a natural rainfall, which carries air and traces of atmospheric plant nutrients to the plant roots growing in this special loose soil. Most plants grown in intensive raised beds, according to the BD/FI folks, should be watered from above with a fine spray. Exceptions are the rot- and mildew-prone tomatoes, squash, peas, and melons, which should be watered at soil level.

Reconciling this daily watering with the claim that the method saves water seems contradictory at first, until you remember that much irrigation water, spread as it is over a wide area, is lost to evaporation. These intensive beds are usually watered about two hours before sunset to avoid the evaporation and mildew problems that might be associated with earlier or later waterings. In addition, the cultivated area is small, making it practical to use waste water left from household use if necessary. At any rate, enough water should be given to produce a moist zone 2 inches deep.

Where to Find More Information on Intensive Gardening

How to Grow More Vegetables than You Thought Possible on Less Land than You Can Imagine, by John Jeavons, (published by Ecology Action in 1974) is available from Ecology Action/Common Ground, 2225 El Camino Real, Palo Alto, California 94306

Another source of information on intensive gardening is

Success with Small Food Gardens Using Special Intensive Methods, by Louise Riotte, published by Garden Way Publishing, Charlotte, Vermont 05445

Jeavons closes his book with the recommendation that the reader try at least one small intensive raised bed—say, 3 by 3 feet —as an experiment. See how much you can grow in an intensively planted bed. Once the plot is dug, it should be easy to tend and, if you can keep the area free of encroaching grass, it ought to be very productive.

Protein Patch

The small farmer's proudest dinnertime boast is his casual remark that "the whole meal came off the place." While most of us depend on some home-raised animal products to round out that meal, it is possible for a determined gardener to make the same boast—that a complete, balanced meal was grown in the garden row. You needn't be a virtuoso gardener to grow a meal that supplies the family's protein requirement and tastes good. While you may not plan to dine solely off the garden—few of us do— you might be surprised to find out how much high-quality protein can be grown from seed.

In any discussion of vegetable protein, the soybean must come first. Its protein content measures an amazing 34.1 grams per 100-gram edible portion for dried soybeans. Even the immature green soys contain 10.9 grams of protein per 100-gram edible portion. Soybean protein is more complete than that of any other vegetable, approaching meat in its value.

The soybean plant is a frost-tender legume that should not be planted much before June 1 in the average (is there such a thing?) northern garden. You can safely move that date up a week or so. Those who live in the far north should consider soybeans a gamble. If your growing season falls short of one hundred days, choose one of the earlier-maturing soybean varieties, such as Fiskeby (70 days), Envy (75 days), Early Green Bush (85 days), Prize (85 days), or Butterbean (90 days).

Like most legumes, the soybean draws heavily on the soil's reserve of lime. We try to give our soybean rows an extra dusting of dolomite lime before planting. To increase both the yield and the amount of nitrogen left in the soil by the plants, treat the seeds with inoculant powder (one that is specific for soybeans; they require a different strain of *Rhizobium* than that used to inoculate garden peas and beans).

The usual method of planting soys is to scatter seed 2–3 inches apart in a shallow furrow, leaving 3 feet between rows. If you're feeling adventurous, you might like to try growing a 3–4-inch-wide row of the 2–3-foot-high bushy beans—a more efficient way to use the space as long as you keep the plants thinned to a 3-inch spacing. To hasten germination, soak the seeds in lukewarm water for half a day before planting.

Pods start to form on the soybean plants in late August, after blossoming. They are ready to pick—for green soybeans—when the pods are swollen with the beans. Try a few to see whether they're large enough to be worth your while before picking a lot. To pick, you can either pluck the largest pods from the plant, leaving the smaller ones to develop, or cut the entire row with a sickle and pick off the pods in comfort while sitting in the waning September sun. Save the stalks for your animals. Our goats love them, and the hens pick out every last soybean that we miss.

The fine hairs covering the pods insulate the mature bean within from damage by light frost. The leaves are more vulnerable.

Processing the green soybeans takes some time; consider it as a well-earned gardener's rest. Half a bushel a day is our usual quota. Steam the beans in one inch of boiling water in a tightly covered kettle for 5 to 8 minutes. Turn them out onto a cookie sheet to cool, and pop the beans into a dish, saving the pods for the goats, sheep, or cows.

Some of our favorite garden meals depend on green soybeans: Sautéed zucchini, corn pudding, and buttered green soybeans; Baked sweet potatoes, steamed green soybeans, and sliced fresh tomatoes; Soup made with onions, corn, green soys, and potatoes; Tossed green salad mixed with toasted sunflower or pumpkin seeds and cold cooked soybeans; Salad made with cold cooked soybeans, potatoes, and homemade dressing.

The easiest way to save dry soybeans is to cut the plants when the pods have dried but before they shatter, place them on a clean sheet, and thresh them by stepping on them or flailing them. Store the beans, well covered, in a cool, dry place.

Dried soybeans make good baked beans, but since they are so low in starch they don't mush up and thicken the gravy as the traditional navy beans do. When using them for baked beans, we generally mix them half-and-half with regular dried beans. A handful of the beans adds substance and staying power to almost any soup; the dried beans, sprouted, are more nourishing yet.

No doubt you already grow peas and snap beans in your garden. In frozen or fresh form, peas rate at 5.1 grams protein per 100-gram portion, beans at 1.7 grams per 100, and limas at 6.2 grams per 100. For the dried legumes the protein content zooms to 24.2 grams per 100 for raw dry peas, 22.3 for dried beans, and 20.4 for dried limas. You may want to put in an extra row of beans or some Wando heat-resistant peas to eat in dried form. Simply leave the pods on the vine until the plants are dry but not brittle. Then hang or spread the plants until the seeds are thoroughly dry. Thresh them out and store them, well covered, in a cool, dry place. Pole beans and tall-growing peas dry faster than low-growing

The figures for protein content were taken from the *USDA Handbook of the Nutritional Contents of Foods*. Some authorities credit soybeans with a protein content as high as 40 per cent.

bush types because there is usually better air circulation around the pod.

Pumpkin seed kernels are a tasty by-product of the orange fruit we use for pies. There are varieties of pumpkin and squash, though, that have been bred to produce seed without hulls. These kinds are just as tasty as usual pumpkin seed and far easier to eat. The seeds are delicious as a snack or a garnish—toasted, for example, and sprinkled on a casserole or served with soup. They can be used to complement the less-complete protein of rice, corn, beans, or wheat.

Choose from:

LADY GODIVA PUMPKIN
A pale yellow, green-striped pumpkin bearing large, delicious, shell-free seeds. The flesh is coarse and not useable for the table, but perfectly good for barnyard animals.

Triple Treat Pumpkins from Burpee bear medium-sized orange-fruits with good edible flesh and hull-less seeds.

EAT-ALL SQUASH
A New Hampshire* development bearing squash that resemble small butternuts with good sweet flesh and hull-less seeds on five-foot vines.

SWEETNUT
A bush-type squash, also* from New Hampshire, with edible flesh and naked seeds. A good choice for the small garden.

Plant the seed in hills four feet apart in good warm soil. Mulch only after the soil is thoroughly warm—just before the vines start to wander—and elevate the fruit on cans or boxes to hasten ripening, if you're in a race with Jack Frost. A dark mulch is particularly efficient at absorbing solar heat and warming the soil. We prefer recycled makeshifts—such as old carpet with a black rubber back, reversed—to the admittedly effective shiny black plastic.

Other garden plants such as corn, potatoes, peanuts, sunflowers, and small grains (occasionally grown in small patches for hand threshing), may also contribute significant amounts of protein to a meal, especially when combined so that the amino-acid deficiencies of one food are offset by the complementary amino-acid content of another food. For more information on combining different vegetable-protein foods, read *Diet for a Small Planet* by Frances Moore Lappé. And keep on hoeing. The vegetables we raise are more than side dishes.

* No longer commercially available

WHERE TO GET SEEDS

Early Soybeans
Hakucho, Altona—Johnny's
    Selected Seeds
Early Green Bush—Stokes Seeds,
    Inc.
Pickett—Park Seed Co.
Kanrich—Charles Hart Seed Co.

*Midseason and later varieties
carried by:*
Johnny's Selected Seeds
Henry Field's
Burpee Seeds
Thompson and Morgan
Burgess Seed Co.
Nichols Garden Nursery
Gurney Seed and Nursery Co.

*Hull-less-seeded Pumpkin
(Lady Godiva)*
Burpee Seeds
Joseph Harris, Inc.
Stokes Seeds, Inc.

Comfrey

When we started homesteading in earnest, we set aside a corner of our acre for a comfrey patch. Disenchantment with the sort of gimmicky tool that promises to perform six functions—but does none of them well—had, perhaps, left us with a certain skepticism about any claim that a single thing will serve a long list of purposes. We had heard and read convincing accounts of the many ways comfrey could be used, though, and were impressed by reports of its high nutritional value and its healing properties.

Could it be folklore? Wishful thinking? A natural-living fad? We decided to plant enough comfrey to give it a thorough test. Our order of 150 roots arrived in late fall, and we planted them—3 feet apart each way and 3 to 4 inches deep—with a raw wind in our faces. The root cuttings, which come in 2- to 6-inch lengths, produced strong plants the following spring. Some one-inch nubbins broken off from larger roots even grew into good plants. Once established, the extremely deep-rooted perennial crowns grow rosettes of somewhat hairy, long leaves, which may be harvested every two or three weeks from May until fall frost. The roots don't spread, beyond producing neat offsets encircling the original crown, but they do persist strongly, so comfrey should be planted in a permanent patch, not in the annual garden bed. It thrives in most soils and is rarely visited—and scarcely ever damaged—by insects. Ordinary care such as mulching or tilling between the crowns, and occasional applications of manure and limestone, helps to promote rapid regrowth after cutting.

During the first season of growth (the spring following planting) we began harvesting the leaves in July. In subsequent years, we made our first cuttings in May. The roots, incidentally, may be planted at any time of year that the ground will admit a digging fork. We've even gotten away with transplanting whole plants in the height of summer, by taking a large ball of earth, trimming the leaves from each crown, and watering generously after replanting.

Repeated trials of comfrey in different forms, and for different purposes, have revealed that it is indeed useful, in at least six ways.

If you've ever spent the afternoon stretching fence with sleet needling your parka, shivered in the cold barn while a first freshener took her time delivering, collected maple sap in a steady drizzle, you know how comforting it is to return to a warm house with a teapot simmering on the woodstove. Comfrey tea, rich in the water-soluble vitamins and minerals in which comfrey abounds, will fortify you for the next round of wind-whipped tree planting or wood chopping. Alone, its flavor is rather bland, but mixed half and half with dried mint, it comes on tasty and refreshing.

This column was published in September 1977. In July 1978, the Henry Doubleday Research Association, a British gardening organization, reported a statement by alkaloid expert Dr. C.C.C. Culvenor of Australia that comfrey, in company with ragwort, crotolaria, borage and heliotrope, contains pyrrolizidine alkaloids thought to be capable of causing liver damage. Most herbalists took this news calmly and many continued to eat comfrey and to feed it to their animals. (Topical application was never questioned.) Many others, however, stopped eating comfrey until further studies could be done.

The most recent word from researchers, among them Dr. C. R. Crout of the University of Exeter, would seem to support the nonchalance of the traditional herbalists who continued to eat their comfrey. In earlier studies the substance was injected, but in actual practice it is either ingested or used topically, never injected. Extensive experience in animal feeding—not only with goats, which have rumens, but also with rabbits, pigs and horses, which lack rumens, would seem to indicate that the alkaloids that caused concern are destroyed or changed in the process of digestion.

HRDA Director Lawrence Hills' conclusion is that "as long as we stick to traditional methods and quantities, we are in no more danger from comfrey than were our ancestors."

TEA

VEGETABLE Unique among land plants as a source of vitamin B-12, comfrey also contains an amazing 21 to 33 per cent protein. Cook it like spinach, snip the leaves into soup, mix them with stronger-tasting wild greens, toss finely cut leaves into a salad, or eat the tightly rolled leaf, with midrib removed, as finger food. The root is good to eat too, either boiled in stew or made into chutney with apples, onions, vinegar, sweetening, and raisins.

FODDER We've fed comfrey to pigs, rabbits, goats, and chickens, and have read reports of its successful use with cows, sheep, and geese as well. For young pigs, up to 50 pounds or so, I whir the leaves in the blender with a cup or two of water. Older pigs get the leaves chopped or cut into ribbons with knife or scissors, moistened and well coated with dry powdered feed. If they haven't gorged themselves first on too much stale popcorn or sour milk, they eat it readily. Some goats relish green comfrey, others sniff the air to see what you might have in your *other* hand. All our goats have made short work of dried comfrey; in fact, a sick animal will sometimes accept the dried leaves when nothing else—not even apples or burnt cookies—will tempt her. Comfrey will not cause bloat or scours in young animals as some leguminous greens will do.

MEDICINE Its content of allantoin, a recognized healing agent that promotes cell growth, probably accounts for comfrey's effectiveness in promoting healing of both skin lesions and bone breaks. To treat an injury, soak the affected part in an infusion of the leaves, preferably fresh, or make a poultice and apply it warm. Drink the tea three times a day to aid in the knitting of broken bones. Be sure to include plenty of stems and midribs, which contain more allantoin than the leaves. Our son lost the fleshy tip of his index finger while operating a cement mixer the summer we were building our barn. Skillful plastic surgery restored the skin surface, but the surgeon warned he'd probably lack a fingernail. After daily soakings in warm comfrey tea, supplemented by applications of vitamin E oil, the nail grew back and the finger healed virtually unscarred. While it is impossible to determine exactly how much credit is due the comfrey treatment, it most certainly did no harm. We've also used comfrey poultices with some success on severe outbreaks of poison ivy, and routinely on the miscellaneous cuts and scratches that crop up regularly in a normally absent-minded family.

SOIL CONDITIONER Since comfrey roots reach depths of 8 to 10 feet, far below the range of the gardener's spade, they improve soil in two ways: (1) by bringing up minerals from the hard, but by no means infertile, subsoil, and (2) by forming channels that help to break up heavy clay and aerate the soil.

FERTILIZER AND COMPOST ACTIVATOR With its high protein content, comfrey is, obviously, a good source of nitrogen. It also contains significant amounts of potash and phosphorus. A solution of the leaves in water may be applied, just like manure tea, to growing plants and new compost piles. In the *Comfrey Report*, British comfrey expert Lawrence D. Hills describes the successful use of wilted comfrey leaves, put in the furrow under some soil at the rate of 1 to 1½ pounds of leaves to each foot of row, in fertilizing potatoes. Yields were comparable to those achieved with chemical fertilizers. For gardeners who lack a ready source of manure, that should be good news.

Sources of Comfrey Plants or Root Cuttings

Gurney Seed and Nursery Company
Nichols Garden Nursery
North Central Comfrey Producers

Compost

Although it might occasionally seem otherwise, compost is not the exclusive province of those who have made a deliberate choice to garden and live naturally. People were making compost long before they really grasped all the implications of what they were doing. For many of our grandparents, adding to the compost pile was just another routine household task like turning the mattresses and beating the rugs. (Then, of course, most town and many city dwellers had vegetable gardens, and farmers hadn't yet decided that it was more "efficient" to plant a single field crop and then buy their vegetables.) Even before people took a hand in the process, in fact ever since the world as we know it began, leaf-fall, fruit-drop, and tree-rot have contributed their slow but effective sheet-composting enrichment to the earth beneath.

It's only now that we are beginning to study and understand how the process works. The first thing we learn is that *we* aren't doing the composting. The active agents are micro-organisms—bacteria and fungi that work—each within its own temperature range—to reduce the rough matter we've piled up into an elemental form more readily available to plant roots. Our role is to gather the materials and arrange them in the right relationship to each other.

When you build a compost pile, it's important to provide the right conditions for these micro-organisms to do their work. The aerobic bacteria are the ones you want to encourage. They are able to break down organic matter more completely than the anaerobes, which thrive in the absence of air.

The first step in starting a compost pile, therefore, should be to lay down about a six-inch base of fine brush or coarse weeds to trap some air at the bottom.

The layers in your pile should consist of about six inches of green matter like weeds, leaves, pine needles, seaweed, fruit rinds, vegetable skins, peanut shells, tea bags, and such, topped by a thin layer of manure and a sprinkling of soil, then another six inches of green matter (either fresh or dried), and so on. Thin rather than thick zones of different materials make the full range

One acre composted is worth acres three,
At harvest thy barans shall declare it to thee.
Thomas Tusser, 1558

of necessary nutrients more readily available to the bacteria doing the work. Do not add fat or greasy scraps to the pile; they tend to coat the green matter and prevent decomposition.

In order to support the bacteria working in your pile, you should supply them with enough nitrogen to enable them to break down the carbonaceous matter in the compost. Practically speaking, this amounts to a good shovelful of manure for each four-to-six-inch layer of green matter. When adding materials like sawdust or straw that are high in carbon and slow to rot, toss on an extra shovelful of high nitrogen stuff like manure, feathers, alfalfa, or soybean or fish meal. You can use blood meal to activate the pile in the same way, but since it is concentrated, add it by the trowelful rather than the shovelful. You don't need any commercial "activator," "compost inoculant," or "stimulator." Like many other things that can be bought, they are not necessary. Your pile is already teeming with bacteria. All you need to do is to provide the conditions for the bacteria to thrive: moisture, air, and food.

Every eight inches or so, give the pile a sprinkling of water. You want it to be moist, but not sopping wet. Bacteria need moisture in order to live, but too much water drives out air and encourages the less desirable anaerobes.

Pile size can vary according to your convenience—but, generally speaking, it should be about five feet square and five feet high. Smaller piles cool and dry faster, but larger piles may admit too little air to the center and they are difficult to turn.

How do you turn a compost pile? By forking it apart and putting it back together again, putting the coarse material from the sides, which hasn't started to rot yet, in the center of the newly formed pile. The easiest way to turn a pile is to have an adjoining compost enclosure into which you can toss the partly decayed material, thus mixing and aerating it in the process of relocating it. Lacking an empty bin, you can fork the finished compost out onto a tarp, or right onto the ground, and rebuild the pile by forking it back into your enclosure. For more thorough mixing, turn the compost out into two piles and use the ingredients of the pile that you've taken off the top of the first heap to start the bottom of the new heap. You'll top the new pile, then, with the stuff that was on the bottom of the old one.

As you add successive layers, you might want to make a "stand-pipe" of some sort to incorporate air into the interior of the pile. There are several ways to do this, all suggested by Stu Campbell in his helpful book, *Let It Rot.*
(1) Bury a few old bean poles in the heap and withdraw them when you're done.
(2) Build in a metal rod or fence post and rotate it from time to time to make an air shaft.
(3) Ventilate the pile with a perforated plastic drainage pipe, a cylinder of wire mesh, or a bundle of cornstalks.

In most cases, it's wise to enclose the pile—preferably with some sort of air-admitting arrangement like snow fencing, straight saplings stacked log-cabin fashion, scrap-wood boards, concrete blocks, or heavy wire fencing.

A day or two after you've assembled your compost heap, it will start to heat. You'll know, then, that your resident bacteria are busy digesting the carbon compounds in the vegetable matter and giving off energy, in the form of heat, as a by-product. If your pile doesn't heat within a few days it may be too dry, or the layers may be too thick, or there may be too much high-carbon stuff like sawdust or straw and too little manure.

If you suspect that the pile is on the dry side, pour four to eight buckets of water over it. (Less for a small pile, more for a large one.) In case you've put a lot of slow-to-decay stuff like sawdust or straw in the pile, make that manure tea rather than plain water. If the pile *still* doesn't heat in a week or so, and daytime temperatures are well above 40°F (cold weather may retard heating even in a well-built pile), then it may be necessary to fork the pile apart and add more manure as you rebuild it. In most cases, though, the manure tea treatment should do the trick.

Ingredients for compost can be found everywhere—not only in the country, but in cities and small towns as well. This year's garden leftovers will nourish next year's growing plants. And so the year turns.

Crop Supports

When vining or climbing vegetables are well supported, they'll yield more fruit of better quality. Providing support for climbers can help to increase the amount of produce you'll harvest from a limited piece of ground. Vines that are able to stretch up into the sun and breeze are less likely to be bothered by mildew and other fungus diseases, and fewer of their fruits will rot on the ground. Here are some plant supports that you can easily construct with very modest expenditures of time and money.

Pole Beans

Both snap and lima pole beans start producing later than their shorter counterparts, but they bear for a longer time. Some of the best-tasting limas, such as King of the Garden, must be grown on poles. Take your choice of bean drapery arrangements, depending on whether you're better supplied with string, poles, or standing stalks.

TEEPEE
Choose three or four beanpoles of equal length, about eight feet long. Ram the heavier ends a few inches into the ground—it helps

to prepare holes first, using a crowbar—then tie the poles together at the top. Early cultivation is a bit more cumbersome with this method, but the teepee is stable in wind, and if your soil is rocky or hard, teepee poles are easier to set than single poles that must be buried deeper.

STRING   Used baler twine is fine for supporting beans. Stretch the twine between the tops and the bottoms of eight-foot poles that are set a foot deep in the ground and spaced six feet apart. Then tie vertical strings between the top and bottom strings. Some gardeners zig-zag an additional string between the top and bottom strings for more support. Bean vines climb string readily, but if the top string is not firmly anchored, the weight of the vines might drag it down.

POLES   Where wind isn't too strong, single poles placed three to four feet apart will do. Poles should be sound wood or they may break at ground level in a high wind. In windy weather you might need to direct the vines occasionally; plants have been known to wander off and join the colony on the next pole.

SHEEP FENCING   Sheep or other wide-mesh fence is an adequate support, but not as good as string or poles because the bean vines tangle and jam up when they travel horizontally, as such fencing may encourage them to do.

SUNFLOWER AND CORNSTALKS   These plants, well-rooted, make good bean supports. You can tie three sunflower stalks together to form a teepee. If you're planting beans to climb this year's corn, wait till the corn has sprouted before you plant the bean seed, so the stalk can get a head start.

CONTAINER GROWING   Gardeners who are short of space can raise pole beans in buckets! A recent release from the National Garden Bureau shows a ten-gallon tub with a tall center pole. Twelve bean plants are climbing strings stretched between the top of the pole and the edge of the bucket.

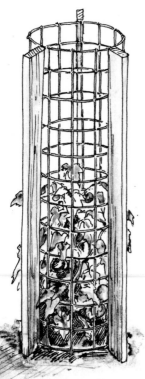

Peas

Weak-kneed vines with skimpy roots but strong, clinging tendrils, all pea plants need some support. For the short varieties, up to 24 inches tall, you can use two or three strings stretched between posts, netting or chicken wire held up by poles (better), or twiggy brush (best). Tall varieties need netting, fence wire, or brush.

The beauty of brush, besides the fact that it's free, is that its support extends in three dimensions, fanning out, leading the pea plant along so that the foliage remains open to sun and air and is thus less prone to fungus attack. Use recently cut brush; its resilient twigs will give with the wind. Old brush is brittle and breaks easily. If you can, set aside well-shaped branches when working in the woods in late winter. Put them in the garden when pea plants are several inches high. If you're too early, the branches will blow over before you need them; if too late, the peas will grow tangled and roots may be damaged. I always wait until after a good rain to poke the branches into the ground so I can set them deeper. Sharpening the end of each branch to a point helps.

Brush alone is enough support for the dwarf and midheight

Tomato cylinder

peas, but for taller varieties such as Sugar Snap and Mammoth Melting Sugar, I like to string about five levels of baler twine, reaching up to six or seven feet high, between steel posts placed every eight feet in the row. The twine catches and holds the plants when the west wind is strong.

If you tie a tomato plant to a single stake, you'll have to keep tying up the main stalk and pruning off suckers as the plant grows. Some of us never get back to do that follow-up work. Here are some alternatives that enable you to avoid the ritual of tying and pruning.

CYLINDERS

Cylinders of concrete-reinforcing wire set around tomato plants are excellent supports. Clip off the horizontal wire on one end, leaving prongs that can be poked into the ground. In high-wind areas, or in sandy soil, drive a few stakes inside the cylinder to anchor it.

FRAMES

Scrap-lumber frames can be set right over young plants. The frames are generally square with four uprights, three to four feet tall, tied together by four braces on the top and four on the bottom. Mature plants lounge all over them, and fruit stays shapely and undecayed when kept off the ground.

Tomato frame

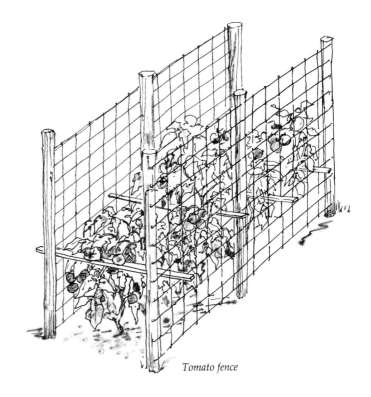

Tomato fence

FENCED TOMATOES   You can simply plant your tomatoes by the back fence or next to a fenced compost pile. For more control, try nailing four-inch-mesh hog wire five feet high to sturdy stakes, then drive the stakes into soft soil. Set up two parallel rows of this fencing about two feet apart, one on each side of your tomato row. Then slide thin sticks or slats through the wire, each end supported by one of the fences, to brace the plants as they grow.

Cucumbers

Cucumbers are really climbers, and they'll give you more fruit per square foot of row space if you can raise them up. Plant seeds by a fence or let them ramble on strong plastic netting. You can also make A-frames of hog wire nailed to two simple rectangular wood frames that are hinged together at the top. They provide excellent support for cukes, and they're easy to store. They work well for tomatoes, too.

Cantaloupes

The vines can manage to climb a fence or strong netting, but the heavy fruits need help to hang on. Support them with slings of scrap fabric tied under the fruit and through the fence.

Simple and inexpensive supports such as these can make your garden more orderly and convenient as well as more productive. Gather materials for supports now, and you can have them put together in time to prevent your climbing and vining plants from encroaching on neighboring rows.

Cucumber A-frame

Pole-bean string

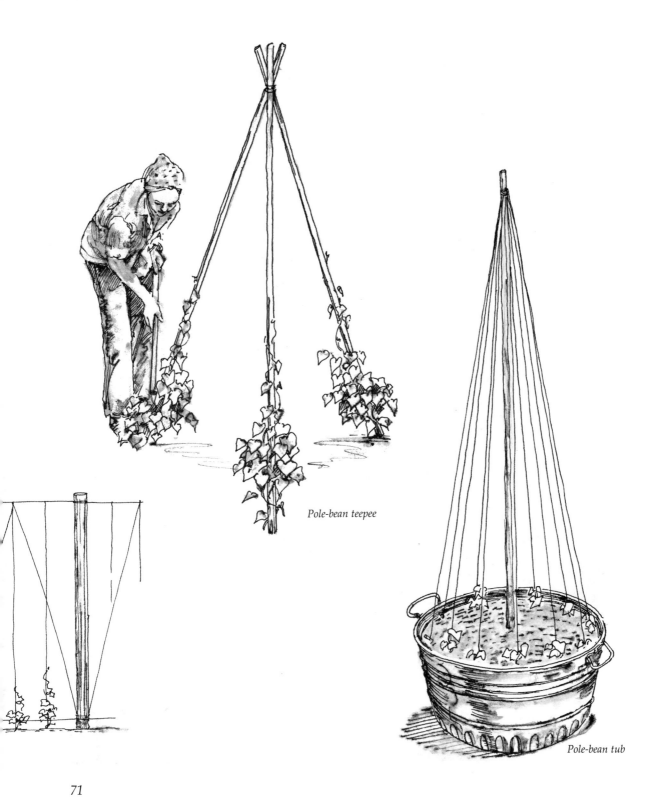

Pole-bean teepee

Pole-bean tub

71

APRIL

Onion Snow

We meet our neighbors in the post office, all of us back in boots again to slog through a late snow. "It can't last," we tell each other. April snow seldom stays long on the ground. Whether we have bought our onion sets or not, whether we've planted them yet or not, we consider this our onion snow. It is as much a sign of spring as the peepers in the woods. The snow is there, no doubt about it, but we see beyond it—as we were unable to do in January.

We are ready to spread manure, dig the ground, dust off the rototiller, and find the twine and stakes we set aside with such finality last fall. It may be just as well that this late snow holds us back a bit; by the time it melts, we'll be another week into the month and less likely to make the easy, eager mistake of digging and planting too soon.

We've had a bag of onion sets waiting hopefully on the kitchen counter for some weeks now. Onion sets, as you know, are tiny, dry bulbs grown from seed the previous year, raised in a "ghetto" row where they are deliberately crowded and underfed to produce stunting. The sets you plant this spring will grow into bunching onions in six to eight weeks, and into mature bulbs in about fourteen weeks. The smallest onions—dime size, on up to three quarters of an inch in diameter, will produce the best bulbs. Larger sets tend to grow into thick-necked plants that go to seed and spoil quickly.

Onions like to begin their growth in cool weather and mature when it is hot and dry. They are not harmed by frost. The sets may be planted as soon as the soil has dried sufficiently to permit easy handling. Clay ground that has been worked too early will form a hard cast around the little bulbs, and clods that are too large will surround the potential roots with air pockets instead of soil. Onion roots are short and fairly skimpy, so they need all the help they can get. On light, well-drained soil, push the sets well into the soft ground, letting the wispy tips protrude. On heavy soils, the bulbs do better with shallow planting; firm the little onions well into the ground, but leave the top half of the bulb uncovered.

A two-pound bag of onion sets will plant about fifty feet of row, and yield about three quarters of a bushel of mature onions. The sets may be planted in single rows, wide rows, or beds. Bulbs that will be used to produce mature onions should be set three or four inches apart. Those that will be harvested as scallions or bunching onions may be set as close as two or three inches. Rows, in both cases, should be twelve inches apart for hand cultivation, or as wide as you need for your tiller or hoe. If you pull every other bulb when harvesting green onions, the remainder of the crop will have plenty of room to develop fully.

Onions thrive best in soil that is near neutral or slightly alkaline. Yields on strongly acid soils will be low. Dolomite lime and wood ashes help to sweeten acid soil.

The maturing bulbs require twelve to fourteen hours of sun a day. The sun should strike the bulb, so heavy mulching of the maturing plants is not advisable, although many gardeners make use of a light mulch of grass clippings or newspaper early in the season. Onions need a good supply of moisture but the soil should be well drained. Weeds that shade the plants and compete for moisture and nourishment must be kept under control—and the only way to do that in the double rows we grow is to hand-pull them.

Perhaps you'd like to try your hand at raising your own onion sets. If so, just scatter the seed thickly in a row at least four inches wide. Instead of thinning to the usual two-to-four-inch spacing, allow the plants to crowd each other and do not fertilize them. When the tops turn yellow in mid-summer, dig up the little bulbs and let them dry in a loose heap in the sun. Sort them and keep only the three-quarter-inch and smaller sets for your next year's crop.

Onions grown from sets are the pungent American type that form medium-sized bulbs and keep quite well. European onions —the Spanish, Italian, and Bermuda varieties—are, as a group, sweeter, larger, and shorter-lived in storage than the native tear-jerkers. Still, they usually keep well into February for us—unless we eat them first.

To grow sweet onions, you can either purchase bunches of southern-grown transplants to set out in May (they are a bit less frost-hardy than the sets), or you can grow your own transplants from seed sown indoors in midwinter. Only fresh onion seed should be used; viability after a year of storage is uncertain. The seeds germinate most readily at 65°F but will generally perform well within a range of 45–85°.

When the young plants are about six inches high, snip off the top two or three inches of the slender green tops and keep them clipped back to encourage root development. Transplant the seedlings at least once, selecting the strongest plants from the many grasslike specimens crowding the flat. Give them a light, well-drained, fertile soil, preferably under lights or glass, and keep them cool until the outside weather has settled sufficiently to set them out.

Space sweet onion plants in the garden row four or five inches apart—in rows about a foot apart. Before planting southern-grown transplants, I usually soak the roots of the clump in water for a day. Each bunch of purchased transplants is a handful as pulled from the field and it may contain from fifty to one hundred plants. You'll probably need two bunches to plant a fifty-foot row. Poke each little quill of a plant into the soft earth just enough to anchor it well—no deeper than an inch. Firm the soil around the roots, and sit back and wait for the first weeds to sprout.

Onions are versatile, both in the range of foods they improve and in the growth stages at which one can harvest them. We use our home-grown onions in five ways:

(1) The green tops are delicious snipped over potatoes or eggs or into soups. Since bulbs from which the tops are repeatedly stripped will never amount to much, we grow a row especially for this purpose.

(2) Scallions or bunching onions—tender green onions pulled before they form a bulb

(3) Fresh, fully bulbed onions eaten straight from the garden in summer

(4) Dried bulbs, stored in a cool dry place for winter use

(5) Pickled onions—the small worthies that would otherwise get lost or grow into thick-necks next year end up in the pickle jar.

It's a rare day when I don't use an onion in preparing at least one (four-person) meal. If that is true for you, too, you can safely devote two hundred feet of garden row to this tasty staple.

Early Crops for Cold Climates

Most gardeners are optimists at heart. When the growing season is short, we soon learn to be realists, too. Gradually we learn what we can do to coax early crops from cold soil. For those determined realists who have not lost their optimism, here are some suggestions for outwitting an unforgiving climate.

Encourage and Protect Early Crops

Protect individual plants from frost with cloches (bottomless plastic or glass jugs), purchased wax caps, or tunnels made of sheet plastic stretched over wire or bent saplings.

Warm the soil around the plants by mulching with black plastic or old dark carpet or by putting discarded tires around individual plants. Cultivating around plants helps to warm the soil, too.

Burgess Seed and Plant Co.
  905 Four Seasons Road
  Bloomington, Illinois 61701
Burpee Seeds
  300 Park Avenue
  Warminster, Pennsylvania 18974
Johnny's Selected Seeds
  Albion, Maine 04910
R. H. Shumway Seedsman, Inc.
  628 Cedar Street
  Rockford, Illinois 61101
Stokes Seeds Inc.
  P.O. Box 548
  Buffalo, New York 14240

Choose Cold-hardy,
Early Varieties

Make early plantings in that part of your garden where the soil is loose and well drained. Heat reflected from buildings and stone walls also helps to moderate temperature.

Pre-sprout seeds for a head start. Most plants require more warmth for germination than for seedling growth.

Time and position your soil-improving additions judiciously. If you make early plantings in recently manured ground, put at least one inch of soil between the seed and the manure, or the seed may decay in the slowly decomposing organic matter. A buried layer of manure will often produce heat, which may hasten seed germination. But too much available nitrogen in the soil early in the season may produce sappy growth, which is easily damaged by frost. Studies made on potatoes reveal that they absorb a large proportion of their total phosphorus requirements quite early in their development. Essential elements such as phosphorus (supplied by bone meal and wood ashes) must be right in the soil, waiting, to do the young plant the most good.

Here are some proven-cold-resistant varieties of the vegetables we can never get soon enough. Check your favorite seed catalogues for more. (Plant scientists are working hard to develop more cold-

In the tables that follow, under Eggplants, Peppers, and Tomatoes, the number of days indicates times from planting out to first crop.

CORN

Polar Vee (Stokes)	53 days
Earlivee (Stokes, Johnny's)	67 days
Spancross (Burgess, Shumway)	60 days
Early Sunglow (Burgess, Shumway)	62 days

BEANS

Royalty and Royal Burgundy may be planted two to three weeks earlier than other beans. Both are widely available.

EGGPLANTS

Dusky Hybrid (Burpee)	60 days
Early Black Egg (Johnny's)	65 days
Hybrid Mission Bell (Shumway)	68 days

PEAS

Alaska, at 52 days, is extra early, but Sparkle, 55 days, has better flavor. Both are widely available.

PEPPERS

Staddon's Select (Johnny's)	70 days
Earliest Red Sweet (Stokes)	55 days
Ace (Johnny's and Stokes)	50 to 60 days
Early Thickset (Park)	48 days

POTATOES

Irish Cobblers are early, with excellent flavor. Alaska Frostless are late-bearing but frost-resistant. (Alaska Frostless set tubers deep, so they don't need hilling. They are available from Northern Lights Greenhouse, 1600 College Road, Fairbanks, Alaska 99701.)

TOMATOES

Burgess Early Salad Hybrid (Burgess)	45 days
Early Girl Hybrid (Burgess, Burpee, and others)	45 to 60 days
Sub-Arctic Maxi (Stokes, Johnny's)	48 days
Sub-Arctic Midi (Johnny's)	59 days
Earlirouge (Johnny's)	67 days
Pixie Hybrid (Burpee)	52 days

hardy vegetable varieties—a process in which they must often work with wild strains of these vegetables in order to breed in the desired genes. All the more reason for preserving these dwindling pockets of genetic diversity.)

Corn seed won't germinate when soil temperature is below 50°F. If you're eager for early corn, you can warm the soil, plant cold-resistant varieties, and pre-plant enough seeds for a small plot of corn in individual peat pots. Sow seed in the pots about six weeks before your normal outdoor corn-planting date. Keep the seedlings under lights or in a sunny window, and let them harden off before you plant them out. When setting out seedlings, plant the entire container, covering it well; disturbing the roots may kill the plant. Young corn sprouts are fairly frost-resistant; foot-tall plants are more likely to be killed by frost. Rake leaves around taller early plants if frost threatens. When planting early corn directly in the row, cover with no more than one inch of soil. The untreated seed many of us prefer to use is prone to rot in cold soil but does well once the soil warms above 60°F.

TOMATOES

Cold-country gardeners have found it possible at last to have tomatoes before September with the introduction of the cold-resistant Sub-Arctic strains. They are less disease-resistant than later varieties, but they yield an early crop. Plant them out as young, well-hardened seedlings, before they develop blossoms. More mature seedlings are more vulnerable to frost damage. Sub-Arctics need no staking or tying and may be planted 12 to 18 inches apart.

Seed expert Rob Johnston reports that it's possible to increase the number of flowers and fruits on the first two or three clusters of early-tomato varieties by chilling the young seedlings just before the first true leaf appears. Expose the seedlings to night temperatures of 50° to 55°F for three weeks. For maximum production, most early varieties need a good supply of phosphorus (from rock phosphate or bone meal) in the soil.

POTATOES

For early planting, select old potatoes—those you dug in summer rather than fall—and bring them up from the root cellar to sprout at room temperature, or about 60°. When sprouting starts, put the potatoes in a cool (but not freezing) place and keep them exposed to light. Older potatoes with single sprouts grow faster than newer tubers with multiple sprouts. A sprout one inch long is ideal for planting. Let the cut seed-potatoes dry for several days so they will be less likely to rot in cold ground. As noted above, ready availability of essential soil minerals promotes good early crops; phosphorus for root and tuber development, potassium for tuber size.

Knowing what and how to plant will give you good grounds for optimism in this new growing season. With persistence and care, you can beat old Jack Frost and feast well, early, on some of your favorite vegetables.

Extra Nutrition from the Garden

The harvest of vegetables produced by a garden is commonly computed in terms of pounds, or bushels, or quarts. There's another way of looking at it, though. The value of home-grown vegetables can also be considered in terms of the nutritional value to be found in each pound of food. Some crops have more vitamin, mineral, protein, or roughage value than others. Furthermore, certain varieties of popular vegetables have been bred especially for high vitamin or protein value. These super-vegetables are worth knowing about. While they may not, in every case, replace your current favorites, the choice of several varieties from the following list could significantly increase the food value you reap from a given square foot of land. That's something to keep in mind as you savor the seed catalogues and think ahead to another planting season, beyond the snow, sleet, and mud.

TOMATOES

Even if your food-producing plot is merely a strip of ground by the south wall of the house, you probably grow tomatoes. Most gardeners do. Here, then, are four varieties that will contribute extra vitamins as well as flavor to your meals.

Doublerich, which bears medium-sized, fairly solid red fruits of acceptable flavor, contains 50–60 units of vitamin C in an average serving (about 100 grams). That is at least twice the vitamin C content of regular tomatoes.

Jubilee, an orange tomato of excellent flavor and quality, is smooth, round, solid and heavy-yielding. It is said by seedsmen to contain more vitamin A and C than the average tomato, but exact figures are unavailable.

Caro-Red, on the other hand, has been analyzed by its developers at Purdue University, who have test-tube proof that the tomato contains ten times as much pro-vitamin A (beta-carotene, from which vitamin A is formed in the body) as regular tomatoes. A 100-gram serving of this rather small tomato with reddish-orange flesh will provide around 9,000 units of vitamin A, putting it in a league with sweet potatoes and spinach as a source of this important vitamin.

Sweet 100, a new variety introduced last year, produces long, fruit-laden clusters of cherry-sized tomatoes that are very rich in vitamin C and have an unusually sweet flavor. If you order this one, you'll want to have some stakes lined up too, for the weight of these pendant fruit clusters makes strong staking a necessity.

SWEET POTATOES

With their bright orange flesh, sweet potatoes are generally recognized to be good sources of vitamin A, but the *Allgold* variety is unusually high in vitamin A. It is a delicious, early, deep yellow-orange potato that, like all sweets, withstands drought and does best on relatively low-nitrogen soil. Order plants in spring for delivery in late May or very early June. If you live in the South or warmer parts of the West, you can plant earlier, whenever settled warm weather arrives, or about two weeks after the average date of your last frost.

All carrots, like all sweet potatoes, contain significant amounts of vitamin A, but the champion in this respect is *Juwarot,* a deep reddish-orange, fine-flavored root that averages twice the usual amount of vitamin A—249 milligrams per kilogram as opposed to 120 milligrams per kilogram found in other carrots.

CARROTS

Sweetheart, a cross between the sugar beet and the Detroit Dark Red, was developed at the University of New Hampshire. It contains almost twice as much natural sugar as other garden beets, with no difference in texture or flavor. Since I always preserve beets by pickling them, I like to grow Sweetheart beets for canning so that I need only a little sweetening to balance the vinegar.

BEETS

Sometimes, paradoxically, it's lack of a substance that makes a vegetable more nutritious. That's the case with the *Monnopa* variety of spinach, which contains only a trace of oxalic acid. (Normally present in rhubarb, spinach, and some other greens, oxalic acid combines with the calcium in a person's blood, making it unavailable to the body.) If you've been concerned about this one drawback of an otherwise excellent food plant, you might want to try this new low-oxalic-acid variety of spinach.

SPINACH

Soybeans in general contain more complete protein than any other vegetable. The new *Fiskeby* surpasses them all with a 40 percent protein rating. Most other soybeans contain around 35 percent protein. Not only will 100 of these beans sustain you from dinner until breakfast as well as five ounces of prime beef, they'll also bear early in the season (often within two months), tolerate crowding, and produce heavily. Listed as a 58-day bean, Fiskeby may be planted as soon as danger of frost is past and replanted in June for a fall crop.

SOYBEANS

Unusually high in protein compared with other shell beans, the tiny, dark red adzuki has an excellent nutty flavor and a generous yield—about 18 pounds per 100-foot row, according to the Vermont Bean Seed Company. It may also be eaten as a snap bean when young. Originated in Japan, the plant adapts well to a wide variety of climates.

ADZUKI BEAN

Potatoes baked in the skin contain an average of 20 milligrams of vitamin C per 100-gram portion. Although potatoes are not generally relied on as a principal source of vitamin C, they actually do contribute important amounts of that vitamin to the winter diet. So when you send for seed potatoes or choose them at your local hardware store, you might want to remember that *Katahdins* rate high in vitamin-C content, while *Irish Cobblers and Sebagos* contain somewhat less of the vitamin.

POTATOES

The hot pepper, perhaps because it is closer to the wild form, is richer by far in both vitamins A and C than the sweet pepper. A 100-gram serving of raw, red (mature), hot peppers contains 369 milligrams of vitamin C and a whopping 21,600 units of vitamin

PEPPERS

A, compared with 204 milligrams of C and 4,450 units of A contributed by the same amount of sweet red peppers. Most of us, of course, are able to consume more sweet peppers than hot ones, but those "welding rods," as a friend of ours calls them, remain a remarkably concentrated source of these two important vitamins —well worth working into the menu.

SOURCES OF VITAMIN-RICH VEGETABLE SEEDS

Doublerich Tomato Burgess Seed and Plant Company, Box 3000, Galesburg, Michigan 49053

Earl May Seed and Nursery Company, Shenandoah, Iowa 51603

Nichols Garden Nursery, 1190 North Pacific Highway, Albany, Oregon, 97321

Olds Seed Company, Madison, Wisconsin 53701

George Park Seed Company, Greenwood, South Carolina 29647

R. H. Shumway, Rockford, Illinois 61101

Caro-Red Tomato not available from commercial sources as far as I can tell. Now it's up to gardeners to keep this seed strain alive.

Sweet 100 Tomato widely available

Farmer Seed and Nursery Company, Fairbault, Minnesota, 55021

Gurney Seed and Nursery Company, Yankton, South Dakota 57058

Harris Seeds, Moreton Farms, Rochester, New York 14624, others.

Allgold Sweet Potato Farmer, Gurney, Fred's Plant Farm, Box 1507, Route 1, Dresden, Tennessee 38225

Juwarot Carrot Thompson and Morgan, Box 24, 401 Kennedy Boulevard, Somerdale, New Jersey 08083

Sweetheart Beet Farmer

Monnopa Spinach Thompson and Morgan

Fiskeby Soybean Nichols, Stokes Seeds, 7180 Stokes Building, Buffalo, New York 14240

Johnny's Selected Seeds, Box H, Albion, Maine 04910

Adzuki Bean Johnny's, Dr. Yoo Farm, Box 290, College Park, Maryland 20740

Space-Saving Techniques

Space-saving gardening techniques make sense, even for the country gardener who may have plenty of land at his disposal. Breaking more ground isn't always practicable. Our kitchen garden, for example—situated on the south side of the house within easy reach of both doors—is right where we want it. But since it is bounded on four sides by obstacles to enlargement—the house, an English walnut tree, a tractor lane, and an underground pipe that shouldn't be disturbed—we have chosen to intensify the kitchen garden rather than extend it. Perhaps some of the techniques we used to increase the productivity of a given piece of land will help you to get more out of your own garden space.

By "intensifying the garden," I mean that we make our plantings close together, leaving no idle spaces. As much as possible, we keep every square foot of the garden full of thriving, producing plants (except for the week we spent on the Maine coast, the summer we built the barn, and the month when *everyone*—bless their hearts!—came to visit us. We plant our vegetables in closely spaced rows or in wide strips, and we keep planting successive crops as early plantings wane.

In order to get away with such intensive cultivation, we feed the soil as well as we can. Early each spring we spread barn bedding (largely chicken manure with some goat manure) over the patch. Over this we spread dolomite lime, about a pound to every 20 square feet—more than usual, but our soil is very acid. Every two or three years we add rock phosphate and granite dust. We try to spread a bag of greensand (a sand containing glauconite, available at organic gardening centers) every other year for further mineral enrichment. Throughout the growing season, we give manure tea to individual plants that need a good supply of nitrogen. And we mulch the garden heavily, from spring through fall (waiting till June, when the soil is warmer, to mulch heat-loving vegetables), to keep weeds down and moisture in, and to feed the soil gradually as the mulch decays.

Wide blocks of vegetables make much more efficient use of garden space than single rows. Wide-row planting involves setting out one- to four-foot-wide strips or whole beds solidly planted to one vegetable. The plantings must be carefully hand weeded and thinned in the beginning, but once established they tend to shade out weeds and retain soil moisture.

Another good way to wedge a few more vegetables into a given space is to let some of them grow up. Plant pole beans and limas, and train climbing cucumbers, squash, and Malabar spinach—to name just a few possibilities—on netting or fencing to make good use of vertical space. Even an old tree stump at the edge of the garden can support a rambling squash vine.

Succession planting will give you a productive garden all season. As soon as a row or section is harvested, plant another crop in its place. Set out young plants of peppers and tomatoes between plants of lettuce, spinach, or radishes that will mature and be eaten before the later-maturing warm-weather plants spread and fill in the spaces. Interplanting pumpkins and corn, parsley and grapes, lettuce and berry bushes, will produce more food in spots where only weeds might have been.

Then take another look at the kinds of things you are planting. It's easy to get in the habit of wasting garden space by growing a vegetable that may go begging when harvest time comes, especially if that vegetable is easy to grow, is a sentimental favorite, or is a cool-weather crop that may be overplanted in early spring to satisfy an acute case of spring fever. Zucchini, beets, and turnips are frequently overplanted. You can waste space in a lettuce or radish planting, too, if you plant too much at once. It is far better to make frequent small plantings for continuous picking of these vegetables at their best.

Some vegetables, like Brussels sprouts, occupy garden space for most of the season but aren't ready for the table until after frost. Others, like broccoli, may be harvested from early summer until late fall. Still others—parsnips, salsify, and the like—also occupy the garden row throughout the season (their flavor, like that of Brussels sprouts, is best after frost), but they can be stored so well right in the row, when well covered, that they may be counted on as a fresh winter vegetable. (Dig during a January thaw and plan your menus around parsnips!) Each gardener has different priorities, but anyone planning for maximum yield in a limited space will need to give some thought to balancing out the properties of the vegetables he chooses to grow: those that need a full season of growth to reach the harvest stage, those that bear for a good part of the season, those that mature quickly—leaving space for another crop to follow, those that take a lot of space, and those that stay within bounds.

It is important, too, to encourage your garden plants to keep producing for you by picking all ripe fruits. As you know, a growing plant that has ripened seed on the stalk has accomplished its purpose in life. There is little need for it to produce more fruit, and the plant becomes more fibrous as its seeds mature in fruit already formed. Don't let your vegetables go to seed. Pick the fruit as it forms—especially those of okra, cucumbers, zucchini, and eggplant.

If you run out of room in the garden patch for all the food you want to grow, plant vegetables in unorthodox places. Odd corners of your place—beside the compost pile, by the garage—can turn into productive growing space if well spaded and planted to vigorous vegetables like squash, pepper, cabbage, and tomato transplants. Make use of the beautiful form and texture of well-grown vegetables by combining them with ornamental plantings. Edge a rose bed with lettuce or parsley. Plant hot peppers as front-yard accent plants instead of geraniums. Border the front walk with strawberries or cherry tomatoes.

The Purple Vegetable Patch

Purple vegetables are considered a novelty, but they're not new. There is some evidence, in fact, that the purple forms of some vegetables are the predecessors of more recently developed green and white varieties. At any rate, there are good reasons for planting a purple patch. Several of the purple forms of vegetables that are more commonly grown in green or white are especially hardy, insect-resistant, and easy to grow.

Take purple cauliflower, for instance. If you've avoided growing cauliflower because it's a nuisance to tie up the leaves for blanching, you might want to try one of the purple varieties, which need no blanching. The head is a deep, velvety purple that resembles a head of tight broccoli buds and the florets turn green when cooked. (Purple headed cauliflower isn't solid enough for shipping, so you won't find it at the store.)

Early Purplehead is ready 85 days after transplanting. *Royal Purple*, with a somewhat more compact and highly colored head, takes about 95 days. Both varieties are easier to grow than white cauliflower; they are less neurotic about being transplanted and they stay in good condition in the garden row for a longer time. Start seeds in May to obtain transplant-sized plants to set out in June. Space the plants about two feet apart in rich garden soil. Fall-maturing heads are best because cauliflower likes cool, moist weather.

The purple beans we've been growing for the past ten years have long since won over the doubters who thought they'd be tough and flavorless. They are, on the contrary, tender and delicious and, because the seed is less prone to rot in cold wet soil, they may be planted several weeks before other beans. Here in south central Pennsylvania I routinely plant purple beans by April 26 (three weeks before our last frost) and put the first fresh beans of the season on the table about June 24. (Although the seed is hardy, seedlings are as frost-sensitive as other beans. Mine have survived frost under a light covering of hay, though.)

Purple bean plants produce lavender-purple blossoms, which are fully as pretty as any sweet pea. The bean itself is a deep, dark purple, stringless, and full of good beany flavor. The bean turns green when it's steamed for two minutes—a built-in timer for freezing. The surprising deep-purple beans are easy to find when picking. We've always grown the variety *Royalty*, but the new *Royal Burgundy* may prove to be even better. Plants are more upright, less vining in their habit, and consequently the beans stay straight and clean.

Then there's purple kohlrabi—a maverick's maverick vegetable. Only the more adventurous gardeners seem to grow white kohlrabi, and even fewer plant the purple form—but enough, apparently, to keep it in the seed catalogues. Thank goodness. We lose more than we realize when catalogue offerings become homogenized to the common taste. Purple kohlrabi has the mild flavor and crisp texture of the usual white variety, but matures in 55 rather than 50 days from seed. The bulb has greenish flesh under the purple skin. Leaves and stems have a purplish cast, too. Plant kohlrabi seeds in early spring when you sow carrot seed, and thin the seedlings to stand 6 inches apart. Harvest the crisp above-

SOURCES OF SEEDS FOR
PURPLE VEGETABLES

Early Purplehead cauliflower
  Stokes
  Burpee
  Farmer Seed and Nursery

Royal Purple cauliflower
Royal Burgundy beans
  Stokes
  Burpee
  Olds Seed Co.

Purple kohlrabi
  Stokes
  R. H. Shumway
  DeGiorgi

Dark Opal basil
  Park Seed Co.
  Olds

White eggplant
  Farmer
  Grace's Gardens

ground bulbs when they're 1 to 2 inches in diameter. Serve the bulb sliced raw in salad or cooked, and eat the greens, too.

Basil, one of the most popular herbs, may be had in either a green- or purple-leaved form. Purple basil is a good garden landscaping plant—handsome between an edging of parsley and a row of tall yellow marigolds. The leafy stems are attractive in bouquets and of course the fragrant leaves marry well with tomato dishes of all kinds. Plant basil seeds in May, around the time of your last frost. They do well in full sun, on soil not excessively supplied with nitrogen. For best flavor, pick them just before they blossom.

Should you decide to plant a whole patch of purple vegetables, you'll probably want to include some eggplant. Set the seedlings out in the garden when all danger of frost has passed. The plant likes plenty of heat, abundant moisture, and rich soil. Eggplants that have grown steadily, unchecked by wilting, will produce best. Since flea beetles can be hard on the young plants, dust with diatomaceous earth to control them. (Perma-Guard is one preparation.)

Eggplant is, of course, expected to be purple, but you might (or might not) want to know that just as there is a purple cauliflower, there is also a white eggplant. If you get carried away, you could plant a purple-and-white checkerboard garden. True, few of us have time for such conceits. We're lucky to get our rows in straight. All these purple possibilities give us more choices, though, and that's one of the many good reasons for having a garden.

How to Grow Watercress

Watercress enjoys a well-deserved reputation for enhancing the flavor of bland foods like cream soups, chicken sandwiches, and lettuce salads. The pungent-leafed plant is, in fact, considered a special luxury by some, especially if a good wild bed of cress or a well-supplied greengrocer are not near at hand. Even if you *can* find it in a store, though, the flaccid rubber-banded nosegays of shipped-in watercress are a far cry from what you can grow yourself.

Although watercress does require certain definite conditions in order to flourish, it is not a difficult plant to grow. Once started, it produces year after year. As far as I can determine, the mature plant is practically immune to insect or disease problems. The only predators that have ever bothered our full-grown cress plants are our Muscovy ducks, who eat it down to water level each fall after frost has killed other greenery. The yearly shearing doesn't seem to hurt the plants, though, for they return each spring, and we gather bunches of the round-leafed, crisp-stemmed delicacy all summer while the ducks are busy elsewhere.

Watercress grows wild in the shallows of fast-moving streams. It has a decided preference for limestone areas and well-aerated water. In its natural habitat, it is nourished by leaf mold formed from water-borne leaves trapped by its network of roots. It does not do well in deep shade. Anyone wishing to start a planting of watercress would do well to duplicate these natural conditions as nearly as possible. If you have water on your place, choose the shallow edge of a bubbling stream or a spring-fed pond inlet for your planting spot, rather than a placid stream or a still pond where the water contains less oxygen. Even a slow-moving stream will support a respectable clump of watercress, though, and you can help things along by placing several large rocks or logs upstream to make the water more active, and therefore better aerated. The lime requirement may be less critical if the plant's other needs are met, as long as the pH (measure of acidity or alkalinity, with 7 as the neutral point) is no lower than 6. Certainly our soil is more acid than the limestone areas where watercress flourishes naturally; but our introduced planting has done very well.

Even if you have no stream or pond, you can still grow some watercress—enough for regular garnishes and occasional bowls of soup, at any rate. You have, in fact, at least four options, and perhaps you'll think of more. A season or two of experimenting will show you which alternative works best in your situation.

Plants grown in clay pots set in pans of water do well in a partially sunny location (4 to 8 hours of sun a day) as long as at least a half inch of water is maintained in the pan. Better yet, change the water every other day (water that has been standing contains less oxygen than freshly drawn water). Cress I raised from seed last year produced small but regular cuttings when grown in an 8-inch-diameter clay pot on the front porch.

Some gardeners report good results from garden plantings of watercress. The secret is to sink a leaky bucket or a juice can with a perforated bottom in the center of a group of eight or ten plants. Put a generous handful of compost mixed with powdered limestone around the perimeter of the can, below soil level. Keep at least one inch of water in the can at all times, and fill it when the level sinks low. As the water seeps out of the sunken irrigator can, it carries nutrients to the watercress in a reasonable imitation of natural stream action. If your soil is heavy clay, add more compost or leaf mold and perhaps even some vermiculite around the roots of the watercress plants to promote better aeration. Although the plants require a constant supply of water, they'll suffocate in dense, poorly aerated clay. Garden-grown watercress will sometimes winter over if well mulched.

Pots of watercress may be grown in the damp, partly shaded

area under greenhouse benches, where they are subject to a daily drenching when the plants and seedling flats above them are watered.

Early spring plantings of watercress will grow well in a cold frame until around the time of the last spring frost. Water them every other day and be sure to prop open the glass top of the cold frame on the occasional hot, sunny day, lest the plants suffer from overheating.

To start your watercress bed, you can raise plants from seed, transplant established plants from another bed, or set out rooted cuttings.

SEED

Although I've done some transplanting from mature plantations, most of the watercress now growing at the edge of our pond has been raised from seed. The seed is very fine and easily overplanted. Use great restraint to scatter a stingy pinch of the tiny seeds over the premoistened surface of an 8-inch-diameter clay bulb pot (shorter than the ordinary flowerpot). Gently press the seeds into the soil. They do not need to be covered. Set the clay pot in a pan of water and keep water in the pan at all times. The seeds germinate well at room temperature—70–75 degrees—and the seedlings thrive in cooler temperatures—from 50 to 65 degrees. When the true leaves appear, transplant the seedlings into additional pots, about eight seedlings to an 8-inch pot, and keep these pots in pans of water, too.

SOURCES OF WATERCRESS SEED

Burpee Seeds
DeGiorgi Company, Inc.
Joseph Harris, Inc.
Charles Hart Seed Company
J. H. Hudson
Natural Development Company
R. H. Shumway, Seedsman
Stokes Seeds, Inc.

The only insect problem I've ever had with watercress was a severe infestation of flea beetles in a potted planting that I had carelessly allowed to dry out. Flea beetles like dry conditions. I've never seen any on my pond watercress.

Start several weeks before the last spring frost date to set the seedlings outside for increasingly longer exposures to the sun and outdoor conditions. The young seedlings will withstand a light frost, so once they're hardened off as described above, they may be planted out a week or even two weeks before your spring frost-free date.

When planting the seedlings on the banks of a stream or pond, dig them into the soil just above the water level. You might want to position rocks or pieces of log around each young plant to prevent washouts when spring snow-melt and rain swells the streams. You can also sow seed directly on the banks of your pond or stream, but in my experience you'll get faster results and more plants by growing the seedlings under protected conditions.

TRANSPLANTING

Easy! Simply pull up clumps of the rooted plants from a well-established bed and relocate them in your chosen spot. Water-to-water transplants are the most satisfactory. Dig them into the soil just above the water level in your pond or stream. The stem will soon branch and sprawl in the stream and form more roots in the water. An established bed will also spread by self-sown seed.

To transplant a water-grown plant to garden soil, I'd first keep it in a tub of water for three to seven days, gradually adding fine soil and compost to make a thick muddy mixture, before committing the roots to the solidly surrounding soil.

ROOTED CUTTINGS

You can root cuttings you've foraged or begged from a friend. You can even root purchased sprigs, provided the stems are sound. Just pop the 4- to 6-inch tall cuttings into a glass of water. Leave at least the top inch of leafy stem exposed to air to absorb the carbon dioxide the plants need. Keep an eye on them. Roots should begin to grow within a week. When each cutting has several roots one to two inches long, it is ready to plant out.

In Praise of Garden Greens

Savory spinach soufflé; crisp, crunchy caesar salad; creamy sorrel soup; homey, tangy coleslaw: There's no end to the list of delicious dishes that begin in the garden. Growing greens will do more than enhance your reputation as a cook, though; leafy greens are one of the most healthful foods you can serve. Rich in vitamin C, folic acid, calcium, and fiber, green vegetables offer exceptional food value with few calories. They are worth the attention of even the busy and space-shy gardener, for most of them grow quickly and compactly, and they are seldom wiped out by bugs or disease, as cukes, beans, and squash can be. The following greens sampler should help you to choose which kinds you want to grow this year. May they do you good!

LOOSE-LEAF LETTUCE

Early, easy and nutritious, leaf lettuce may be planted as soon as you can scratch a furrow in the ground. Space plants 8 inches apart so they can develop fully. Crowded plants grow more slowly. Good varieties include Black Seeded Simpson, Oak Leaf, and Salad Bowl. Matures in 41 to 50 days.

BUTTERHEAD LETTUCE

Bibb, Boston, Buttercrunch, and Kagran are good soft-headed varieties, with a nugget of folded, butter-colored leaves at the center of a rosette of green, crinkled leaves. Buttercrunch can stand some heat, and Kagran does even better in warm weather. Like the loose-leaf lettuces, Bibb and Boston go to seed quickly when days turn warm. Plant the butterheads as soon as you can work the ground in spring, sowing seed every two weeks until mid-May, and again in mid- to late summer for a fall crop. Allow 8 to 12 inches between plants, and keep them well watered. All lettuce plants have skimpy roots and can't range far for moisture. Matures in 58 to 64 days.

HEAD LETTUCE

The paler leaves of head lettuce have a lower vitamin content than the leaves of the more loosely wrapped varieties, but they have a crackling crispness that makes them excellent additions to the salad bowl. And they're fun to grow. Start seeds early indoors and set out plants four to five weeks before your last frost. Give them several doses of manure tea or diluted fish emulsion to promote leafy growth. Matures in 60 to 80 days.

ROMAINE This glamorous member of the lettuce family is no harder to grow than the others. It has the sweetest flavor of any lettuce. The flat leaves fit well into sandwiches and are indispensable in caesar salad. Start plants early indoors, and set out and fertilize as you would head lettuce. Matures in 60 to 80 days.

ESCAROLE AND ENDIVE To grow these as spring crops, you'll need to start them early indoors. Endive has a fringed leaf and a pungent flavor. Escarole leaves are broad, rounded, slightly frilled, and somewhat milder. Both become bitter and go to seed in warm weather, but they're wonderful in fall. Some plants survive the south-central Pennsylvania winter in my cold frame. Start seed in July or August for the fall crop. They like rich soil and a steady supply of moisture, but are generally less sensitive than lettuce. To blanch the centers, tie up the heads when dry. (If the leaves are wet, they may rot.) Matures in 85 to 98 days.

COLLARDS Although associated with the South, collards are hardy plants that do well in northern gardens. In fact, frost improves their flavor. The three-foot-tall plants bear spoon-shaped leaves, which are usually served cooked. Plant seeds in late spring for a fall crop, spacing plants 2 feet apart. Pick individual leaves as needed. Ordinary garden soil is fine. Matures in 80 days.

KALE This super vegetable is a favorite in our family. The extravagantly ruffled leaves have a good, mild flavor after frost, cook up quickly, and are extremely hardy. You can pick kale all winter; mulch or snow cover helps to keep it green in the North. Start plants for the fall crop in June, spacing them 18 inches apart in good soil. Kale's generous vitamin content—one of the highest among vegetables—makes it worth growing even in small gardens. Matures in 55 to 65 days.

CHINESE CABBAGE Both of the two basic forms—Bok Choy, with loose, chardlike leaves, and Wong Bok, with solid, cylindrical heads—go to seed in warm weather, so they should be grown as early spring crops. Start plants indoors in March, or—better—treat them as fall crops from summer plants spaced 18 inches apart, and fertilize monthly when they're heading up. Frost improves flavor. Matures in 60 to 80 days.

TURNIP GREENS Grow these for good, quick greens—as early as thirty days for Shogoin or Tokyo Cross, which also produce roots in another forty days. Or grow one of the nonrooting varieties, such as Twilley's Hybrid or Seven-Top, just for the vitamin-rich tops. Plant seeds in earliest spring and again in late summer for a fall crop. Space plants 4 to 6 inches apart. Matures in 30 to 40 days.

CORN SALAD This is an oldie that's long on dependability, if not flavor. Limp, round, mild-flavored green leaves mix well with more pungent greens. Corn salad thrives in ordinary soil and is pest-free. Plant it in March for May picking, or in August for fall and winter. It's very hardy. Matures in 60 days.

One of the easiest vegetables to grow, this leafy member of the **SWISS CHARD** beet family, planted in spring, will put greens on your table through summer and fall. Often, some plants will survive the winter to provide early greens the next spring. Chard has a strong, deep root, thrives in ordinary soil, and is seldom bothered by insects or disease. Plant up to a month before the last frost, and thin plants to stand 10 inches apart. To encourage tender new growth, cut back in midsummer. Matures in 50 to 60 days.

An obliging perennial, sorrel thrives in acid soil, which needn't **SORREL** be rich, and it doesn't mind light shade. Plant seeds in early spring and thin seedlings to 8 to 12 inches apart. The tangy leaves taste best in cool weather. Sorrel is most often served cooked in soup or raw in salads, mixed with lettuce or spinach. Matures in 60 days.

Regular spinach is a short-lived crop in spring, but it's so tender **SPINACH** and good that it's worth growing. Plant seeds as early as possible in spring and again in August for fall crops, which last for weeks after the first frost and often survive the winter with protection. Spinach likes well-limed, rich soil, cool weather, and abundant moisture. Fertilize fall spinach as you would head lettuce. Matures in 42 to 50 days.

This is a vine with thick-fleshed, triangular leaves of excellent **NEW ZEALAND SPINACH** flavor. Although the plant grows most rapidly in warm weather, the seeds germinate best when the soil is cool, so they should be planted early in spring after soaking overnight. Thin seedlings to 15 inches apart in rows 3 feet apart. New Zealand Spinach will give you greens in summer and produce until frost and even a bit beyond if covered. Matures in 70 days.

Another hot-weather green with mild flavor and a vining habit, **MALABAR SPINACH** Malabar spinach should be supported on a fence, netting, or stretched string. You can either plant seeds when soil has warmed or start seedlings indoors and set them out a week or two after your last frost date. Pick individual leaves. Matures in 70 days.

Seed-Starting Hints

If you've ever planted parsley, you're familiar with the problem of the slow-germinating seed. Some other vegetable seeds can be tricky too—either erratic, heat or cold sensitive, prone to rot, or of low vitality. Most seeds will respond well, though, when given the germinating conditions that suit them best. Here is a list of seed-starting hints to help you to germinate some of the trickier seeds successfully, both indoors and out.

SNAP BEANS   Most snap bean seeds will rot in cold, damp soil and therefore should not be planted before the last frost. The exceptions are the purple varieties Royalty and Royal Burgundy, which may be planted three weeks before the last frost, since their seeds are less prone to rot in cold ground.

LIMA BEANS   If you've had trouble getting limas to germinate, here are some clues: Wait until weather is thoroughly warm to plant lima seeds; they're likely to rot in cold soil. Acid soil may retard germination. Presoaking can hasten germination, but soak the seeds for only an hour or so; they tend to split if submerged longer. Finally, poke the seeds into the soil eye-side down, so the root, which emerges from the eye, will grow down and the seed leaves will point up. Limas, it seems, are easily confused.

BEETS   Beets are usually easy to grow but can be temperamental about germinating since they are very sensitive to toxic substances in the soil. Highly acid soil may inhibit germination, too. And, more than the seeds of other vegetables, beet seeds need close, firm contact with the soil. Walk lightly down the just-planted row, or press the loose soil over the seeds with the back of a rake or hoe.

CABBAGE   Don't plant cabbage seeds too close together. Cabbage often seems to germinate 100 per cent and the crowded seedlings soon grow spindly. For summer plantings of fall cabbage, I sow seed in flats, not in the garden, because flea beetles can be devastating to young cole crops in summer.

CARROTS   Carrots aren't difficult, but they're *slow* and easy to overplant. To speed things up, you can pour hot water over the just-planted seeds. Wider spacing may be achieved by mixing the seeds with sand or dry, used coffee grounds, or by shaking them from a large-holed shaker. Don't plant carrots *too* early. In tests reported by Dr. J. F. Harrington, carrot seed germination was 43 per cent at a soil temperature of 41°F, 93 per cent at 50°F.

CELERY   Celery seed germinates best at 60° to 70°F. Temperatures higher than 70° tend to retard germination, but leaving the seeds uncovered and exposed to light can help to overcome this problem of hot-weather dormancy. Oddly enough, alternating temperatures —warm days and cool nights—help to promote celery-seed germination.

CUCUMBERS   Cukes need considerable warmth for germination—70° to 90°F —but once sprouted they grow well at lower temperatures—65° to 75°F. To get an early start, plant seeds indoors in peat pots and set them out when frost danger is over. Make a second, main planting directly in the ground when weather is warm.

LETTUCE   While they are simple to start in cool weather, lettuce seeds may surprise you by refusing to sprout in midsummer. This protective mechanism tends to insure that the plant will have a chance to grow in the cool weather that suits it best. There are three effective ways to persuade lettuce to sprout in summer heat:
(1) Use old seeds, in which hot-weather dormancy is weaker.
(2) Refrigerate the seeds for several days before you plant them.

(3) When planting, press seeds well into the ground but don't cover them. Exposure to light promotes lettuce-seed germination when the temperature is higher than ideal.

Most vegetables require more warmth for germination than for growth, but New Zealand spinach is an exception. This hot-weather green grows best in midsummer, but should be planted in spring because the seed germinates most readily at cool temperatures—ideally less than 55°F. Presoaking the seeds helps, too. **NEW ZEALAND SPINACH**

Okra seed, in Dr. Harrington's tests mentioned above, did not germinate at all at 50°F, while 74 per cent germinated at 59° and 92 per cent at 77°. Okra thrives in heat and should be planted outside only in thoroughly warm weather. Some northern gardeners start plants indoors. Soaking seeds for twelve hours before planting hastens germination. **OKRA**

Parsley can take as long as four weeks to germinate in cold soil, but you can knock a week off its germination time by keeping the packet of seeds in the freezer for two weeks before planting. To further encourage germination, pour very hot water over the just-planted seeds before covering them with soil. **PARSLEY**

For some reason, seeds of this delicious cold-hardy vegetable are very weak in germinating power. Use only fresh seed saved from last year's crop or purchased from a current catalogue, and plant it thickly. Germination is very slow—at least three weeks—so you may want to include a few radish seeds to mark the row. **PARSNIPS**

Peanut seed may be planted without shelling. If you prefer to remove the shell, don't split the peanut or remove the red skin. **PEANUTS**

Regular pumpkins sprout readily from seed, but the naked-seeded varieties such as Lady Godiva, Streaker, and Triple Treat are rather fragile because they lack the thick, protective seed coat. They break easily and tend to rot in cold, damp soil, so treat them gently and either start them indoors or wait until steadily warm weather before planting them outside. **PUMPKINS**

All watermelons like it hot, both for germination and for growth, but the ones to watch are the seedless varieties, which lack the vigor of the regular seedy kinds and are quite sensitive to cold temperatures. If you're planting seed for seedless watermelons, sow it more thickly than usual. **WATERMELON**

MAY

Six Ways to Improve Your Garden Soil

Most gardens, my own included, have room for improvement. Enhancing soil quality will not only boost plant health and vegetable yields, but also influence the flavor, nutritional content, and even the storage life of certain vegetables. In *The Small Garden Book,* Milton Carleton writes: "Gardening IS soil management." No matter where you garden, you can use some of the following suggestions to make poor soil good and good soil better.

Increase Humus Content

This is the single most effective soil amendment, and in one way or another, it affects most of the other things you'll do to improve your soil. Humus—decayed organic matter—loosens tight clay soil and holds nutrients in sievelike sandy soil. Decomposing organic matter releases ethylene gas, which suppresses some fungal diseases, and carbonic acid, which helps dissolve elements in the soil that are necessary for plant nutrition. Humus acts like a sponge, absorbing from five to ten times its weight in water and releasing moisture gradually as needed. (Good topsoil, in comparison, can soak up only about half its weight in water.) Soil rich in humus encourages earthworms, which further improve the ground by aerating it as they burrow and by contributing their rich castings—as much as 25 tons per acre per year in rich soil. The soil's supply of organic matter is oxidized—and therefore used up—more quickly under frequent cultivation, so it's necessary to restore the supply continuously.

Here are some ways to boost your soil's humus content toward the ideal 5 per cent level: Mulch with organic matter such as leaves, hay, sawdust, and corn cobs. Plant green manure crops in unused garden rows and turn them under while still green and succulent. (Rye, clover, alfalfa, buckwheat, oats, soybeans, and vetch are all good green manures.) Put compost in the furrow or hole when planting seeds and plants. Turn under a layer of manure in the garden each spring. Save and compost every scrap of once living matter that comes your way: feathers, eggshells, coffee grounds, weeds, fish heads, fruit and vegetable discards, and so on.

Avoid Compacting Soil

Use the lightest equipment possible to work your land. A rotary

93

tiller compacts less than a tractor, and a hand cultivator less than a tiller. Let soil dry before working it or stepping on it. Spread boards or mulch in paths to help absorb weight of foot traffic. Heavy or repeated pressure on soil presses out air, and plant roots grow best in aerated soil. According to Dr. Albert Trouse of the USDA's National Tillage Machinery Laboratory, quoted in *Getting the Most from Your Garden,* soil compaction can cut a plant's ability to function by 25 to 50 per cent. One of the best features of the intensive, raised-bed garden is that soil stays loose because foot traffic is confined to surrounding paths, and vegetables are not planted in places that were footpaths last year. Thus, soil-tilth improvements can be maintained from season to season.

Prevent Erosion

Loss of topsoil didn't end with the Dust Bowl days: tons of irreplaceable topsoil wash and blow from our land each year. To keep your topsoil on your own place, mulch bare rows, plant cover crops like winter rye to hold soil over winter, run rows parallel to a slope, and increase the soil's humus content so more water will soak in instead of running off. Gardens on steep slopes should be terraced. Where strong winds blow, plant windbreaks to shelter your garden. Avoid growing corn repeatedly in the same spot. Improve soil drainage in wet spots to reduce washouts in heavy rains. Use diversion ditches and even drain tiles to divert run-off pouring onto land from above.

Adjust Soil Acidity or Alkalinity

Most eastern soils tend to be acid. Alkaline soils occur mainly, but not exclusively, in the West. Most garden vegetables prefer a pH of 6.5 to 7—slightly acid to neutral. In highly acid soil, necessary elements may be abundant but unavailable to plants. Raising soil pH to a less acid level will unlock those tied-up elements. To increase soil pH by one unit (ten-fold), apply 2½ pounds of ground limestone to each 10- by 10-foot section in sandy soil, up to 6 pounds per 100 square feet for heavy clay. To decrease soil alkalinity, sulfur is often used, applied at ½ pound per 100 square feet in light soil, up to 2 pounds per 100 square feet in heavy soil. Sulfur is not acceptable to many organic gardeners, who may prefer the slower but safer practice of applying acidifying mulches, such as pine needles, oak sawdust, and acid peat moss, and using an acidifying fertilizer, such as cottonseed meal. Compost usually helps to neutralize extremes of soil acidity or alkalinity. According to Gene Logsdon's *Gardener's Guide to Better Soil,* your soil pH is probably about right for vegetables if clover germinates and grows well in it.

Rotate Crops

Growing a variety of vegetables enhances good health—both yours and your garden's. Every vegetable you grow demands something different from the soil. Keep changing your garden layout so the corn you grew last year is succeeded by a healing crop of soybeans, tomatoes by squash, beets by lettuce, and the soil will not be depleted of any one nutrient in any one place. Crop rotation also helps control the transmission of soil-borne diseases.

Encourage Helpful Soil Microbes

There are millions of bacteria and fungi in a single spoonful of ordinary soil, and the overwhelming majority of them are helpful. When you feed your soil, you are really feeding the unseen, teeming population that helps break down organic matter and releases elements in a form plants can use. Mycorrhizal fungi, which look like fuzzy threads and live on plant roots in abundant organic matter, help plants absorb more necessary elements from the surrounding soil. Helpful micro-organisms in the soil are harmed by the use of seed treated with fungicides. Superphosphate releases sulfuric acid, and ammonia-containing fertilizers are oxidized by bacteria to form nitric acid. In both cases, the increased soil acidity discourages soil bacteria. While it is true that liming can help to buffer this acidity, possibly to the point where its effect is minimal, my own preference is to avoid using such substances in my own garden. My garden is doing very well without them. In any case, regular dependence on chemical fertilizers that supply isolated elements but no humus cannot help but have an adverse effect on soil life, and therefore on soil health.

We are just beginning to comprehend the staggering complexity of the soil and its life. Many basic questions remain unexplored. You're working with marvelous stuff.

Planting Guide

When can you safely plant your spring vegetable seeds and set out your seedling plants? Most gardening books give planting dates for various vegetables, and these guidelines—which are based on the average year in a particular temperature zone—are generally helpful.

I've heard experienced gardeners wonder out loud, though, whether there *is* such a thing as an average year. We gardeners must make the most of conditions that confront us *this* year, average or not. Although we respect the planting timetables, we sense that adhering to a rigid formula won't always work. We need help for this season, which may be drier, wetter, colder, or balmier than last.

Another way to gauge the advance of spring is to watch the budding and blossoming of nearby trees and flowers. When daffodils blossom, the earth has reached a certain stage in the progression of the season. When you look at the whole picture, you can learn to read a variety of natural signs. The leafing-out of trees, blooming of bulbs, even apple petal-fall and the return of certain birds are clues that tell you the time is ripe. They're not always perfect guides, any more than those zoned maps and time charts are, but they help to indicate good planting times for many vegetables. This lore, based on observation and experience, and gathered from old and recent books and from seasoned gardeners, can be very useful. You might also ask your neighbors and local master gardeners what they consider dependable seasonal planting signs. Observe, experiment, and draw your own conclusions. At the very least, you'll experience more fully the subtle changes in unfolding leaves and blowing blossoms, so often missed in the spring rush to clean out the barn.

SNOWDROPS When snowdrops bloom, plant peas, lettuce, and onion sets if the ground can be worked.

CROCUSES Crocus bloom signals safe planting for seeds of carrots, lettuce, spinach, and radishes. (Milton Carleton, author of *Vegetables for Today's Gardens*, prefers to sow carrots when maples are leafing out.)

EARLY TULIPS Early tulips in bloom tell you the ground is ready for beets.

MAPLE TREES When maple blossoms are freshly opened, plant your Swiss chard seeds. Milton Carleton suggests planting tomato seeds right in the garden row when maples are in bloom.

SUMMER TULIPS Midseason tulips open? It is safe, then, to plant cabbage seedlings, which sometimes form fibrous heads if set outside while weather is very cold.

DAFFODILS Daffodil bloom is your cue to plant seeds of parsnip, salsify, and Hamburg-rooted parsley.

APPLE TREES Apple blossom time is when it's safe to plant seed of bush beans and sweet corn and to set out started leek seedlings. Some old gardening books advise planting squash and pumpkin seeds now, but I prefer to wait until later, at least until petals fall and sometimes until late irises bloom.

PETAL-FALL Apple blossom petal-fall indicates that conditions are right for planting seed of asparagus, pole beans, cucumbers, eggplant, and peppers, and for setting out celeriac plants.

OAKS Oak leaves of mouse-ear size show the correct soybean-planting time.

BARN SWALLOWS "When the barn swallows are back, then it's all right to set out your tomato plants," maintains Jesse Webb of Dillsburg, Pennsylvania, who has planted many, many gardens.

PEONIES Peonies should be in bloom when you plant melon, lima bean, and okra seed. They all need warm soil.

While you were looking, really looking, at what was going on around you as spring progressed, did you notice that cold spell while the blackberries were blooming? That's blackberry winter. According to Indiana farm writer Rachel Peden, blackberry winter usually falls about three weeks after the onset of spring fever. Around our house we have to hastily retrieve the warm jackets we've banished to the attic in an early burst of spring enthusiasm. We keep them on the edge of the rack, though, because blackberry winter usually lasts less than a week.

Transplanting

The year I grew my first garden, I transplanted radish and cucumber seedlings. I had a lot to learn. Other gardeners, books, and the plants themselves soon taught me that there are some plants you just don't transplant. Included in this group of hard-to-move plants are those that have deep taproots or too few small feeder roots, those with succulent stems (and roots), and those that appear to weather the uprooting but respond by going to seed or producing poorly. Most root crops should not be transplanted. The three exceptions—beets, turnips, and celeriac—may be moved with care when quite young. Other vegetables that suffer or die when moved include corn, cucumbers, gourds, melons, squash, pumpkins, and snap beans. Chinese cabbage often goes to seed if uprooted, and cauliflower, while it may be transplanted with care, has a tendency to produce worthless button heads if allowed to dry after transplanting.

There is, on the other hand, an even larger group of vegetables that not only tolerate transplanting, but often actually thrive on being moved. Plants that do well when transplanted as seedlings include asparagus, broccoli, cabbage, cauliflower (with extra care), celery (careful here, too), chives, eggplant, endive, leeks, lettuce, onions, peppers, and tomatoes. Most of these plants have finer, more abundant surface roots than those mentioned above. When some of those roots are broken in unearthing the plant, the remaining roots are stimulated to produce a network of new feeder roots, a process that strengthens the plant.

There are other good reasons for transplanting seedling plants. If you've planted seeds in a flat, it's quite likely that the young plants will begin to crowd each other when they're two to three inches tall. They'll develop long, weak stems unless you give them more room. Transplanting to a richer mixture is necessary, too, when seeds have been started in a nutrient-free medium like vermiculite. And finally, the process of moving seedlings gives you an opportunity to evaluate them and choose the best ones. Look for sturdy green leaves, symmetrical development, and a compact, well-developed root system. There is some evidence that seedlings that sprout early will turn out to be vigorous, high-yielding plants.

Although transplantable plants (except cauliflower, eggplant, and celery) may be moved three or four times before you set them out in the garden, most gardeners content themselves with transplanting young plants twice: first moving seedlings to better soil and wider spacing indoors, then transferring the well-developed plant to the outdoor garden. Some gardeners perform the first uprooting when the seedlings are very small—just after the first pair of leaves (cotyledons) has unfolded. I do this when working with rare or expensive seeds in order to try to save each one, but I prefer to wait until the seedling has developed its first set of true leaves, so that differences between the plants will be more pronounced, aiding me in selecting the best. In any case, it's a good idea to get the first transplanting done before the third set of true leaves develops.

Whether you're transferring a plant indoors or out, it's important to select the best seedlings if you can't use all that have sprouted; protect tender stems from bruising; guard roots from drying; water well and observe the transplanted plant; provide shelter to minimize wilting.

Before uprooting plants indoors, assemble all the equipment you'll need: new flats or other containers, potting soil, newspapers, watering can, and your favorite miniature digging tools. Some gardeners use popsicle sticks to pry out seedlings; others swear by pencils or old screwdrivers. I'm accustomed to a slim-handled discarded fork. Try to keep a ball of soil around the roots when you dig up the seedling. When roots are long and thready, this is hard to do. I often clip unusually long roots (like those of onions) back to a length of one to two inches to promote more compact, bushy root development. Do not dip the roots in water; this misguided practice clumps the roots together unnaturally. Roots should be spread out to go their individual ways. Try to hold small seedlings by the leaves, not by the easily bruised stems, when transplanting. Immediately replant each seedling in its new place before digging up another. Space leafy transplants three inches apart in their new quarters. (One inch is enough for onions and leeks.) Water the seedling well, then fill in around it with more potting soil. Firm the soil gently around the roots. Roots need contact with soil, but they also need a certain amount of air, so avoid flooding the planter with water or tamping the soil in a hard mass around the roots.

If you're working with a plant that has unusually long, trailing roots, it's difficult to avoid the error of tangling the roots or doubling them back on themselves. One way to increase root contact with soil in such cases is to put the plant into an individual container. Use a pot or can in which you've put a small amount of soil. Turn the pot on its side, insert the plant roots and spread them out on the soil that extends down the side of the container, and fill in with potting soil as you gradually tilt the pot back to an upright position.

Outdoors, dig a hole large enough to accommodate the plant's roots without crowding. If possible, do your outdoor transplanting on a damp, drizzly, cloudy day. Sun and wind can dry recently uprooted plants unmercifully.

Indoors, seedlings are less likely to suffer from transplanting shock, but it can happen. If you've watered the plants well but they are still wilted, cover the flat with a plastic bag or a tent of damp newspapers and keep it out of the light for a day.

Vegetables in Containers

"Vegetables," our agronomist friend insists, "don't know or care where they're growing." Maybe so. I remind him gently that they *do* know when they're getting what they need. Either one of us, I suppose, could point to a well-grown container garden to support his contention. It may seem unnatural to grow a tomato plant in a bucket, but the fact is that the confined tomato performs very well indeed, as long as its basic needs for soil, water, air, sun, and warmth are taken care of.

It is even possible, in fact, to tailor growing conditions to the requirements of certain finicky plants. If conditions on your patio are exactly to its liking, eggplant, for example, may surprise you by outyielding its cousins in the garden row. Gardeners with space problems aren't the only ones who can profit by planting some crops in containers. Many vegetable plants, such as hot peppers and cherry tomatoes, are appreciated for their ornamental value when grown in pots. Others—especially the herbs—are handy to have in clay pots on the porch, conveniently close to the kitchen. Potted or bucketed plants may be moved from one spot to another to make the most of the daily quota of sun that falls on your piece of earth. You can even bring them indoors when frost threatens. And you can tend a special individual plant more directly and more intensively than if it were among many in the garden plot.

On the other hand, though, vegetables growing in containers are highly dependent on you for care and protection—much more so than those grown in the garden. They are more vulnerable to the adverse effects of heat and dryness since their roots are confined in a small area. They are also more likely to suffer severely from overwatering if the container is poorly drained. While superb care can produce admirable results, even a few days of neglect can be disastrous.

Large clay pots are perfect to use for planters. Crocks, sections of drain tile, and small barrels also work well. Practical containers for large plants include picnic coolers and baskets. A motley collection of baskets or large cans may be "slip-covered" by setting them inside a wicker wastebasket. Gardeners have even grown vegetables in pipe elbows, children's dump trucks, cookie jars, bean pots, antique stoves, and leaky roasting pans.

You might want to put your heavier containers on casters for ease in moving, or plant directly in a child's wagon or an unused wheelbarrow, which can then be rolled where you want it. A more temporary arrangement, good only for a single season, is a bushel basket lined with plastic. Don't overlook the possibility of raising lettuce, herbs, and cherry tomatoes in window boxes, which may be placed around the edge of a patio or hung on the wall.

Once, when I was young and foolish, I planted a spring salad garden in a foot-deep, yard-long antique pine dough tray that I'd purchased at auction for a dollar. It worked beautifully. I kept the dough-tray planter on our wide, sunny back step and was able to plant lettuce and onions in it several weeks before the garden soil had warmed up enough to dig. The arrangement lasted for several years, but of course eventually the nailed-together sides separated and the bottom began to rot since there was no air space under it. I cringe now when I remember my disrespectful treatment of that fine old primitive piece. I should never have used it for a planter. (But the lettuces were delicious.)

You'll need good soil for your container garden, because the plant roots cannot travel far in search of more nourishment. The following mixture should serve well for any vegetables you plant: one part compost, leaf mold, or peat moss; one part garden soil; one part perlite or sharp sand. For proper root development, vegetable containers should be at least 8 inches deep; 5 inches will do for some herbs like thyme. Containers up to about a foot in diameter and 10 inches deep should have 2 to 3 inches of gravel on the bottom to trap excess water. Larger containers holding several gallons of soil need at least a 5-inch layer of gravel. Sometimes, especially in clay pots that have a fairly large hole, soil will wash down through the bottom opening if the plant has not yet grown enough roots to hold the soil together. You can prevent this by inserting a small piece of wire screening over the hole before putting in the gravel.

Choose a place for your potted vegetable garden where the plants will receive at least six hours of sun a day. Fruiting and heat-loving crops like eggplants and tomatoes should have considerably more sun (at least ten hours) and often benefit by growing near a south wall.

Soil in containers dries quickly in the hot summer sun, so you will have to water your captive plants at least three times a week, and often once a day when the temperature is high and the plants are producing fruit. Mulching the surface of the pot will help to retain soil moisture. Fertilizer, too, must be brought to the plant; it can't be assumed that the limited amount of soil can meet all of the plant's needs.

Here's a good complete fertilizer formula used in a roof-top garden studied by the Institute of Local Self-Reliance and reported by Miranda Smith in *Self-Reliance:* one tablespoon of fish emulsion; one tablespoon of liquid kelp; one teaspoon of blood meal mixed with one gallon of water. Or use compost or manure tea. Apply fertilizer weekly for most vegetables.

Which vegetables can be grown in containers? More than you might suppose. Start with the varieties with which you're most familiar and gradually branch out and try some unexpected ones. The following vegetables should do well, with good care.

LETTUCE
Plant a container of lettuce every week or two and you'll have a crop all season long—even in summer heat, if you remember to move the pot away from the midday sun for three or four hours (or shade it). Lettuce has a shallow root system and needs plenty of water.

PEPPERS
Decorative and easy to grow. They don't need rich soil. Temperatures under 60° or over 90° slow down fruit production.

HERBS
Keep the soil on the lean side, feeding about every three weeks, and take care not to overwater. Chives, marjoram, thyme, basil, dill, rosemary, and savory are good choices.

TOMATOES
Begin with cherry tomatoes, which thrive in one gallon of soil, bear quickly, and need minimal support. If you're running out of floor space, small-fruited tomatoes do well in hanging baskets. Raising standard-sized tomatoes in tubs is a more ambitious undertaking, but you should have no problem if you give them at least 5 gallons of soil and stake them well, or tie the vines to a trellis.

EGGPLANT
Eggplant will either be great or awful. If you have a good sun-drenched spot for it, feed it twice a week, water it faithfully, give it your largest tub of soil (at least 5 gallons), and *never* let it wilt, you might have to look for new eggplant recipes to help you use up your crop. If it doesn't get enough heat or water, though, the plant might only have a single fruit, if that.

SPINACH
Spinach is a good choice for container planting because it must be started early to get a good crop before hot weather, yet garden soil is often too wet to work at the time when spinach can be planted. Spinach is a glutton—feed it two or three times a week!

CUCUMBERS
Cucumbers need warmth and plenty of moisture, especially while fruiting, but when they're on the porch right under your nose, you can pamper them. Let them climb a trellis, porch railing, or patio fence. Feed them weekly.

ZUCCHINI
Give it a 5-gallon container of soil, plant the seed, and step back. Full sun and weekly fertilizer should bring on the zucchini.

ROOT VEGETABLES
Start carrots, beets, and radishes early in the spring, choose short, stubby varieties and give them at least 8 inches of soil. Some midday shade won't hurt, especially in midsummer. You can grow ten carrots, five beets, or about fifteen radishes in an 8-inch diameter pot.

Growing Asparagus

My aunt Margie, whose way with a good story is a gift to be envied, could hold you spellbound with her tale of the day her old asparagus bed, underlying her recently hard-surfaced driveway, responded to the warmth of spring by erupting through the black asphalt with its hopeful green spears. That was not some Freudian dream; it really happened. Asparagus persists. A bed of this delicious perennial vegetable can bear for twenty or thirty years.

You'll have better picking if you treat it right, though. Assuming that you want to encourage your asparagus, and you have another place to put your driveway, a little extra care taken at planting time will reward you over the years with better harvests of this marvelous vegetable that comes just when we need it most—after the long winter.

Years ago, when blanched vegetables were in vogue, it was the custom to plant asparagus in a one-foot-deep trench. Each crown sends out roots that ultimately range five to six feet deep and nearly as far on each side. The plants are very long lived and, once established, may be harvested for five to ten weeks each summer. Given such persistence and productivity, it seemed only appropriate to make the planting of asparagus a heroic task—by digging up great quantities of soil and gradually replacing it over the crowns during the plant's first season. Deep planting of asparagus certainly does no harm, and may well prove to be worthwhile when the plants begin to bear. In heavy clay soil, deep digging gives you a chance to modify the soil directly under the roots to the more friable loam that asparagus appreciates. You can even break up the soil on the bottom of the trench with a rototiller. I'm sure you won't be sorry. Another advantage of deep planting is that you can rototill directly over the dormant crowns of the plants in early spring to kill weeds, while mixing in manure and lime.

For the traditional deep-planting method, dig a trench about twelve inches deep and eighteen inches wide. Place mounds of mixed compost and topsoil at intervals of twelve to eighteen inches in the trench. Some gardeners allow the loose soil to settle for a few days before planting the roots. Arrange an asparagus crown on each mound, spreading the roots equally around the sides and pressing them into the soft soil. Cover the crown with about three inches of loose soil. Firm the soil well over the crown. Fill in another inch or so of soil above each root each time you weed the bed during the summer.

Perhaps you've noticed, though, that wild plants and seedling plants in your garden grow close to the soil surface, wherever the seed landed. Planting asparagus crowns three to four inches deep and even one to two inches deep is now considered acceptable.

Those delving roots are strong; they find their way down in any case. If this method is your choice, dig a shallow furrow, arrange each crown at twelve- to eighteen-inch intervals with roots spread as much as possible, firm loose soil (not clods) over the crowns, and mulch heavily once the first spears are up. Since you can't run the rototiller over this bed, you will need to weed it regularly, especially during the first few years when the top growth is spindly. The heavy mulch will protect the crown, discourage weeds, and enrich the soil as it decays.

Plant asparagus roots as early in spring as your soil can be worked. We favor one-year roots and would never buy any older than two years. Older roots lose too much vigor when transplanted. Young ones soon catch up.

Whether your planting is deep (six inches), shallow (three to four inches), or surface (one to two inches), your rows should be about three feet apart—slightly wider if you intend to run the rototiller between them. You may also want to plant a soil-enriching cover crop like clover, rye, or soybeans between the rows of asparagus; if so, you'll need space enough to till that in, too. Plant your asparagus beds about four feet away from berry bushes and other perennial plants. We keep our asparagus in a separate bed from our much-worked-over kitchen garden. It borders a larger plot where, along with raspberries, gooseberries, and blueberries, it can grow undisturbed.

Asparagus flavor varies little, if any, from one variety to another. Mainly, you should look for a good rust-resistant strain like Mary Washington, Waltham Washington, or Paradise. If you are buying roots at a nursery, look for crowns with many potential shoots and at least ten roots, six inches in length. One hundred crowns will amply feed a family of four. We always soak the roots in water overnight before planting them. Unlike other vegetables, asparagus has male and female plants. Generally, the male plants produce more, but thinner, spears.

If you want to prolong your harvest of asparagus, you can either plant your roots at different levels (six to seven inches, four to five inches, and two to three inches); mulch thickly in some areas, thinly in others; or progressively rake mulch off the rows in early spring.

The asparagus-picking schedule goes like this: no picking the first year, ever. The few spears you would get would not be worth the strain on the new roots. They need every bit of that ferny top growth to store food for future effort. Let the fronds mature and go to seed in the fall. The second summer, you can harvest finger- or thumb-sized spears, but none smaller. Thin spears come from roots that need more growing time. By the third year, if the tops made three to five feet of growth the previous season, and if the spears are thick, you can cut for four or five weeks. If you've planted one-year roots, wait until the third year to cut from them, and then take only three cuttings. Overcutting too soon will weaken the roots. You need to observe your plants as well as this timetable. When the spears become small and sparse, stop cutting for that year. After the fourth year, you can harvest asparagus for 8–10 weeks.

A well-maintained asparagus bed is kept free of weeds, mulched or cultivated regularly, and given a generous yearly helping of manure and lime, preferably in the fall. Asparagus thrives on lime and puts out enough new green growth every year to justify heavy applications of manure or compost. Historically a seaside plant, it will tolerate salt better than many other vegetables. If you garden on the coast, you'll want to make room for asparagus.

Once your bed is in full production, you may even have a surplus of asparagus to store for winter. It freezes beautifully. Uncooked spears make a fine addition to a green salad. It is also a pleasure to munch on right in the patch; the raw vegetable, we think, tastes best when eaten outside, like Thoreau's wild apples. And, of course, the cooked spears may be served on toast, in soup, or under cheese or butter for days on end around here without offending anyone. I find it difficult to imagine having too much asparagus.

Oriental Vegetables

Vegetables are supremely important in Chinese and Japanese cuisine. Those ancient cultures have developed many subtly varying strains of food plants; leavy greens that cook quickly, spicy roots, pungent herbs, multipurpose cabbages. The oriental custom of stir-frying mixed vegetables with small amounts of meat is now recognized as offering a sensible diet, low in saturated fat and sugar, yet high in vitamins and fiber. For us Westerners, to whom vegetables often mean peas, corn, and beans, these new foods can make meals more interesting and nutritious. Here are some easy ones to grow:

HEUNG KUNN

Chinese celery. Less succulent than our familiar Pascal celery, but easier to grow, this is an excellent seasoning plant, available all summer to add flavor to soups, stews, and casseroles. The leaves are good dried, too, as a flavoring in winter dishes. The plant is shallow-rooted and may even be grown indoors as a houseplant—a good addition to a kitchen-window-sill herb shelf.

Start seeds indoors in early spring and plant the seedlings outside a week or two before your last expected frost, after hardening them off for a week. Space the plants 8 to 10 inches apart in the row. In rich soil with a good supply of moisture, Chinese celery will produce a steady succession of stalks for cutting all season. It withstands light frost about as well as leaf lettuce does, but heavy frost will kill it.

Chinese mustard greens. These tasty greens fit neatly into a garden-succession plan, because they may be planted early—usually in April, when the soil is ready to be worked—and they grow to picking size in only five weeks. The flavor is rich but mild, without the hot or bitter taste found in many mustard greens. Pluck whole plants and enjoy them while they're young and tender, because they shoot to seed quickly when the weather turns hot. In May the plants are sometimes attacked by flea beetles, pinhead-sized jumping black insects. Diatomaceous earth, available commercially as Perma-Guard, usually foils the beetles. **GAI CHOY**

Japanese radish. In the Orient, the radish is a staple, not just a salad and appetizer food like our summer radish. The largest of these radishes are served as cooked vegetables; small and medium sized varieties are also pickled or served raw, either sliced or grated. Smaller varieties mature in six to eight weeks; larger ones, like the prodigious, cabbage-sized Sakurajima, take as long as five months. While not as delicate and crisp as our quick-growing summer radishes, these are more versatile, and most of them keep well in winter storage. Sow the larger, long-season radishes in spring, medium varieties like Mino Early and Miyashige (fifty days) in early summer. Deeply dug, humus-rich soil will produce good-quality roots. These deep rooters are a good crop to follow early lettuce. **DAIKON**

Chinese spinach. Another good succession crop, this nutritious member of the amaranth family dotes on hot weather. Plants set out to follow an early radish crop will be ready to pick in midsummer, when few other garden greens are available. I've transplanted young seedlings 1 inch high by taking a good clump of soil with them, watering well, and shading them for several days, but larger seedlings usually don't survive transplanting. Another way to get a head start with *hinn choy* would be to plant seeds in peat pots and set the whole pot in the ground. Many gardeners prefer to plant seeds directly in the ground. They should be planted in rows 12 to 15 inches apart, and the seedlings should be thinned to stand 4 to 6 inches apart. Seedlings of the amaranth family vary widely, and you may find some with reddish streaks or leaves wholly tinged with dark red. *Hinn choy* has a mild flavor and is an excellent vegetable for braising with more pungent greens, and, of course, it blends well in almost any soup. You can cut the top leaves from the plant and come back for another cutting from the side branches in a week or so. **HINN CHOY**

Edible chrysanthemum. If you like to keep your family guessing, serve a salad into which you've snipped a few *shungiku* leaves and ask them to identify the pleasantly aromatic flavor. This edible, annual member of the chrysanthemum family bears yellow, daisy-like flowers, but its flavor is best before it flowers. Use *shungiku* as **SHUNGIKU** you would herbs or mint, by the sprig rather than the basketful. Sow the seeds in early spring and thin the plants to 4 inches apart. Plants grow bushier and produce more leaves when their tops are harvested first, leaving side shoots to develop later.

BOK CHOY   Chinese cabbage, also called *pak coi*. There are two forms of Chinese cabbage: *wong bok*, which forms a solid head, and *bok choy*, which is leafy, with white-ribbed, loosely grouped stalks. *Bok choy*, the lesser known, is a good cut-and-come-again vegetable; you can harvest individual leaves over a period of weeks. All Chinese cabbages go to seed when days are long. It's best, therefore, to treat *bok choy* as a fall crop, planting seeds in summer and thinning to 12 inches apart. Seedlings are difficult to transplant successfully. Count on two months from seed to harvest.

GOW CHOY   Chinese chives. This pungent, flat-leafed perennial has a flavor stronger than chives, closer to garlic. Avoid long cooking, which makes it stringy. Plant seeds two weeks before the final frost. Space plants 10 inches apart. Seedlings don't mind light frost, and well-established plants live through the winter unmulched here in south-central Pennsylvania. Feeling adventurous? Try eating the flower buds as the Chinese do.

SEED SOURCES

Grace's Gardens
Johnny's Selected Seeds
Tsang and Ma International

Pick Them Early

Before we begin to take for granted once again the luxury of eating fresh-picked garden vegetables daily, perhaps a few picking hints are in order.

First, here are several general principles to keep in mind:

(1) Young, rapidly growing vegetables generally contain more vitamin C than those that are mature. Vitamin A content, on the other hand, increases in some vegetables (peppers, for example), as they complete their growth.

(2) Pick vegetables fresh for each meal. Food value is lost when vegetables are kept overnight in the refrigerator.

(3) When possible, pick above-ground vegetables at the end of a clear, sunny day. Some studies have shown that vitamin content is at its height then, and plants apparently use up some of their vitamin C at night.

Now, a few guidelines for harvesting each spring vegetable at its best.

ASPARAGUS   Snap off six- to eight-inch spears at ground level. Cutting shorter stalks is wasteful, although most of us will admit to having occasionally sacrificed overall volume of yield for a few early short spears of this spring-tonic vegetable. Do cut the spears, though, before the scales on their tips begin to branch out. Pick stalks that are pencil-size and larger; thinner ones should be left to strengthen the plant. Some gardeners maintain that asparagus shoots are most tender when picked early in the day.

An established bed may be harvested for eight weeks, a three-year-old bed for three weeks, and a two-year-old bed for no more than one week (and then only the thumb-size or larger shoots should be removed).

BROCCOLI Your first harvest will be the central head, which may be as small as two inches or as large as eight inches. In any case, cut the cluster of green florets while it is still compact and well before the buds separate and begin to flower. Smaller florets will then grow in the leaf axils. Keep cutting them to encourage continuous production. Although a broccoli plant will usually bear from spring through fall, I like to make a late spring planting for a fresh fall crop.

CABBAGE For sauerkraut or cole slaw, cut the heads as soon as they are solid. For soup or cooked cabbage, cut alternate heads in a closely planted row whenever they are large enough, even if they're not firm yet. Watch the cabbage row in rainy weather and try to use the heads before they split. After you've whacked off the central head, small sprouts will usually form at the edges of the stump.

CANTALOUPE If the cantaloupe separates cleanly from the stem when you lift it gently, it's ripe. Other clues: full, fruity aroma; pronounced embossing of netting veins; color changing to yellow-green. Cantaloupes picked before they are ripe will not gain any sweetness off the vine, but they will soften.

CHARD Start cutting when leaves are seven inches high. Keep cutting the old leaves to encourage new growth, but choose the younger leaves for table use. Chard has a deep, vigorous root that can support season-long growth even if the plant is repeatedly sheared.

ENDIVE AND ESCAROLE Eat the thinnings any time. When the main crop plants are ten to twelve inches in diameter, blanch them by tying the outer leaves together over the crown. In two or three weeks, the hearts will be pale and tender. Watch for rot in wet weather.

FENNEL Cut for salad or stewing as soon as the base bulb forms at least a two-inch clump. The young ferny tops are good in salads. Cut the tender stalks before they go to seed; old ones are tough and stringy. Tender thinnings are good to eat right in the garden.

KOHLRABI This bulbous member of the cabbage family is at its best when small and tender. Start picking when the bulbs are two inches in diameter. Large, old specimens become woody. If plants are crowded and you want to pick a mature one growing between two that are still not ready to harvest, cut below the bulb. Kohlrabi roots entangle with their neighbors, and younger plants may suffer shock if closely planted older roots are pulled.

LETTUCE Eat thinnings and outer leaves any time. Lettuce tends to be crisper in the morning before the sun hits it.

Leaf lettuce: individual leaves may be picked whenever they are large enough.

Butterhead lettuce: pick when a soft head forms.

Head lettuce: at its best when it has formed a fairly solid head, but I always start picking while heads are still somewhat loose so as to get the most out of the row before hot weather toughens it or rain splits and rots the heads.

PEAS The lowest blossoms on the stalk will develop into pods first. Pick the pods daily, choosing those in which the peas have filled out the pods. Rough-surfaced, pale, or yellowed pods are over-mature. Cook or freeze the crop as soon as possible after picking.

RADISH Summer radishes should be picked as soon as they're large enough to be worth washing. Those left in the ground past maturity will be tough and bitter.

RHUBARB An established bed may be harvested for two months in the spring. Take no more than a third of the stalks from a plant at each picking. And the stalk should be pulled, not cut.

SPINACH Cut the first large outer leaves as soon as they've grown big enough to be worth your while. Dick Raymond, in his book *Down to Earth Vegetable Gardening*, recommends shearing the whole plant off close to ground level to prevent its going to seed quickly. Since bolting is also determined by plant sex, though, there's no way you can gain complete control over spinach's exasperating tendency to bolt to seed. Most plantings are a mixture of male, female, and self-fertile plants. The male spinach plants are the first to form seed stalks. Just start picking this shortlived plant early, and enjoy it while you have it!

SUGAR PEAS Pick the flat pods of older varieties like Mammoth Melting Sugar before the peas begin to bulge. The new Sugar Snap is sweetest when the pods begin to swell with peas. Harvest the crop daily. Sugar peas lose quality rapidly in hot weather.

TURNIPS Thinnings make good soup or stewed greens. The tops are really richer in vitamins than the roots. Start pulling the roots when they are an inch and a half to two inches in diameter. Those that grow larger than three inches soon become coarse.

Some Unresolved Gardening Problems

I really shouldn't complain about gardening problems. After all, our garden does take care of us year-round. Of course, it requires a steady but not unreasonable amount of planning and tending, but in return I can count on a generous harvest of tender lettuce, sweet peas, juicy tomatoes, peppers, squash, cabbages, and so much more. I've got plenty of reasons for contentment. Still, I must admit that I've never found satisfactory solutions to a number of gardening dilemmas—obvious annoyances like certain bugs and weeds, as well as other abiding vexations. I suppose every gardener must have a personal list of problems. What follow are a few of mine:

Squash borers, squash bugs, and cucumber beetles. The borer is the most insidious of these insects; the first symptom of borer damage is often a drooping plant. Although I follow the usual preventive measures—burying onion skins in the planting soil and tossing soil over stem joints to encourage auxiliary rooting—sooner or later the borers always get my squash plants. Now, I can —and do—replant zucchini, and much of the winter squash is usually ready to pick before the plants fold up from borer on-slaughts; but just once I'd like to see them continue to grow vig-orously and large-leafed all season long.

Squash bugs, those ugly gray insects that suck plant juices, aren't hard to pick by hand—if you have all day. Dusting with rotenone or diatomaceous earth helps too, especially if you spray the undersides of the leaves, where the shield-shaped insects lurk. But have you ever tried crawling down a 50-foot row of squash plants and spraying *both* sides of the leaves?

Cucumber beetles damage plants most severely by spreading wilt. Planting wilt-resistant varieties, interplanting with radishes, and dusting with rotenone reduce their threat. Still, I usually make a second planting of cucumbers in June or early July in order to have cukes all summer. If cucumber beetles were to become ex-tinct, I would not miss that sinking sensation I feel when I first see those small yellow-and-black beetles in June.

Another vexing question is how to have garden lettuce ready to pick during tomato season. Now, I know how, theoretically: You keep the roots cool, give the plants some light shade, and plant a heat-resistant variety like soft-leafed, light-green Kagran (available from Johnny's Selected Seeds). I've done all those things, and they work; but I want *more* lettuce. For those of us who like to make a meal of a tossed salad in hot weather, a crisper lettuce leaf and a more dependable supply in the dog days would be a real break-through.

Weed control in the asparagus patch has so far eluded my inge-nuity. The row runs north to south, you see, and the west wind bends the tall stalks toward the east. By midsummer the mulch or manure we spread next to the row has started to sprout weed seeds, and the strip must be rototilled. But how do you rototill when your path is blocked by bent-over asparagus foliage? I need a flunky to hold the greenery back as I progress down the row, or a strong third arm to hold a stick out ahead of me. A weed-free mulch would help, of course, but we use what we have around here, and buying enough straw to cover a space 4 feet wide by 150 feet long goes against the grain. I *could* let the hay rot so weed seeds would sprout and die, but enough would still survive to require tilling, I'm sure.

Cantaloupes are fickle. When days are steamy and nights are hot, they reward you with flavor that truly does match the catalogue descriptions. We planted Burpee's Ambrosia two summers ago and raved about it. Last summer was cool, though, and our cantaloupes—from the same seed, raised the same way—were what we euphemistically call "fruit salad quality," deteriorating in early September to "pickling quality." The hens, we discovered, liked them better than we did, and we shared our crop with them quite freely. I don't want to move south, but I do wish I could be assured a tasty, sweet cantaloupe crop every year.

Cabbage splits in wet weather. You can often prevent that annoyance by twisting or pulling on the stalk to break feeder roots so the head absorbs less water. When rain is heavy and continuous, though, even that ploy fails. I use just-split heads for slaw, and those that have been split a week for kraut, and I cut off older heads so small new ones will sprout around the stump. Still, I'd like to find a way to carry a row of cabbages intact throughout a rainy season.

Birds eat sunflower seeds right off the stalk. Now, it's true that we use many of the smaller sunflower seeds to feed our birds in winter. But we want them to eat according to our plan, see? They're supposed to eat weed seeds in summer and entertain us at the bird feeder in winter. For them to strip sunflower heads of unripe seeds in balmy August is unfair. It's difficult to hold a grudge against those brilliant, darting goldfinches, but we *are* tempted to bag the sunflower heads or cover them with net. It's just that so many other garden tasks clamor for attention in late summer that we never quite get around to it.

If, on the same day, I plant a seventy-day corn, an eighty-day corn, and an eighty-eight-day corn, they will all start to bear in the same week. Don't ask me why; it must be Murphy's Corn Law.

I know who's to blame for this final problem, and I know why it happens, but that doesn't make it any easier to deal with: I grow too much! Thirty-six tomato plants for two people? Five kinds of beans, four kinds of peppers? The garden's my lab; I try out new and unfamiliar varieties each year, so there's good reason for my extravagance. But if you come around here during lettuce or zucchini or cucumber time, you won't escape without a bagful of something green!

JUNE

Volunteer Vegetables

As I weed my way down the rows of early lettuce, I find that not every out-of-place plant is a marauding thistle, bindweed, or crabgrass. There are surprises there in the row—plants seeded by birds, blown in by the wind, tossed by a passing peach eater, or buried under the mulch by the cook (who is also the gardener). These volunteers that spring up all green and vigorous, right in the middle of the path, cause a break in the rhythm of my hoeing. They made it through the winter on their own. Often, in fact, they seem more prosperous than some carefully nurtured crops, perhaps because only the strongest of the seeds have survived the random conditions of their planting.

What shall I do about them? Hoe around them? Transplant them? Grub them out? What do you do about volunteer vegetables in your garden?

The easiest solution, of course, is to weed them out along with the foxtail and mallow, and to continue to order the garden by the neatly drawn plan on paper rustling there in the breeze under your trowel.

But suppose you can't resist a free plant, a gamble, or a persistent spark of green life that keeps saying "tomatoes" in the bean patch. Suppose you want to give them a chance, or a try. Which volunteer vegetables are worth keeping? Which are likely to disappoint you?

At one time or another, we've found all of the following vegetable volunteers in our garden. Gradually we've learned a little about how they were pollinated and how they perform, so that we now know which ones we want to keep when they turn up.

LETTUCE

Self-sown lettuce is very useful. It is usually vigorous, often matures between your regular plantings, and may easily be transplanted if you find it between rows. Volunteer leaf lettuce comes true to variety because it is almost invariably self-pollinated. It is so good, in fact, that you may want to let a late-summer stalk of leaf lettuce flower and produce seed, just to see what will happen. (You can save the seed too, of course.)

POTATOES

When I find the unmistakable dark green crumpled foliage of the potato plant growing in the kitchen garden, I usually let it be.

> We are apt to covet the things which we cannot have; but we are happier when we love the things which grow because they must.
> *Liberty Hyde Bailey*

It co-exists quite well with most other vegetables. Potato volunteers generally originate in peelings, or in small spoiled potatoes buried in the garden. This vegetative reproduction assures that the new potatoes will be the same variety as the originals. How much closer can you get to "something for nothing" than harvesting a handful of new potatoes from a plant that grew out of the eyes in a potato peeling?

TOMATOES Like lettuce, tomatoes are generally self-pollinated. Seed from any non-hybrid variety like Rutgers, Sunray, or Marglobe will come true to the parent plant. Seedlings from hybrids will be unpredictable and are generally inferior to the parent. Tomato seed seems to survive any treatment short of fire, and sometimes I wonder about that. You can feed tomatoes to your hens or pigs and get them all back again next year, in triplicate. After tending my sheltered hybrid seedlings for two months, I am always struck by the irony of finding a fistful of tomato seedlings at the edge of the patch. They have waited there all winter until the time was right.

I usually allow a few tomato seedlings to grow from Sunray, cherry, or plum tomatoes. Transplanting does them no harm. Volunteers are worth keeping for two reasons: they often reach their peak of productivity late in the season when early plantings are giving out; and the later-started, more compact vines are easier to protect from fall frosts.

ASPARAGUS Asparagus self-sows readily, and the new plants are just as good as the originals. Transplant them while small, filling gaps in your established bed; add to your present planting, or give them away. Keep them well weeded and allow yourself a cutting when they're three years old.

SUNFLOWERS Sunflowers often produce volunteers—there are always a few that the blue jays miss. They usually can't be transplanted well, though; it is best to keep only those that spring up in places where they won't be in the way. Sometimes it happens that a sunflower appears just where you always needed one but didn't know it— by the bird feeder or alongside the woodshed. For good big seed heads next fall, thin the volunteers to three feet apart and give them manure tea or a rich mulch of barn bedding.

DILL The seedlings appear as feathery, pungent wisps of green, scattered around the original plant or blown across the garden by the wind. They don't intrude much on other plants, and we're always glad to see them. The long tap root makes transplanting chancy.

PEAS Peas generally come true to variety, but they don't volunteer as thickly as tomatoes or lettuce, probably because gardeners manage to harvest most of the seed pods, and those we miss contain only a few potential plants. Volunteer pea plants will thrive and produce crops, but since they are generally out of step with the other pea plantings, and there are usually only a few of them, they are not likely to be worth saving. What can you do with eight peas?

PUMPKIN AND SQUASH Both the tough-skinned winter keepers and the tender summer

114

varieties cross so readily that all kinds of combinations are possible. Don't worry about the squash (*Cucurbita pepo*) having crossed with melons (*Cucumis melo*). These plants will cross freely, but only within their own species. Your tender-skinned summer zucchini, though, may cross with a hard-rinded Hubbard squash, yielding a hard-fleshed vegetable that doesn't keep well . . . or any of a thousand other variations. Some pumpkin-squash crosses are good. All are edible. Some are palatable. And some will even come true—like the Hallowe'en pumpkins we raised last year from a volunteer vine nurtured by the chicken manure in which it grew. So the answer to this one is you never can tell. If you have enough garden space and like a little mystery, let them grow. You can always feed the crop to the animals if it isn't something you want to eat. If your space is limited, though, you could grow a lot of "sure things" in the space taken by one pumpkin vine of uncertain parentage.

Succession Planting

It's a good place, the June garden. The annual rite of "putting in the garden" is mostly finished. Peas are blossoming, tomatoes set out, spinach and lettuce ready to eat. Bean seedlings sprout. Early cabbage is heading. All signs point ahead.

But some rows, those nearing their peak of production, will decline in a few weeks, when weather turns hot. Spinach will bolt and toughen, lettuce go to seed, radishes turn woody. What will replace them?

Weeds, most likely, in plots where the garden is "put in" once and for all in the spring. That needn't happen, though. Even a small patch can produce a continuous vegetable harvest. The secret is succession planting—just another term, really, for planning ahead and using every inch.

Succession planting involves the planned—or impromptu—replacement of a finished row or plant with seed or plants of another variety. You've practiced this method whenever you've set out late cabbage plants to follow the peas, or planted midsummer snap beans after a planting of early lettuce. The idea is to keep each row full of producing plants.

Effective succession planting depends on combining the following considerations, a strategy that can become as full of double consequences as a chess game:

Time Required for Maturity

Catalogues figure maturity dates from seed-planting time, except

115

for tomatoes, celery, eggplant and such, which are usually counted from the setting out of started plants. Sixty-day cabbage may be followed by bush beans or limas, but ninety-day cabbage would leave time only for such quick-growing crops as radishes.

Cucumbers, liking warm weather, can follow an early crop of such cool-weather crops as lettuce and radishes. Spinach should be planted early or late, but not in midsummer heat. And so forth.

Generally, it is best to alternate leafy kale, lettuce, and cabbage crops, heavy users of soil nitrogen, with root crops which need less nitrogen but plenty of potash. When possible, spread compost between crops. Legumes may be grown after any leafy crops to help restore depleted soil nitrogen.

The average date of the first frost in your area will determine how much leeway you have in planting third crops or using a late-maturing vegetable as your second crop. Such frost-resistant vegetables as cabbage, turnips, broccoli, and kale will extend your harvest, but they should be ready to use by frost, not just half grown.

Soil in June is warmer than it was in May, and often drier. In planting succession crops, make a deeper furrow than in earlier plantings and water the furrow first, before planting the seed. Then rake dry soil over the seed, avoiding the surface caking that discourages seedlings. Always firm the soil well, too. Seed left in a dry air pocket won't germinate.

The following early-maturing vegetables may either be followed by a second crop, or used as second crops to follow other vegetables: Bush beans, beets, cabbage, carrots, radishes, lettuce, turnips, kohlrabi, spinach, endive, broccoli.

And here are some other good second crops, better planted late than early: corn, cucumbers, okra, kale, rutabaga, summer squash, Chinese radishes.

Even among such vegetable as tomatoes, peppers, and Brussels sprouts, which occupy the row throughout the season, you can reap more from a row by interplanting—sowing a short-term crop of radishes, say, between the widely spaced plants. The radishes will mature by the time tomatoes start to sprawl. We have also pulled alternate lettuce heads in a row and planted bush bean seed in the spaces. By the time the beans were up, we were cutting the remaining lettuce. Planting lettuce between broccoli works well too; the growing broccoli shades the lettuce from the hot sun.

Cover crops make good succession plantings too. If your larder is filling up, and you really have enough radishes, consider sowing your idle row to a good green-manure crop like buckwheat, clover, or rye that will enrich the soil when turned under. Some gardeners also plant cover crops *between* vegetable rows. In order to suppress weeds effectively when using this method, plant your

Best Temperatures for Vegetables

Soil Requirements of the Plant

Average Fall Frost Dates

cover crop thickly. Rows should be at least three feet apart, too. Another practice followed by many soil-building gardeners is the sowing of a crop of winter rye between rows of corn after the last cultivating. This has the additional advantage of preventing winter erosion on the cornbare land.

Our garden, begun as neat straight rows, ends the season as patchwork, with a few turnips tucked into the cabbage row, a bed of lettuce at the corner where the dog had dug up a zucchini plant, an end row beginning as kohlrabi and ending in rutabagas.

This is the time to plan for that continuous feast and select seed for your succession crops. We like to keep the seed packets ready in a small basket on the kitchen counter. See what combinations you can work out on paper or in the garden; then, as time permits, you can replant a corner, a gap, or a whole row.

Corn, the All-American Vegetable

Corn was domesticated by the Indians, in a gradual process of selection by which, ultimately, they developed five separate strains: popcorn, flint corn, dent corn, flour corn, and sweet corn. If man changed corn, though, the development of an agriculture based on corn also changed man. Former nomads found themselves remaining in one place to tend their corn crops, with the result that a whole civilization came to be built around the culture of corn. The Mayas and Aztecs, in fact, devised their calendars because they needed to plan their corn plantings systematically.

Corn quickly became a staple in early colonial and later pioneer settlements. In many pioneer homes, Gertrude Harris reminds us in her book *Foods of the Frontier*, having enough food meant having enough corn. A practical colonial pastor, Reverend John Campanius, even revised the line, "Give us this day our daily bread," in the Lord's Prayer to read: "Give us a plentiful supply of venison and corn." At first, colonists depended primarily on the sturdy, coarse cooking corn, which stored well and cooked into hearty, filling hot dishes.

By 1799, sweet corn seed had become more widely available for home gardens, and in the following century named varieties were sold through seed catalogues. Despite the fact that corn was exported to Europe shortly after Columbus completed his voyage here, sweet corn remains a distinctly (although not, of course, exclusively) American food. One well-known British seed catalogue for 1978 lists only four kinds of sweet corn (but *six* kinds of Brussels sprouts!). As recently as 1950, when my husband came to this country from Poland, he considered sweet corn a marvelous revelation; in the Central Europe of his experience, corn was field corn, grown only for animals.

Thanks then to the Indians, who purified and propagated the sweet-corn strain (and ate some fresh as a luxury, while storing much of it in dried form), and to Luther Burbank, who increased the number of rows on a cob from eight to twelve, and thanks to many unknown breeders and backyard gardeners, we can grow corn today that is sweeter and more tender than any ever grown in the history of the grain.

Indeed, there are so many sweet-corn varieties that the process of selection can be difficult for a new corn grower. Stowell's Evergreen, introduced in 1845, is the oldest strain still commercially available. Other good open-pollinated corns include Country Gentleman and Golden Bantam—an early twentieth-century introduction which, with its yellow kernels, was radical for its time; all other sweet corns were white.

There are so many hybrid sweet-corn varieties offered that it would be impossible to discuss them all here, except to mention three different kinds that are widely grown. The sweetest corn of all, and one of the largest and latest, is Silver Queen. If it were an earlier corn, many people would probably plant no other kind. Close behind Silver Queen on our family's rating scale are the yellow and white corns—Butter and Sugar, and Sweet Sue. The newer, extra-sweet varieties offered by many catalogues have been improved recently. Some, like Kandy Korn and Garden Sweet (Stokes) no longer require isolation from other concurrent-tasseling corns to prevent loss of sweetness. Illinichief must still be planted at least 600 feet from other tasseling corn.

North American Indians planted corn when the oak leaves were about the size of squirrel ears, and that's still as good a guide as any. If you prefer to go by the calendar, aim for a week before your last expected frost. If you elect to gamble an extra-early planting in hopes of winning early pickings, choose one of the early or extra-early varieties, some of which are also bred for good performance in cold soil, like PolarVee and Northern Vee (Stokes) or Blitz and Spring Gold (Harris). When using untreated seed in early plantings, sow it much more thickly than the recommended 2–3 seeds per foot if the soil temperature is below 60°F. Thin later, as usual, to 8–10 inches apart for the shorter early varieties and 12–16 inches apart for the larger late kinds. Row spacing should be 30–40 inches depending on plant size and method of cultivation. One pound of seed is enough to plant 800 feet of row at the usual rate. Cover the seed with 1–2 inches of loose soil, firmed down with the back of the rake.

To produce well-filled ears, corn plants need neighbors on all sides, because the pollen is carried from the tassels of one plant to the silks of another by the wind. When you consider that each thread in the tuft of silk at the top of the ear originates in an embryo kernel on the cob, and that each individual silk must receive a grain of pollen if the kernel is to develop, you may find yourself marveling at the random chanciness of a process that yields so dependable a result. When you picture the path of the pollen grains, you will see why corn should be planted in a block at least four rows deep. If you've allotted 300 feet in your garden for corn, you'll have more complete pollination—and thus better-filled ears—if you make the plot short and wide rather than long and thin: 15 by 20 feet, not 30 by 10.

Perfection doesn't last long in the corn patch; sweet corn continues to mature on the stalk and in hot weather quickly becomes tough and starchy. The sugar in sweet corn starts to turn to starch after picking. So it makes much more sense to plant small blocks of corn at intervals—about every two weeks—than to make a main planting too large to deal with comfortably in a short space of time. We sometimes plant early, mid-season, and late varieties at the same time but we also make several other plantings to stretch out the season. The planting you count on for freezing should, in fact, be a fairly late one—maturing as close to September as possible—for the most efficient use of freezer space. It's fun to gamble at the end of the season, too, by planting corn for a summer's-end treat. To do this, count back at least 10 weeks from the average date of your first fall frost, and plant a quick-maturing variety. When planting 80 days before frost, I use a 65-day corn, because cool nights that begin right after Labor Day slow corn growth considerably.

Corn likes plenty of sun, rich soil, abundant rain (especially as tassels are forming), and hot weather. You can't manipulate these conditions as you might wish to do, but you *can* plant the seed in well-manured soil away from trees, give it a side-dressing or two of manure tea as it grows, mulch or irrigate it if you have a small patch, and keep down weeds that rob the corn of moisture and nutrients. Weed control should begin early, with hoeing or roto-tilling several times before the corn is knee high. Avoid chopping too close to the roots, which extend at least a foot to the side of a two-foot-tall plant. The "tillers" arising from the base of the plant should not be removed; although their value to the plant is not entirely understood, there are more good reasons for leaving them on than for taking them off.

Most of us have a certain amount of competition for our home-grown sweet corn. The two most common insect problems in the northern states are the corn borer and the corn earworm. You can prevent cornborer damage by planting your main crop relatively late in the season after borer activity has passed its peak and by plowing or tilling under the corn stalks and stubble in which the borer likes to take refuge over the winter. Direct attack methods include capturing the moth of the borer in light traps, applying *Bacillus thuringiensis* (available commercially as Dipel or Thuricide) to infect the borer larvae and, if you have a small garden, probing below the borer's entrance hole in the stalk to crush and remove it. Ladybugs eat borer eggs.

The earworm works its way from the silks, where it hatches, down into the ear, eating all the way. Squirting a few drops of mineral oil into the silks when they've begun to dry (indicating that pollination is complete) will cut down on a lot of earworm activity. Also, be sure to crush any of these larvae you may find while husking corn, or they'll live to lay more eggs.

Japanese beetles sometimes infest corn, occasionally damaging the silks enough to interfere with pollination. Inoculating your lawn with milky-spore disease provides an effective long-term method of control, but if the beetles are on the rampage and you must do something *now,* arm yourself with a large can of water and knock the beetles off the plants into the can. (My husband likes to toss these hand-picked beetles to the bass in our pond.) If you want to be sure the beetles don't survive, float a thin layer of kerosene on top of the water in the can.

I've been surprised that we haven't had coons raiding our corn. I can only conclude that they're finding food elsewhere, because we do see their footprints by the creek. Those little marauders have an uncanny way of sensing *exactly* when the corn is at its best —neither young and watery nor old and tough with doughy kernels, but at the just-right milk stage, when the milky juice in the kernel seeps through the cut you've made with your fingernail . . . if you get there before the coons.

Some of the more ingenious coon-spooking devices I've heard about include: walking barefoot around the patch, planting pumpkins or squash around the perimeter of the plot, erecting a wobbly, hard-to-climb fence, leaving a portable radio on all night, dusting the ears with red pepper, and draping highly seasoned work clothes on plants at the edge of the plot. The fact that there are so many remedies would seem to indicate that no one of them is a sure-fire cure, but perhaps one of these or a combination of several will work for you, as it apparently has for others.

Meanwhile, it's time to pace off the corn patch and count out the seed, so that by midsummer you'll have basketsful of sweet, tender ears to be happily slathered with butter and eaten in company with your favorite people.

Globe Artichokes in the North?

Somewhat to my surprise, several enterprising New England gardeners have successfully grown the thistlelike globe artichoke—even to the point of feasting on the fleshy-petalled flower bud that makes all the effort worthwhile.

John and Nancy Chilelli of Bennington, Vermont, planted three mail-order globe artichoke plants (from Gurney's, in Yankton, South Dakota) in their garden right after Memorial Day last year. One plant died, but the other two flourished, and went on to produce a total of seven globes, three of which they harvested at twelve inches in diameter—eating size and then some.

In response to my request for more information on their growing methods, John and Nancy replied that they had planted the artichokes in light loamy soil that was rather consistently moist, but at the same time well drained. Cucumber vines planted 2 to 5 feet away spread a leafy mulch close to the plants. The Chilellis fed their plants every two weeks. And they had a lot of fun surprising John's parents with the impressive results.

The Chilellis were kind enough to send me a photograph of one of their globe artichoke plants. The handsome vegetable has two buds, one almost edible size, borne in the center of a thistle-leafed crown. Amazing but true, and needless to say, there are even more ambitious plans for a larger planting of globe artichokes in the Chilelli garden this year.

Even farther north (ten miles south of Quebec, in fact) Geoff Hewitt of Franklin County, Vermont, coaxed one of his three first-year plants into producing a globe a little larger than a baseball. After planting his globe artichokes, Geoff cut back the outer leaves, once they had grown to a height of about 14 inches, in order to stimulate growth of the plant's central crown. The plant that produced the edible-size globe—despite three frosts between August 31 and September 10—also bore two marble-sized buds. Geoff planned to protect each of his plants with both mulch and inverted plastic trash cans over the frigid winter.

When Eliot Coleman was gardening in Harborside, Maine, he grew globe artichokes from seed (Grande Beurre from Thompson and Morgan in Somerdale, New Jersey) planted in late February in a friend's heated greenhouse. Eliot grew twenty-five plants and gave away nineteen. The remaining six were moved from the greenhouse, which had auxiliary heat, to a sun-heated greenhouse, where they endured cool nights for a few weeks. Having lost a crop of celery when it shot to seed after an early chilling, Eliot had a hunch.

"I figured that if I could trick the artichokes the same way, they would then produce the part I wanted to eat the first year. Three of the plants did just that. Delicious. Two of the plants gave one big bud each and the third a big bud plus a smaller side shoot bud."

The Coleman artichoke seeds were planted in homemade potting soil, and the plants were fertilized with compost while growing in the garden, in sandy soil with a southern exposure.

"Actually," Eliot continued, "the plants did not grow well by my standards. They had bug holes and no real bloom to them. They may need more lime, or more phosphorus or potassium."

According to Victor Tiedjens, author of *The Vegetable Encyclopedia*, globe artichokes do need a generous supply of potash, which may be provided by mulching with seaweed or spreading wood ashes while the plants are dormant. Lime should also be in good supply. The plant is a vigorous grower and needs a fertile, well-drained soil, rich in organic matter. At the same time, though, it requires plenty of moisture. Buds that form during a dry season will be tough.

Don't let water pool around the crown of the plant, for it is very vulnerable to fungus disease. When setting out seedlings, take care not to bury them too deeply, or the growing center of the plant may rot. After harvesting a bud, cut the stem back to ground level. Disease can start in the stump and work down into the crown. For the same reason, cut off all top growth in the fall so that no rotting stems remain around the plant.

Giving the globe artichoke southern exposure—preferably near a sheltering building—makes winter protection easier. Mound leaves lightly over the crown, hold the mulch down with a basket or crate, and pack manure around and over that. Then cross your fingers . . . but don't hold your breath! Persuading these tender perennials to winter over in northern states is a chancy business at best. Nevertheless, it *has* been done.

SOURCES OF SEED

Charles Hart
DiGiorgi Company, Inc.
William Dam Seeds
Thompson and Morgan
Burpee Seeds
Park Seed Company
Gurney Seed and Nursery
   Company
Comstock, Ferre and Company

The Child's Garden

A sense of delight in growing things can be both caught and taught. The best way to encourage children to take an interest in gardening is to give them their own small plots of land and make the experience of tending those plots as satisfying as possible. That's not always easy. A child's gardening project can turn into a disaster, with weeds overrunning the flowers or vegetables, parents scolding, and the young gardener feeling dutiful but bored. Be careful, therefore, to give your children every chance to succeed. A child who is successful at growing something will want to do it again.

The single most important factor is the size of the garden: keep it small! For most children younger than ten, a 2- by 3-foot bed is quite large enough. Young children usually like to feel that the space is all theirs to do with as they please. They often appreciate having their gardens enclosed or defined by boards or stones. Older children might prefer to have a single row in your large garden, where they may plant what they wish, or they might want to take responsibility for a single crop. Other ways to help ensure good experiences for your children include the following:

Use fresh seed, not that jumble of leftover packets that has sifted to the bottom of the seed box.

Give the children good ground in a sunny spot.

Put markers on planted rows or squares so the children won't accidentally dig them up.

Show them how to thin seedlings, weed, and water plants. Kids need demonstrations, not just verbal directions.

Let them get dirty.

Naturally, you'll want to involve the children in preparing the garden. If they are younger than eight, you'll probably need to do the digging, but young gardeners can rake the soil smooth, break up clumps, and remove stones. They can haul compost in a wagon and dig small holes for seedling transplants. Children ten and older can usually manage the digging for a small plot. No child younger than twelve should be allowed to operate a garden tiller without direct supervision. Tools that are to be used by children should be sturdy and well made.

Most children are quite indignant when their vegetables are damaged by insects. You can help by showing them how to identify the problem and defend their plants. Help them, too, to see that crop failures don't necessarily mean *they* have failed. Adult gardeners have problems too, and we all try again next year.

In general, it's a good idea to encourage young gardeners to grow plants that (1) have large, easy-to-handle seeds, (2) germinate quickly, (3) can stand up to weeds, (4) have few disease and insect problems, (5) bear early, and (6) are fun to eat. At one time or another, our children have tried their hands at the following vegetables.

SNAP BEANS
These are an excellent choice because seeds are large and quick to germinate. Plants are sturdy and bear in about eight weeks.

POPCORN
Somewhat less demanding for rich soil than sweet corn, more resistant to disease and insects, and able to produce well even in fairly dry weather. And, of course, popping and eating the crop is great fun. Plant in blocks rather than single rows.

SUGAR PEAS
Seeds are easy to handle. Pea plants are hardy and pest-free, and they bear generously for several weeks. Good raw or cooked.

TOMATOES
Give your children seedlings you've raised or use seeds of one of the extra-early Sub-Arctic varieties like Early, Midi, or Maxi, which can be planted directly in the ground. (Those varieties can be obtained from Johnny's Selected Seeds.)

123

SUNFLOWERS	Nice large seeds to plant, spectacular plants, colorful flowers, and a nutritious crop of seeds for snacking or for bird feed.
ZUCCHINI	Our son's first cash crop. These have large seeds, grow fast, and produce many pounds of squash. Pick them young so you can use more of them!
PUMPKINS	A single vine will more than cover a 2- by 3-foot bed, but you could try one of the bush varieties or let children plant seeds at the edge of your corn patch. Pumpkins are fun to harvest and use.
CUCUMBERS	Use a disease-resistant variety and keep the plants well watered. Pick daily or every other day to encourage better production.
STRAWBERRIES	If you're thinning your berry patch, give the children some runners to edge their vegetable plots. Let them blossom and bear the first year.
WATERMELON	Mulch well. Small-fruited icebox varieties like Sugar Baby are best.
RADISHES	Quickest of all the vegetables, but use these only in spring and fall. Summer-planted radishes tend to be strong flavored and infested with root maggots, which can be discouraging to young gardeners.

Your children will glow with pride when their produce is served appreciatively at meals. Even a few sugar peas or beans can perk up a soup or salad, and enjoying the harvest reinforces two gardening lessons: "I can grow it!" and "It tastes good!"

Outwitting the Animals

Gardens are for people, but there are wild creatures who consider your vegetable patch as much their territory as the woods and hedgerows. Unlike insect injury, animal damage is often sudden and devastating. An entire row of just-sprouted beans can be wiped out overnight.

In wooded areas, deer can be a serious threat to your larder, but small mammals are often at least as troublesome in suburban and even city gardens as they are in rural sections. Paving over good land for parking lots and developments has eliminated the wild and randomly weedy natural habitat of many small mammals. These displaced creatures are often quick, therefore, to raid the vegetable patches in all of those neatly manicured back yards.

When we moved to our farm, which is surrounded by woods on three sides, we expected trouble with animal depredations. To our surprise, we've lost only a few crops to animals. Rabbits abound, but they apparently find enough wild fare to satisfy them, and I'm sure our dog chases many of them away.

Deer ate all of our sweet corn the first year here, but that was because we had planted it far from the house, near the woods. Ever since then we've planted our corn patch right behind the house, surrounded by open land. Deer seem to prefer not to cross much bare, open grassland. A four-foot-wide strip of chicken wire, laid flat on the ground at the edge of the garden and pegged down in spots, is also a good deterrent. Scattering blood meal or small net bags of human hair clippings might help to fend off the deer —at least until you can get the corn picked. Watch out for the soybeans, too. Deer and rabbits love them.

The versatile raccoons leave charming small handprints in the damp sand at the edge of our stream, but it's hard to appreciate their charm when you find downed cornstalks with gnawed ears. These wily, masked marauders seem to know just when the ears are ready. Planting a barrier of coarse-vined pumpkins around the corn patch should help discourage the raccoons for a time. Some gardeners leave transistor radios on all night in the garden. Rock music is apparently a more effective deterrent than a classical symphony or Muzak. If nothing else helps and you decide to resort to a fence, a simple, two-wire electric fence will do the trick. Or, if you prefer to use a woven fence, make it wobbly, not strung tight, so the raccoons will find it difficult to climb.

Hungry rabbits can be foiled by a few tricks that Mr. McGregor missed. These methods are more effective than throwing a flower pot:

Scatter blood meal along the row. Repeat after rain.

Soak twine in creosote and stretch it around the garden perimeter. Resoak after two weeks.

Put wire cages over rows of special crops. Such cages can serve two purposes. Later, covered with plastic film, they'll protect fall crops from frost.

Skunks are attracted by carrion and food scraps. In digging for this buried treasure they often uproot seedlings. To keep them out of your garden, confine all organic discards to the compost pile and bury dead animals and birds outside the vegetable garden.

They might not be quite as clever as raccoons, but woodchucks are persistent. Old-timers in Lancaster County bury broken glass bottles in woodchuck holes. Mean, but effective. I'd suggest using the same defenses against woodchucks as you'd use against raccoons. If you do decide to fence them out, attach a strip of metal flashing around the top of the fence so the woodchucks can't climb over.

One resourceful gardener, in his search for a way to declare his garden off-limits to animal raiders, decided to mark his boundaries in the same way many wild creatures do. He reported that human urine distributed around the perimeter of the garden is an effective animal deterrent.

The ultimate solution to animal raids is, of course, to fence in your garden. Apart from the expense, a fenced garden can be a nuisance to cultivate with power equipment. And if you keep several garden patches to make good use of special microclimate or soil conditions, as we do, then it is a great bother to fence each one. So most of us resort first to tricks that will reduce, if not eliminate, losses to free-loading animals. None of these tricks is foolproof, but each has worked for someone.

In many cases, you don't need season-long protection anyway, but just a temporary deterrent to get your plants past a certain crucial point. (The newly sprouted bean plants, for example, are most tempting to rabbits.) Animal populations and feeding conditions vary from one year to another, too, and it may be that the rabbits that overran your garden last year will not return.

Vegetables for Gardeners Only

June's the month for gloating in the garden. If you've been raising vegetables for more than a few years, you've probably forgotten how supermarket fare tastes, or doesn't taste. You take for granted the ever-readiness of a row of parsley; the crisp dewy lettuce virtually free for the snatching just outside your kitchen door; the picker's perquisite, green peas just popped from the pod, sweet and crunchy munched right there in the row. In the garden's still-weedless rows of young plants, there is quality you could never buy in a store. Simple freshness gives you a tremendous advantage over shipped-in, wilted and revived vegetables, but there is more to home-grown vegetables than that. You can enjoy the luxury of picking each food at its moment of perfection. And you can include in your menu foods that few stores are able to stock.

As I survey the rows of onion spears, carrot fuzz, ruffly lettuce, and clambering pea vines fanning out from my sink-side view over the kitchen garden, I reflect on how good we have it, we gardeners. We can pick our vegetables when they're scandalously young, because there are plenty. Have you ever tried June peas, plucked when they've just begun to plump the pod, with virtually skinless potatoes stolen from the row's end hill? And young beets, pulled before the roots reach two inches in diameter, so tender and delicious that they need no sauce or even butter? When you grow your own asparagus, you can snap off the crisp spears before the scales even think of opening on their way to flower. Who cares if they're only five inches high? More will be along in a day or so. Raw asparagus, too, is surprisingly sweet and delicate, another picker's reward to be savored on the way back to the kitchen. Once you've sampled fingerling zucchini, you may find yourself treating these eager prolific plants with new respect. Gather the fruits when they're only three to four inches long and thumb-thick. Split them, brush with butter or dot with snippets of bacon, and broil briefly until brown and tender but still solid. This, we've decided, is what zucchini is all about, and we no longer feel guilty about interrupting the squash before it reaches arm size. In fact, we're also spared, to an extent, that other form of zucchini guilt—having a surplus that we don't have time to process but can't bear to waste. Some zucchini still grow large, it is true, but they weigh more lightly on our conscience since we've given ourselves permission to eat the young fruits. And we even manage to pickle some.

For the most part, it's only in a garden that you'll find truly ripe produce, matured right on the plant. Red peppers are sweeter and contain more vitamin A than green ones, but they don't keep long, so they are not easy to buy. Not until we began raising our own did we realize that a red bell pepper can be as sweet as an apple. Commercially grown tomatoes are picked green (often even white) and ripened in storage. Those labeled "vine-ripened" were probably left on the vine until the mature-green stage, or at best until they began to color up, but certainly not until truly ripe. Juicy, red tomatoes can't be shipped: they can only be grown at home. So enjoy yours. They're special. Sweet corn, too, is a revelation when you begin growing your own after years of buying it, even if you've gotten it from a farm stand. When you cook corn within a few minutes after picking, you capture the natural sugars before they can turn to starch. It's so good that you can make a meal of corn—just corn, with a tall glass of milk.

Then there are the vegetables that exist only in seed catalogues and home gardens, nowhere else. I'm thinking of the turnip Des Vertus Marteau, of which the Epicure Seeds catalogue says "You've just found a brand new vegetable." And they're right. This turnip is buttery-sweet, tender, and delicious. The Sugar Snap pea, offered by most seed companies this year, has also been hailed as a new vegetable—one with a pod that remains eating-tender even when the peas have attained full size. We gardeners can grow special, small, solid cucumbers just for pickling, squash with edible seeds that don't need hulling (Eat-All and Lady Godiva), salsify for hearty winter soups, and dainty, lavender-flowered chives. Our family especially prizes the delicate green tops of very young onion sets snipped over potatoes and soups. To get them that young, we must grow our own.

Wary as I am of declaring any one path to be the only way, I can't seem to escape the conclusion that to be sure you are serving the very best at your table you must raise it yourself. Enjoy it all, fellow gardeners. The weeds are coming, but in June we still think we'll be able to control them. And if that asparagus patch still exists only in your mind's eye, it's not too late to plant some from seed, for good eating in the future.

SOURCES FOR VEGETABLE SEEDS

Turnip, Des Vertus Marteau
Epicure Seeds
Squash, Eat-All
Farmer Seed and Nursery Co.
Pumpkin, Lady Godiva
William Dam Seeds
Gurney Seed & Nursery Co.
Geo. W. Park Seed Co., Inc.

JULY

Drought Insurance

Some of the influences that affect the garden are beyond our control. Random and inexplicable occurrences happen, and sometimes it doesn't rain for weeks on end.

And yet, what you do *does* make a difference. Attentive, careful husbandry helps plants to weather the stress of heat and drought.

The crucial growing weeks in the vegetable garden are just ahead. Who knows what they'll bring? Generous rain to keep us complacent and make the weeds grow, or dry weather to sharpen our gardening skills and increase the value of each juicy tomato? If you manage your garden as if there were a drought just around the corner, you'll have some insurance against the loss of your vegetable crops.

Increasing your soil's content of organic matter is the single most effective gardening technique to help plants keep producing despite lack of rain. Decayed organic matter acts like a sponge. It holds water and plant nutrients in reserve for the plants to draw on in times of stress. Adding humus to heavy clay soil provides more open pathways for the penetration of fine feeder roots. When improved by organic matter, sandy soil retains water for a longer time. Good humus-building practices include tilling under green manure crops like clover, rye, or soybeans; digging in manure; putting compost in the planting hole with transplanted seedlings, and sheet-composting right in the garden—tucking vegetable trimmings and such under a layer of mulch. ADDING ORGANIC MATTER

Mulching conserves ground water in several ways. As the mulch decays, it adds humus to the soil. But more immediately, a good carpet of mulch shades and seals the soil surface so that precious water is not lost by surface evaporation—the most devastating cause of plant stress in hot dry weather. Plants lose some water by transpiration through their leaves, it is true, but the water lost by evaporation from bare soil is considerable in summer. Blanket the soil between rows and plants with hay, leaves, straw, old sawdust, discarded carpet, pulled pea vines, grass clippings, wood chips, or what-have-you. Mulch spread over moist soil is most effective. MULCHING

Planting the garden with water conservation in mind is another defensive strategy. Some plants suffer more than others when PLANNING FOR WATER

129

water is short. It makes good sense to group moisture lovers like eggplant, celery, cucumbers, cauliflower, and lettuce close to the hose or the rain barrel. If dry summer weather is the rule rather than the exception in your area, try keeping your garden small. Build up the soil so it's good and rich and plant the rows very close together, or make intensive raised beds, so that you can more easily tend both plants and soil. Planting a windbreak—either shrubs or annual garden plants like kochia, corn, okra, and such —can cut down on the loss of garden water in a windy spot. When making summer plantings, hoe a fairly deep furrow, run a stream of water down the furrow, scatter your seeds, and then firmly tamp fine dry soil over them. Plant summer lettuce where it will receive some light shade.

WATERING   Your watering technique can help or hurt your plants too. After the initial watering-in at transplanting time, avoid giving your crops small frequent doses of water. This only encourages the development of a vulnerable shallow root system. Deep-rooted plants are able to find water even when the top few inches of soil are dry. If you must water, soak the soil slowly and deeply—down to a good four inches.

Ideally, most garden plants need about an inch of water each week. If you take it upon yourself to make up any deficiency between the actual amount of rainfall and the ideal, it's important to realize that the common rotary sprinkler takes several hours to deliver an inch of water, and a good deal evaporates before it ever reaches the soil. More effective methods of delivering water to the plant's root zone, where it matters most, include: running a canvas or perforated plastic hose between the rows to soak the soil; sinking large bottomless cans and leaky or bottomless buckets between plants and periodically filling these reservoirs with water from the hose; irrigating with lengths of metal drainpipe set in a shallow trench between the rows. Drill holes in the bottom of the pipe and fasten the sections together with asphalt cement or caulking. If low ground-water levels necessitate the conservation of well water, consider resuming the time-honored practice of emptying dishwater on special garden plants. Pour the water around the plant's root zone, not on its foliage. Most garden plants, except acid-loving watermelons, potatoes, and blueberries, will thrive on this treatment, unless the water contains concentrations of boron, sodium, chlorine, or other strong cleaning agents.

Excess watering leaches nutrients from the soil. Mulching and digging-in decayed plant matter, on the other hand, will improve your garden whether the season is wet or dry. Every year is different. One always hopes that the current year won't be *too* different. We wish you all the rain you need, and all the mulch you can use.

Dealing with Fungus Diseases

If you have some plants that appear to be diseased, suspect a fungus. Fungi are the most common disease-causing microorganisms in the garden. (Bacteria and viruses are next.) The symptoms of fungus disease are not always clear and specific. Sometimes symptoms that appear to be caused by deficiency of some nutrient, by drought, or by an overdose of fertilizer may in fact be signs of a fungus disease.

Here are some of the many common fungus diseases you should watch for:

BEANS

Plants infected by *bean anthracnose* have cankerlike black spots on the pods. The fungus lives over the winter on dead bean vines and can be carried by affected seeds. *Bean rust* causes small bumps on the undersides of the leaves, which turn yellow and drop off. Pods are spotted with brown patches.

CABBAGE

Cabbage plants are subject to a disease called *cabbage yellows,* which is caused by a fungus that lives on in the soil for as long as twenty years. Symptoms include yellowing and wilting of plants, unevenly formed heads, and bitter flavor. The fungus thrives in warm weather, so early crops often escape injury.

CARROTS

Black rot is a disease that causes irregular shallow sunken patches on carrots. *Fusarium rot* of carrots can be caused by any of the many species of Fusarium, a genus of fungus; symptoms vary but include spongy texture, surface lesions, and fuzzy fungus growths.

CORN

Corn is attacked by *corn smut:* irregular, bumpy white galls that break open to reveal black fungus tissue. Galls may be found on cornstalks and ears.

CUCUMBERS

Vines affected by *downy mildew* have curled, shriveled leaves, which later turn brown and drop off. *Scab,* which is worst in cool, damp weather, causes black or brown sunken ulcers on the fruits.

LETTUCE

Heads may be troubled by *bottom rot,* which affects those with low-lying leaves more than those that grow upright like the cos varieties. Rusty spots form on the leaves. The head and lower leaves, but not the stem, gradually turn slimy and rot away.

PEAS

Plants affected by *fusarium wilt,* a common pea fungus that enters at the root, have yellowed leaves, and eventually the whole plant wilts.

POTATOES

Tubers with *late blight* show diseased spots on the lower leaves first, starting when nights turn cool and damp. Foliage dies down rapidly. Affected potatoes have areas of brown flesh under the skin. If you suspect late blight, wait to dig your potato crop until two weeks after the tops have died down. That way you'll avoid spreading the spores to the tubers.

SPINACH

Spinach, like peas, may be infected by *fusarium wilt,* which causes plants to turn yellow and lower leaves to wilt.

Fusarium wilt of tomatoes lives in the soil for many years. Leaves wilt first, and then turn yellow as the plant's network of food and water distribution becomes blocked. A cut section of stem shows an abnormally dark surface. *Verticillium wilt,* the other principal fungus disease of tomatoes, causes similar symptoms but is not as lethal. Leaves may show brown patches, and plants will be under-sized.

While you can't do much to cure most fungus diseases after they strike, you can take preventive measures to keep them out of your garden or to keep them from spreading.

Begin with clean seed, especially for beans, potatoes, and to-matoes, in which some fungus diseases may persist in the seed. If you save your own seed, keep seed only from healthy plants. Most commercially raised bean seed is grown in the West where dry air inhibits fungi.

Choose disease-resistant seed, especially for cabbage, cucumbers, and tomatoes. A list of resistant vegetable varieties is available for 67 cents (including postage) from the University of Wisconsin Extension Service, Agricultural Bulletin Building, 1535 Observatory Drive, Madison, Wisconsin 53706.

Use clean soil when making up potting mixtures for seedlings. If you've had fungus disease problems with seedlings, don't reuse the potting soil in which they grew. To sterilize your garden soil, try soaking the bed with water and then covering the ground with clear polyethylene sheeting. Cover the edges of the plastic with soil to seal it all around, and leave it on the soil for three to four weeks. This heat treatment kills many pathogenic fungi.

Keep the crops hopping. Rotation won't control *all* fungus diseases, but it will help to prevent serious build-ups. It will also keep insect pests wondering where their favorite vegetables will turn up next.

Build up your soil with all the compost and other organic matter you can muster. There is considerable evidence that well-nourished plants can resist disease longer than those that receive the bare minimum of nutrients. In addition, soil that contains a generous amount of humus is likely to support helpful organisms that will do their part to keep disease-causing organisms in check.

Some fungi like it warm, and some like it cool, but all require abundant moisture. Many damaging fungi are, in fact, unable to enter a host plant if the plant tissue surfaces are dry. Therefore, anything you can do to increase ventilation in a wet season will help to control fungi. Try trellising and staking plants, watering early in the day so the leaves can dry before evening, even allowing a bit more space between plants in a row. Use new bean stakes if your pole beans were diseased last year. Even if you see no evidence of disease, avoid working in your bean, potato, and to-mato rows when the plants are wet; droplets you carry as you move from plant to plant may contain many spores.

As you work in the garden, hoe carefully and try not to injure plants or roots, for tissue breaks invite fungus infestation. Destroy affected plants at the end of the season—by burning, if possible. If you must dump cull potatoes, carrots, or other vegetables back on the garden, either spread them out where they will freeze or put them in the center of a hot compost pile.

In storage, you can control fungus diseases and their propagation by keeping the temperature low—as close as possible to 32°F —ventilating the area well, and annually cleaning and airing the root cellar and all containers used for storage.

Fungi are everywhere. In damp, misty weather they're likely to affect at least one of your crops. But these preventive measures will help to keep them from spreading and from infecting the next vegetables you plant.

Supersweet Corn

Supersweet corn is the most recent chapter in the old, old story of man and corn. Fossil corn pollen found in an ancient lake bed underneath Mexico City has been estimated to be 60,000 years old. The oldest known fossil ear of corn, found in New Mexico's Bat Cave, dates from about 2,000 B.C. It is small, not much over one inch long. From primitive corn like that, Indians living in Central and South America developed the five distinct kinds of corn we know today by saving and selecting seed. Their patient watchfulness was aided by corn's high mutation rate, which made the chances of developing good new qualities better than might otherwise be expected.

Regular sweet corn was one of those mutations. In this type of corn, a new gene—called *shrunken 1*—interferes with the orderly conversion of sugar to dextrin to starch, which is characteristic of dent, flint, and other corns. Sweet corn has more sucrose and creamy dextrin, and less starch. It was never a staple for the Indians, because it was difficult to store and less vigorous and resistant to disease than other types of corn, but they kept it as a separate strain and grew it for immediate consumption.

Until Golden Bantam appeared in the mid-1800s, sweet corn was white. In the early 1900s, plantsmen began developing hybrid corns, both dent and sweet, that soon became highly uniform and predictable. More recent tinkering with genes has led to the development of the supersweet corns. It all started with the discovery, by Dr. John Laughman of the University of Illinois, that another corn gene—*shrunken 2*—conferred extra sweetness. Corn carrying the *shrunken-2* gene has an inborn metabolic defect that interrupts the conversion of sucrose to starch at an even earlier stage.

Supersweet varieties, such as Illini Xtra-Sweet, Florida Staysweet, and Early Extra Sweet, are not as creamy as regular corns, because they contain less dextrin. The seed is shriveled, which may account for the corn's tendency to germinate poorly and to produce less vigorous seedlings. The *shrunken-2* varieties are fussier about ideal weather and soil conditions than regular sweet corn. An equally serious problem for home gardeners is the necessity of isolating these varieties to prevent cross-pollination that would ruin their quality. Both the *shrunken-2* corns and the more recently developed ADX types will turn starchy and tough—just like field corn—if pollinated by another type, even another sweet corn. And if these new varieties pollinate ears of regular sweet corn, they too will turn starchy. Different varieties tasseling at the same time should be separated by at least 350 to 500 feet. For complete isolation, plant breeders recommend spacing varieties 700 feet apart. If you're depending on isolation by time rather than space, allow fourteen days between the tasseling times of segregated varieties.

In most plants the characteristics of the seed do not affect the grain or fruit in which it is carried, but corn is different. According to Dr. Garrison Wilkes, writing in *Horticulture*, when a single silk of corn is fertilized by pollen from a tassel, not one but two sperm are involved. One sperm penetrates the egg and proceeds to form the seed's embryo, which will germinate into a new plant when the seed is planted. The other sperm, which joins with two endosperm nuclei, develops into the seed's storage material—the sugary-starchy part of the seed. The quality of the kernel is thus determined by the genes in the pollen that fertilizes the silk. That's why you'll sometimes find a few white grains in your yellow corn if it grows close to a bicolor or white variety.

Pennfresh ADX (Agway), which is about twice as sweet as regular corn, but somewhat less sweet than the *shrunken-2* varieties, also has improved seed germination and plant vigor. ADX corn has not one but three mutant genes. Pennfresh has been quite popular with commercial growers.

The recently introduced Everlasting Heritage series has solved the back-yard gardener's worry about isolation of high-sugar corn, as well as some of the fidgeting over poor germination. These sweeter corns—Kandy Korn E.H., Mainliner E.H., Golden Sweet E.H., and others—may be grown near regular sweet corn with no less of sweetness for either variety. Germination and seedling vigor have been improved, and the corn stays in good condition on the stalk for at least three or four days longer than regular sweet corn. These improvements have been achieved by introducing genes that came from an American Indian roasting corn and that also delay starch formation. When I want a sweeter corn, I prefer to use one of the E.H. varieties. Kandy Korn E.H., despite its coy name, is dependable and has fine flavor. Mainliner E.H. is much like it, but with a longer ear.

If you are planting any of the high-sugar varieties, it makes good sense to use them as midseason and late plantings, when soil is warm and germination faster. For early corn use one of the good, fast-maturing regular varieties, such as Early Sunglow, Sundance, and Earlivee. If space is limited and you need to fudge a bit in planting a variety that requires isolation, you might try planting several rows of sunflowers between the two varieties to act as a pollen trap.

For some palates, the supersweet corns are almost too sweet. I don't believe they'll supplant the regular corns, but they're an interesting extra. You can be sure that corn will be the subject of a lot more experimental work in the future. As Luther Burbank once said, "No plant is ever a finished product."

Help for the Weekend Gardener

"Can you help me?" the letter began. "I dearly enjoy gardening, but I am able to work in my garden only on weekends. During the week I'm in town near my job. Is there any way I can have a good garden without watching over it every day?"

Since this plaint of the part-time gardener is shared by those who rent community garden plots at some distance from their homes and also by homesteaders who start gardens on newly acquired acreage, remaining in their town homes while preparing for the transition, a few hints for managing a garden *in absentia* may be useful. Perhaps no solution to this dilemma is wholly adequate, but there are measures you can take to make your intermittently tended garden productive and satisfying.

The single most important thing you can do is to keep your garden area small. While that may sound obvious, I know all too well how necessary it is to curb the spring madness that leads one to enlarge the garden, oblivious that the patch may already be too large for a part-time gardener to care for comfortably. Make your garden small, but make it good—on well-drained soil, in full sun. Dig it thoroughly and rake the soil fine. You might want to try growing an intensively planted bed in which there are no rows at all, just closely planted vegetables in well-dug soil generously supplied with manure and compost. These small plots can be surprisingly productive. They require less mulch and less time spent in weeding than for the same number of plants grown in the conventional row system.

Starting vegetable plants indoors on the windowsill or under fluorescent lights and transplanting them to the garden will give you a head start and more control over plant spacing and seedling quality.

Mulching is very important. When you won't be seeing the garden from Monday through Friday, be sure that the soil surface is covered with a moisture-conserving mulch in case the week's weather is dry. Also, fruit resting on mulch decays less readily than on bare ground. And for early crops like peas, mulch helps to keep the roots cool if weather turns warm.

Another good way to keep certain special plantings well supplied with moisture is to sink a large can with several holes punched in the bottom next to a plant or in the center of a group of plants. Fill the can with water just before you leave your country place. Cucumbers, eggplant, and tomatoes in particular appreciate this treatment in a dry season.

Your choice of plants can make things easier for you, too. Grow only vegetables you really like and will use. Save the experiments for some year when you have more time. If you still need to pare down the list of vegetables you can grow in the space and time available, the garden might include only those vegetables that are difficult to find in your local market, or those that suffer the most serious loss of quality in shipping and storage.

Your use of gardening space and time will be more productive if you grow vegetables that keep bearing over a period of weeks or even months. Swiss chard, peppers, carrots, and New Zealand spinach are a few of the vegetables that produce reliably all summer even if they are not picked frequently. Broccoli, sugar peas, beans, summer squash, cucumbers, and okra are also productive over a long period but must be picked several times a week in order to maintain their productivity. When not picked, they quickly go to seed. If a neighbor would enjoy picking privileges in your garden during your absence, perhaps you can manage to arrive at an arrangement that will give both of you more fresh vegetables than you might otherwise have had.

If no one can pick your vegetables during the week, make the rounds in the garden just before you leave and pick every possible vegetable—even the tiny snap beans, fingerling zucchini, and petite peas. If you anticipate a *two*-week absence, pick off the squash blossoms, too. The plants will be ready with more when you return.

If you must have corn, make small frequent plantings and choose one of the open-pollinated varieties like Country Gentleman or Golden Bantam which ripen over a longer span of time than the more uniform hybrids. Make small plantings of lettuce every three weeks or so in order to have a continuous supply.

If you are determined to have fresh vegetables, you can even plant some in containers and haul them back and forth with you. Herbs, cherry tomatoes, peppers, and the new short-vine Potluck

Hybrid cucumber (Burgess) are good candidates for this kind of experiment. Moving potted peppers from country to town and back again may not be the most practical solution to your problem, but I mention the idea because I'm sure I'm not the only person crazy enough about gardening to try almost anything once.

In your absence, animal predators may consider your garden theirs. If simpler control measures fail, you may need to fence in the garden. Certain natural controls will work against insect pests while you're away, and these can be supplemented by interplanting marigolds and herbs among the vegetables, introducing praying mantises (hang the egg cases in a low bush in early spring), and dusting with rotenone if things get out of hand.

You might want to consider bordering your vegetable garden with a row of colorful carefree flowers like zinnias, nasturtiums, marigolds, calendulas, or portulaca. All season long the flowers will provide you with a bright welcome and a ready source of cheerful bouquets for the house.

Flowers on the table, fresh garden salad for dinner, corn fritters (using up the ears that are past their prime) for Saturday breakfast —all these can be yours with a little planning and planting, even if your heart's in the country and your head's in town.

Eating Garden Weeds

Some of the greenery we grub out from between our intentional plantings is food as tasty and as nourishing as what we plant. Many weeds that are found in cultivated gardens are, in fact, even richer in some important vitamins than tame crops like spinach and lettuce. It won't do, of course, to let the weeds take over and smother our precise rows of garden vegetables. But perhaps if we realized what good foods some of these weeds afford, we'd find a way to use them and even let some of them continue to grow.

Quack grass and cocklebur, thistle and bindweed have got to go, but several other weeds common to disturbed ground are worth picking for the dinner table.

Of the many edible wild plants, the following are especially likely to be found in gardens. These are not the only uninvited edibles you're likely to find among the beans and lettuce, but they are some of the most common and most delicious. They are, moreover, the wild greens that I've most often picked and cooked from my gardens in Wisconsin, Indiana, and Pennsylvania.

Also known as red-root, wild beet, pigweed, or carelessweed, AMARANTH amaranth is an annual that may reach a height of four to six feet if

137

you don't eat it young. When mature, the plant bears panicles of small green flowers at the nodes where the rough, veined, dull green leaves meet the stems. The tip of the plant's taproot is red. Amaranth is related to the garden ornamental cockscomb. According to biologist Edwin Spencer, author of *Just Weeds*, the amaranths have the ability to throw second-generation plants that vary widely in their adaptability to adverse conditions. Hence the folk name "carelessweed"; of the roughly 115,000 seeds that can be produced by each plant, some are sure to fall on ground that is just to their liking.

Young amaranth greens—up to ten or twelve inches high—are tender and very mild-flavored. I braise them in a covered pan for 15 minutes—often with other, more pungent greens. The shiny black seeds that appear later in the summer are edible and, according to Euell Gibbons, quite appetizing when toasted. They were a staple food for some American Indian tribes. Don't use the roots, or the red leaves in the fall, however; they may be poisonous.

DANDELION

Dandelion is a strong-rooted perennial that produces a low-to-the-ground crown of nutritious leaves that are mild to mild-pungent in flavor. Leaf bitterness increases near blooming time. Also called blowball and lion's tooth (from *dent de lion*), the dandelion is so widespread that it needs no introduction. Those who have taken great pains to eliminate the plant from manicured lawns may be amused (or perhaps chagrined) to learn that at least one seed house (Grace's Gardens) sells dandelion seed, for gardeners who want to be sure of having enough. If that sounds preposterous, consider that there is scarcely a part of the plant that can't be eaten. The young tender greens are widely appreciated for their flavor. They are, in fact, sold by the pound in many Pennsylvania farm markets and I know more than one displaced country person who buys them routinely each spring. The flower buds are good to eat, too. The blossoms may be made into a classic wine, and the roasted ground roots may be brewed into a coffeelike beverage.

It is the leaves that we use most often. In fact, I develop a positive craving for them each spring, even though I grew up on much blander, tamer fare and ate nothing wilder than blueberries, wintergreen berries, and elderberry jelly until I came of age. Although spring is the traditional dandelion-gathering time, I find that young leafy seedling plants appear in my garden throughout the growing season, and I always count on having at least a few good pickings of tender new leaves in the fall.

LAMB'S QUARTERS

This common annual, also known as goosefoot, wild spinach, and pigweed (pigs, you see, know what's good), may reach a height of four to six feet in good ground. It is, in fact, an indicator of good soil. The toothed, egg-shaped leaves have an overlay of tiny white granules, especially on the undersides, and they shed water more readily than most greens. As with other edible greens, both wild and cultivated, the plants are most tender and tasty when young—up to a foot or so in height. I have, however, stripped individual leaves from plants that were considerably taller than that and no one complained when I cooked them in the soup.

Lamb's quarters has a delicious mild flavor that many people prefer to that of spinach. It was a common household potherb in Roman and even later times, until spinach was imported from southwest Asia during the sixteenth century. Although garden fashion has somehow passed it by, *Chenopodium album* is sold even today in gourmet shops in London.

I have plenty of it in my garden, without the trouble of planting it. It seems to do particularly well among the peas. (I've found that my peas produce best if I let some weeds grow up among them; the extra greenery keeps the soil cool and the shallow-rooted peas are not torn loose from their fairly uncertain moorings as they were when I righteously yanked out all extraneous plants.) The young leaves of lamb's quarters—or tiny whole plants—are good braised, in soups or "spinach" soufflés, creamed or served au gratin, and they may be frozen for winter use—a task for which I never seem to have enough time during pea season.

Lamb's quarters seeds may be gathered, husked by rubbing, winnowed in the wind, and then ground to make a flour that Euell Gibbons recommended as the equal of buckwheat—dark but tasty. Most of our garden lamb's quarters, though, is picked green and eaten before it goes to seed, and I've not yet tried foraging the seed from the many mature plants that surround us in fields and hedgerows. But I was interested to learn that biologists who participated in 1950 studies done on the early Iron Age Tollund Man, whose body was exhumed remarkably intact from a bog in Denmark, identified—in the porridge that had constituted the man's last meal before hanging—seeds of lamb's quarters and other wild plants cooked along with the linseed and barley seeds that formed the bulk of the meal. Such a mixture would far outweigh our packaged breakfast cereals in nutritional value.

Purslane (also called pussley or pursley) is a sprawling, fleshy-leaved annual about two inches high and a foot across. The smooth, rounded, thick leaves grow on branched stems and bear tiny yellow flowers. I can well remember, in my first garden, waiting in vain for these relatives of the domestic ornamental portulaca to produce the familiar bright-hued blossoms. Some years after I concluded that I would have to consider the plant a weed, I found that it is good salad and pickle material. Civilizations older than ours have, in fact, cultivated purslane for centuries. You can pinch off the leafy tips, pickle the fat stems, or cook the whole plant. Purslane may be a nuisance in some gardens but I've never been able to find a great deal of it in any of the garden patches I've cultivated. When I do come upon some, we usually eat it.

When you shoulder your hoe, then, to make order in the vegetable patch, perhaps you'll want to take a picking basket along too.

PURSLANE

The following books are helpful references for identifying edible garden weeds:

Just Weeds by Edwin R. Spencer, published in 1957 by Charles Scribner's Sons, New York. (This book is out of print, but may be available through your library.)

Common Weeds of the United States, prepared by the USDA, published by Dover in 1970.

139

Planting for Winter Storage

Robert Frost's poem refers to foresightedness of a different kind, yet I seem to hear his matter-of-fact intonation, "Provide, provide," whenever I kneel to plant beets.

How was your supply of root-cellar vegetables last winter? July is the time to provide, to plant seeds for an ample supply of good keepers to tide you over the winter to come.

The hardy vegetables you'll plant now needn't be lifted at the first touch of frost. Neither do they require canning or freezing— a relief from the boiling and blanching that attends the putting up of peas and beans. When correctly stored, they can be cooked as needed during the winter.

The list of good keepers reads (with good reason) like a menu for a traditional Thanksgiving dinner: turnips, carrots, beets, cabbage, kohlrabi, radishes, rutabaga. Other good storage vegetables such as onions, parsnips, salsify, and squash must be planted earlier.

Turnips grow quickly. A late planting will provide good greens, tender new roots for fall meals, and good solid eating for the winter. Turnip seed, like that of all Brassicas, seems to germinate 100 percent, so we take care not to sow it too thickly. Turnips thrive in cool weather, developing fine crisp roots during the early days of fall and continuing to grow after the first frost. If you manured and limed the garden in the spring, turnips should do well without further soil enrichment.

If turnips were more difficult to grow they might be better appreciated. Their sweet, crisp flesh is good slivered into tossed salads; they are delicious grated and sautéed until golden; and many country cooks mash a cooked turnip in with the whipped potatoes.

Rutabagas store well, resist frost, and taste as good as turnips do—some folks say better. Prepare them for the table much as you would turnips, but allow them a month longer in the ground.

The best carrots are grown in soil of fine tilth, with plenty of potash. We accomplish this in our patch by digging deeply, building up the humus content of the soil, and spreading wood ashes.

Thinning carrots, especially in a dry summer, may leave the remaining exposed roots vulnerable to damage by the carrot rust fly. We try to avoid the necessity for heavy thinning (we still do some) by mixing the seed with sand or coffee grounds before planting. The coffee has the additional effect of discouraging insect pests. Sometimes we sow carrots in bands 4 to 6 inches wide rather than the narrow, single-file row. Broadcasting the seed over this wider row area tends to make overplanting less likely. This method saves on mulch and garden space too. When the carrots are well on their way, the leaves will shade out much weedy competition, but you must hand-pluck the weeds while the carrots are still tiny, since they can't be hoed out of the wider row.

A few quick-germinating radish or lettuce seeds sown with carrots will mark the row. As with all midsummer plantings, I soak the furrow before planting the seed and pull fine soil over it, firming the surface but not watering again. This prevents surface crusting—a threat to the meek, tentative, feathery carrot tops.

Cabbage keeps well, too. Started plants set out now should head by fall, just when you want them for kraut or storage. A side dressing of manure or manure tea will promote quick, solid, leafy growth. Cabbage should follow a root or legume crop, rather than lettuce or another Brassica.

Winter radishes may be sown in small patches here and there. They do best when their growth is unchecked. You can't change the weather, but you can water them and give them mulch and a bit of noonday shade in hot weather. Winter radishes need cool weather at the end of their growing season. Our favorite keeping radish is the China Rose, ready in 52 days. Black Spanish and Celestial keep well, too. You may want to try these cooked in soups and stews in the Chinese manner.

Kohlrabi do well near beets. The shapes complement each other and their root exudates apparently have a mutually encouraging effect. (Experiments in soil and root science corroborate the intuitive judgments of the experienced gardener.) Thin kohlrabi to stand about 4 inches apart. Thinnings may be transplanted; they'll develop later.

A bushel or two of beets should round out the provisions in your root cellar. As you plant the seeds, remember that they are really corky "fruits," each containing several small seeds. Space them 1–2 inches apart, thinning them later to stand about 5 inches apart.

Unlike carrots, beets can be transplanted. Some gardeners nip off the point of the beet seedling's taproot and clip the tops to two inches when transplanting them.

Beet problems are few. Black, bitter spots indicate boron deficiency, for which some gardeners apply household borax in a solution of ¼ teaspoon to 12 gallons of water. It's easy to apply too much, though. Better yet, take the long-term view and add more organic matter to your soil. Certain plants such as vetch, clover, and muskmelon leaves have the ability to accumulate boron from the soil—a good thing to remember next time you make compost.

The Playful Gardener

Sometimes it seems to me that we're all so terribly *purposeful* these days. Even the games we give our children must be educational, designed to build coordination or sharpen mathematical skills. Who has time for playfulness, dreamy-eyed fiddling, nonproductive exploration? Lucky the child who is allowed to follow some perfectly useless whim outdoors! And lucky the adult who has a young relative or friend with whom to share a leisurely afternoon of creative wandering in the garden.

When I was a child, my mother showed me how to make frogs from the fleshy leaves of the sedum plant. Sitting on the steps of the front porch, smelling the honeysuckle draped over the banister and watching for the first faint fireflies to appear before bedtime, my brother and I patiently pinched sedum leaves until we could make them into frogs. Sedum, also called stonecrop or live-for-ever, is an old dooryard garden plant that grows in many forms. The kind we used for making frogs had a fleshy leaf about an inch long and slightly less than an inch wide.

There is a knack to making frogs; sometimes you must try several times before you get it right. Pick a leaf and pinch it between your thumb and forefinger until the entire leaf surface looks bruised and turns a darker green. Then, after you've thoroughly squeezed the whole leaf, hold it between your thumb and forefinger and use a gentle sliding motion to free the outer membrane from the inside of the leaf without tearing it. This maneuver requires patience and care, but it is not difficult. Just be careful not to puncture the outside membrane, or you'll have a flat frog. Now blow into the stem end of the leaf. When it's inflated, you've fashioned a frog. Can't do it? Ask the nearest child to show you how.

If there's no sedum around, there are always weeds. Puff on a pod full of loose milkweed silk and watch—really watch—where the gossamer parachutes go. Pluck a handful of burdock burs. As children, we would fashion these into tiny chairs and baskets. The hooked barbs of the burs stick together like Velcro. Blow three times on a dandelion seed head, then count the number of wispy seeds that remain. Now you know the hour of day, according to folk wisdom.

Flowers make childhood memories too, especially if the gardener has planted enough of them to allow for liberal picking and playing. A grandmother I know has made friends with her young visitors by being generous with her hollyhock blossoms. They make charming instant dolls. Poke a straight pin through an unopened bud into the stem end of an open blossom to form a head above a silky skirt. Then raid the flower border or hedgerow for materials to turn into hats for the multicolored dolls. Red trumpet flowers can be dolls too. Simply make slits in two of the petals and pull the stems out to form arms. For a little more action, you might try a violet tug-of-war. Hook the flowers together and pull; country lore has it that the winner gets his wish.

If you want to have something to show for your whimsical efforts, start a just-for-fun growing project, like one of these:

THE BUTTERBEAN TENT

You don't need studs and beams to make a playhouse. A small square of garden space becomes a summer hideout when enclosed. The simplest structure is a teepee, formed by ramming the heavy ends of six bean poles into the ground and wiring the tops together. Space the poles 18 to 24 inches apart and plant five climbing bean seeds around the base of each pole. (Or use morning glory, gourds, climbing nasturtiums, or a combination of these and other quick-growing vines.) To form a doorway, wire a sturdy stick between two poles, 3 or 4 feet from the ground, and do not plant seeds in that space. Train the vines around the doorway. A circle or open rectangle of sunflowers will also make a quick-growing house. For extra shade and seclusion, plant pole beans or other vines around the sunflower stalks and train them up and between the stalks.

BOTTLED CUCUMBER

This is a good game for the child who's tired of hearing a procession of visiting relatives exclaim, "My, how you've grown!" Let the youngster select a small cucumber on a healthy-looking vine. Give him a narrow-mouthed jar to pop over the cucumber. Leave the cucumber on the vine and pull a few leaves over the bottled fruit so it won't cook in the sun. Visit the cuke every few days and watch it grow until it's too large to pull out of the bottle's small opening. Then cut off the stem and put the curiosity on display, or pickle it right in the bottle.

PERSONAL PUMPKINS

Small pumpkins grow large before summer is over, and their hard rind heals well over shallow cuts. You can take advantage of this awesome healing power by carving a name in the still-tender skin of a half-grown pumpkin. By September the name will be written large in light tan scar tissue that stands out from the orange background.

There are many other plant and flower games, some practiced for hundreds of years. Perhaps one of these suggestions will recall a bit of long-forgotten lore from your own childhood, or prompt you to invent a delightful new bit of garden nonsense. If we don't pass on this lore, who will? Can you imagine a generation growing up ignorant of the possibilities of hollyhock dolls? What idle things did you do with flowers when you were a child? If there are children around you, perhaps you can make an indolent summer afternoon memorable for them. They may seem to have everything, but they still need freedom to make discoveries, and they need attention from us.

Picking and Pruning for Better Yields

Picking techniques can make a considerable difference in the quality and yield of your vegetable plants. Here are some helpful picking practices that I've learned from experience, from reading, and from listening to other gardeners.

BEANS
Pod development stops about 2½ weeks after flowering. Then during the next week seeds develop rapidly, and the pod gradually toughens. Instead of pulling the beans off, I prefer to snap them off, leaving the stem end on the plant. Then I can simply wash and cook the pods without picking them over to cut off the stems. Avoid picking when the plants are wet so you don't spread bean rust disease from plant to plant.

BROCCOLI
Thorough, careful pruning will give you repeated crops of large heads from your broccoli plants, according to Dr. Peter Cunningham of Guilford, Connecticut, who wrote to report his technique:

"After I cut the first head, I wait a few days and then cut the next tier of smaller heads. There remain many incipient sucker heads. These may be either small, differentiated heads or wisps of stem 1 or 2 inches long with small, curled leaves protecting them. Very small incipient buds, mere nubbins farther down on the stalk, are ignored.

"I pinch out the heads that are actually differentiated; they will not enlarge significantly. Three or four of the 1- or 2-inch shoots are left, and the rest pinched out. And I mean *all* the rest. If you leave eight, they will make small heads, but if you leave three or four, they will grow into sizable heads. After cutting this second crop of large heads, I repeat the process. There will usually be a low side shoot that doesn't look like more than a bud with several leaves. With the stimulus of pinching above, that stalk will enlarge dramatically, grow a big head, and perhaps even lend itself to the entire pinching process.

"As summer progresses, I take off some leaves, too. Later in the season, I remove more leaves. Toward fall, my son Peter (known around here as 'The Butcher'), strips the plants down to a few leaves and young buds. Now all that remains are practically bare stumps, but the plants produce nice heads as usual. I wouldn't recommend such severe pruning until late in the season, but some leaves do need to be taken off as the plants get bushy.

"The temptation is to leave too many buds or to leave on a head 1½ inches wide that you hope will enlarge. It won't. You must start early and clean the plant off, and not let a lot of suckers grow out and turn into little nothings."

BRUSSELS SPROUTS
Snap off all trunk leaves as soon as sprouts start to form. Then begin picking at the bottom of the plant and work upward. Twist off the sprouts or pop them off sideways. When the lower part of

144

the stem is bare, you can mound the soil around the plant to give it extra support if necessary.

Treat the vines gently as you pick, taking care not to twist them or to reposition the flowers, or the newly formed fruits may loosen. Any cantaloupe you pick should be so loosely attached that you needn't tug to get it off the vine. CANTALOUPES

If the carrot rust fly is a problem in your area, don't harvest isolated carrots from random spots in midrow. The fly can lay eggs in the holes and spread through your remaining carrots. Instead, dig steadily from one end of the row. If you must steal a whopper from the middle of the row, pack soil back in the hole. CARROTS

Expect two ears from each stalk, with good weather and good soil. Ears of some new corn varieties, such as Snow Queen, are harder to snap off than others. Use two hands when picking the first ear to avoid bending or loosening the stalk, which could interfere with the development of the second ear. Always leave tillers (extra bottom shoots) on the cornstalks. They help to nourish the plant. CORN

If you push the stem off with your thumb instead of pulling cukes off the vine, you'll be less likely to damage the vine. Pick daily or every other day. Plants quit bearing when fruits become overmature. CUCUMBERS

Pick in the morning while the plants are still dewy; they'll wilt much less. LETTUCE AND OTHER GREENS

Pick daily or every other day. Pods should snap or puncture readily. Leave the stems attached to the pods when cutting. Okra leaves and stems have tiny spines that can sting annoyingly when the plant is wet, so pick when it's dry if possible. Pruning off side shoots above the leafstalks will hasten maturation of the pods. OKRA

Peas have such shallow roots that they're easily disturbed by yanking on the vines. I prefer to snap peas off as I do beans, leaving the stem end of the pod on the plant. Sugar Snap peas are sweeter when the pods are swollen with peas, but when the peas begin to crowd each other in the pod, they're past their prime. PEAS

Cut fruit from the plant, don't pull, and keep some stem on the pepper. Slim peppers and cherry peppers can be snapped off with your thumb. PEPPERS

The old German custom of *gabelling*—forking an early potato or two out of each hill while leaving the hill intact—has been Anglicized to *graveling* here in Pennsylvania. In any case, it's good to know that you *can* sneak a few virtually skinless, tender new potatoes without disturbing the main crop, if you're careful. POTATOES

Let the plant grow six good leaves before you start cutting, but when it has grown that much, use it while you have it. You can either pluck individual leaves or shear off most of the top growth, leaving a 3-inch stub. When days grow longer and nights are warmer, spinach goes to seed no matter what you do. When you notice central stalks elongating and leaves toughening, cut and use all the plants right away. SPINACH

145

The Sun Worshippers

If the August sun is hot on your back as you work in the garden, you can take some consolation from the fact that this intense radiant energy brings out the best in some of our favorite vegetables. Although we can't control the weather, there are gardening measures we can take to encourage generous production from these heat-loving plants.

CANTALOUPE

If you've planted your melons on loose-textured, well-drained soil that slopes a bit to the south, you're off to a good start. Full exposure to sun and generous warmth produces sweet melons. Corn and other tall vegetables should not be planted close enough to cast shade on the melon vines. Scraps of black plastic sheeting placed around the plants will help to heat the soil. I've used pieces of old black-rubber-backed carpet with equally good results. Master gardener Dick Raymond shoves tin cans a few inches into the ground and sets his developing melons on these low pedestals where the air is warmer than at ground level. Cantaloupe vines have shallow roots and should be cultivated with care. Lifting the vines unnecessarily may reduce production by interfering with pollination.

CORN

This grain-bearing grass thrives on heat and moisture. There are gardeners who insist they've heard the corn growing on a hot, still summer night, and I believe them. Corn that is tasseling needs a good supply of moisture. One way to irrigate is to hoe a furrow between the rows and let water from a hose dribble into the shallow trench, then cover it with soil. Corn roots grow close to the surface, so all hoeing and cultivation should be done at a respectful distance of about eight inches from the stalks. Extra side sprouts help to nourish the plant and should be left undisturbed.

EGGPLANTS

You'd think eggplants had feelings—and in a sense they do. They are very sensitive to cold; cold wind or irrigation with cold well water can put them into a sulk. Since eggplants require a steady supply of moisture, it's a good idea to let the watering can stand in the sun for a while. Tobacco users should scrub their hands before touching the plants to avoid spreading tobacco-borne plant diseases.

LIMA BEANS

Full sun and plenty of heat boost lima bean production, so the plants should be kept at a safe distance from shade-casting trees

147

or corn. The shallow roots are easily disturbed, and the plants are especially sensitive to root injury when in bloom. Many gardeners hoe around their plants early in the season and then mulch to control weeds when the soil is good and warm—usually in July. Monthly side dressings of your favorite fertilizer are fine, but should be withheld after the beans flower, until the pods are well formed. Use rotenone to control the Mexican bean beetle, which seems to reduce yield more drastically in limas than in snap beans.

OKRA
Keep the pods picked in order to encourage continued production. A dark, heat-absorbing mulch will help to convince these plants that they're in their native warm country.

PEPPERS
Dry soil and hot, drying winds can cause the blossoms to drop without forming fruit. While there's no final solution to this maddening midsummer problem, it does help to irrigate and mist the plants and to jar them gently to increase pollination. In extremely hot weather, pepper plants may appreciate a bit of light shade at midday. Hot nights may contribute to blossom drop too. The ideal temperature range for pepper plants is 70–80°F during the day, 60–70°F at night. Too little magnesium in the soil can cause leaf drop, and the consequent sunburning of fruit often contributes to premature decay. Dolomite limestone is a good, although slow acting, source of magnesium.

SWEET POTATOES
Control weeds by hand or tiller until the vines begin to travel. Just before they start to ramble, mulch between rows. Do not prune leaves or vines, or the formation of starch—which is stored in the roots—will be reduced. Don't worry if you find skinny little roots when you check into a hill in late August. The roots will enlarge steadily over the next few weeks, until frost.

TOMATOES
Like the pepper plant, the tomato plant likes plenty of warmth, but not super-hot days. Modern hybrids may drop their blossoms when the temperature is more than 90°F. The less highly bred cherry tomatoes are not as sensitive to heat. Night temperatures cooler than 60°F also cause blossom drop. In very hot weather, the plants need more water—up to two inches a week instead of the one inch that is usually sufficient. If weather is favorable and fruits are still slow to ripen, consider the possibility of a phosphorus deficiency. (Rock phosphate is a good, natural, slow-release source of phosphorus.)

WATERMELON
Treat them like cantaloupe, except that watermelon needs more space and tolerates leaner and more acid soil.

Take good care of yourself, too, by doing your garden work early and late. Linger indoors over a noonday platter of the freshest and best from your garden while the sun is at its peak.

Tomato Troubles

Perhaps your only problem with tomatoes is to find a willing neighbor on whom you can dump that latest basket of ripe red fruits, because you've already canned plenty and you're tired of eating them for lunch *and* dinner.

Tomatoes are usually easy to raise, but they can have some annoying problems. In dealing with the most common tomato ailments, we need to remember that there isn't always a sure-fire, direct-action cure for some of them, although there are often preventive practices that can make a difference in next year's crop. Still, it is some consolation to be able to identify the cause of the trouble.

Here, then, is a quick review of some commonly encountered obstacles to tomato perfection, along with their causes and remedies or preventive measures.

Sunscald

SYMPTOMS White or yellow patch of toughened skin on the side of the fruit exposed to the sun.

CAUSE Insufficient leaf cover, sometimes due to dropping of diseased leaves, but also often due simply to position of fruit on normal plant, especially if plant is pruned and staked and weather is hot and dry. Some varieties tend to provide better leaf cover than others.

REMEDY Toss a handful of straw lightly over the exposed fruit clusters to prevent further scalding.

Blossom-End Rot

SYMPTOMS A sunken, leathery spot on the bottom of the tomato. Secondary soft rot sometimes sets in.

CAUSES Uneven moisture—either a dry period following good early-season weather, or excessive rain. Either condition can interfere with cell growth on the fruit's blossom end. This is not a disease, but the natural response of the tomato to less-than-ideal growing conditions. Low soil calcium can intensify the problem.

PREVENTION Mulching helps, by maintaining even soil moisture. Irrigating from below, done in time, may prevent some disfiguration of fruit. Lime the soil. Don't expect total control, though.

Fusarium Wilt

SYMPTOMS Yellowing and drooping of lower leaves, followed by stunted plant and leaf loss. Interior of stem cut near base of plant shows brown discoloration.

CAUSE A fungus, which can live in the soil for many years. The growth prevents water from rising in the plant stem.

REMEDY No cure. Plant wilt-resistant varieties like Roma, Sunray, Manalucie, or Marglobe.

PREVENTION Crop rotation to prevent severe build-up.

149

Bacterial Canker

SYMPTOMS Wilting of lower leaf margins followed by curling and browning of leaves (which usually remain attached to the stem). Often this occurs on one side, causing plant to drop over. Cavities develop in the stem and, in late stages, open "sores" appear on the stem surface.

CAUSE Bacterial infestation, often seed-borne.

PREVENTION If you save tomato seeds, put them in a glass with a small amount of water and stir daily for 3–4 days. Pour off seeds that rise to the top, and the fermented pulp. Dry the remaining seeds.

Rotate tomato plantings—do not repeat plantings of tomatoes, peppers, eggplants, or potatoes in the same spot for 4–5 years.

Tobacco Mosaic

SYMPTOMS Streaking, puckering, mottling of leaves. Fruit not directly affected, but plant can die from leaf loss.

CAUSE A highly contagious virus, which is not killed in the ordinary processing of tobacco, is easily transferred by brief contact with the hands of a person who has been smoking.

PREVENTION No smoking in or near tomato patch, hand-washing after handling tobacco, isolation of tomatoes from related plants that might carry the virus. Try spraying young plants with milk as a preventive measure.

Curly Top

SYMPTOMS Rolling and twisting of leaves, exposing the undersides. Eventual stiffening and yellowing of foliage, occasional purpling of leaf veins.

CAUSE Virus, which also affects beets and sometimes beans, spinach, squash, and peppers, and is spread by the beet leafhopper.

PREVENTION Separate tomato and beet plantings. Stagger tomato planting times, shade plants with slatted or cloth-covered frames. (The leafhoppers avoid dark, confined areas.) Burn diseased plants. Try deep mulching, closer-than-usual planting.

Blotchy Ripening

SYMPTOMS Hard, white tissue inside fruit.

CAUSE Possible shortage of nutrients, especially potassium.

REMEDY Apply balanced fertilizer and/or wood ashes. Dig in greensand and banana peels or cantaloupe rinds to supply potassium for next year's crop.

Poor Fruit Set

SYMPTOMS Too little fruit.

CAUSES Excessive nitrogen supplied to young plants (thus promoting leaf growth over flowering).
Shade.
Night temperatures below 60 degrees or above 80 degrees, with consequent decline in pollen ripening in already-formed blossoms.
Drought.

REMEDIES Fertilize plants *after* fruit begins to form.
Plant in full sun.
Cover plants on cool summer nights.
Irrigate if very dry.

Stunting and wilting of plant, without the canker or interior stem browning characteristic of bacterial canker or fusarium wilt.

Root secretion of juglone, to which tomatoes are extremely sensitive, by a nearby walnut tree.

It's a lot easier to keep tomato plants away from walnut trees than to move the trees.

Large areas of leaf tissue eaten. Occasional fruit damage.

Unmistakable. Large (2 to 4 inches long, ⅜- to ½-inch thick) light green, horned larvae with light diagonal "racing stripes" on sides.

Hand pick and squash larvae or—a poor second—drown them in kerosene. Watch for hornworms bearing erect white rice-grain-sized eggs on their backs. They are carrying parasites (the larvae of the ichneumon fly) and should be left to spread trouble to other hornworms. It's a marvelous example of natural control with which I'm only too happy to cooperate. Simple work gloves still seem to me insufficient protection for hand picking these grotesque pests.

If you've ever read a book on poultry diseases clear through in one sitting, as I have, you're probably immune to the kind of squirmy feeling such a clinical review as this can give you. If not, consider that it's quite unlikely that all these plagues will strike your garden. At least not all at once.

Then again, if you're still canning tomatoes two months from now, and the jars are running out, you might even find yourself wishing for one of them.

Disease and Pest Clinic

August's realities sometimes include problems in the vegetable patch: diseases to identify, pests to discourage, blights to fight. Every garden has its share of these challenges. Some difficulties can still be corrected this season; others require a long-term preventive approach. Here, then, is an August garden clinic to help you identify and treat the causes of some common vegetable-growing problems:

You spread wood ashes thickly over the row and your snap beans still didn't do well? I've made the same mistake. Once I planted beans where a bag of wood ashes had spilled and the result was the poorest bean crop I've ever had. Beans are sensitive to an excess of potash (supplied by wood ashes) in the soil. Regu-

BEETS lar moderate doses of wood ashes should be fine, but unusually heavy applications on bean ground are self-defeating.

Plants with black-spotted roots have most likely been grown in boron-deficient soil. Granite dust is a source of boron.

CABBAGE Heads sometimes crack open after heavy rain. Twist the stems of nearly mature cabbages to break some of the feeder roots and thus decrease water absorption. Plants that turn yellow or fail to thrive may be affected by clubroot fungus, which causes finger-shaped swellings on the root. To control this pesky disease, rotate your plantings, destroy affected plants, and when transplanting discard young plants with knobby or swollen roots.

CARROTS Do the carrots have thick tufts of hairy roots and twisted tops? Sounds like yellows, a viral disease spread by leafhoppers. To avoid the yellows syndrome, sow your main crop of carrots late—after June 1—and dig up your earlier plantings by September, when a second leafhopper hatch may give rise to a new wave of the disease. Also, control perennial weeds (which may harbor leafhoppers), around the garden.

CAULIFLOWER Plants that form tiny button heads before the plant develops fully are probably sulking because their growth was checked at transplanting time. Cauliflower seedlings need careful watering and shading the first week after they've been moved.

CANTALOUPES Do the fruits lack flavor? Blame the weather. Since warmth during the ripening process promotes good flavor, tuck pieces of black plastic under melons to provide more warmth. Soil deficiencies can affect flavor too. Cantaloupes like plenty of lime and potash, but not too much nitrogen.

CELERY STALKS Stalks that split indicate a boron deficiency. *(See Beets.)*

CHARD Plantings that have become a mass of tough, coarse leaves may be renewed by shearing each plant down to a 3-inch stub. New leaves will be ready in a month.

CHINESE CABBAGE Chinese cabbage often goes to seed instead of heading when it's planted as a spring crop. Try switching to early summer planting or growing one of the new varieties, such as Springtime (Stokes), which were developed especially for spring planting. Don't transplant Chinese cabbage; that can make it go to seed too.

CORN Ears that are not well filled were not completely pollinated. Wind carries the pollen, so plant your corn in solid blocks, not in long thin rows. Corn that grows only 2 or 3 feet before forming tassels is suffering from acid soil, dry weather, or lack of nitrogen.

CUCUMBERS Fruits with a bitter flavor may have been affected by cool weather. If the vines stop bearing but are not diseased, hunt under the leaves for the yellowing, gone-to-seed cuke you may have missed; thorough picking improves cucumber production.

EGGPLANT Blossom-drop can be caused by cool nights or by drying winds. Try a heat-retaining stone mulch and regular sprinkling.

ENDIVE AND ESCAROLE If endive or escarole hearts that you've tied up for blanching rot from the inside, the heads may not have been dry when you tied them. Wet leaves spoil when packed tightly together.

152

Lettuce goes to seed in warm weather. You can't fight it. Save the seed for next year and plant a new row of leaf lettuce for fall eating.

LETTUCE

Plants that lose their blossoms are probably reacting to cold wet weather, extreme heat, or excessive soil nitrogen.

LIMA BEANS

These mild peppers from home-saved seed may turn out hot if you've also grown hot peppers. When you intend to save seed, keep pepper varieties 50 feet apart to prevent crossing.

BELL OR CHERRY PEPPERS

Radishes that have woody texture and hot flavor have been affected by heat and low soil moisture. Replant for a fall crop.

RADISHES

Plants sometimes fail to set fruit when shaded, overheated (above 90° during the day, 80° at night), or given too much nitrogen before blossoming.

TOMATOES

The Transplanted Gardener

Whether you're settling in at the country place of your dreams, going along with a company transfer, returning to a simpler home, trying out small-town life, or scrapping everything and building a cabin in the woods, moving is an uprooting experience. There are favorite plants you're reluctant to leave behind. The new place seems to need *everything*—orchard, flowers, bushes, vegetable garden—and there are times when, although you know that starting over offers great opportunities, you wonder where to begin. Knowing what to take with you when you move, and how to do it, can help give you a head start in your new garden.

Transferring plants from one garden to another can be done carefully without diminishing the old garden. If you have fruit trees, for example, you can take scions—twig cuttings—to graft in spring onto established fruit trees or inexpensive grafting root-stocks* at your new place. Some older varieties of fruits, like the Price Engelbert blue plum we cherish here on our farm, grow true to seed and can be propagated by planting the pits or by digging up chance seedling trees. Seeds can also be saved from favorite strains of annual vegetables and from asparagus, grapes, and perennial flowers, as long as they are open-pollinated varieties, not hybrids. Collect seeds from ripe vegetables, dry, package, and label them, and keep them cool and dry until planting time.

Perennials—herbs, flowers such as mums and Shasta daisies, and food plants such as asparagus, rhubarb, and strawberries—often grow in clumps too dense for their own good. You can divide crowded perennial colonies to start new plantations on your new ground. Repot them in perforated cans or light-weight plastic pots before moving day.

Many shrubs, both ornamentals and those that produce food, may be induced to root new plants by layering, or nicking the underside of a young branch and covering it with soil held down by a rock. That works well with flowering quince, gooseberry, currant, brambles, mock orange, and many others. Start layering several months before you move.

Some especially amenable plants, including pussy willow, weeping willow, forsythia, and privet hedge, will root in jars of water. Most of those will also root readily in damp ground, as will roses (cover with a large jar), and grape cuttings.

If you have many started plants to move and no time to replant them properly at your new place, you can save most of them by "heeling in." In a well-drained place, dig a trench with one sloping side. Place the young trees or shrubs close together in the trench with their stems reclining on the slope. Tamp loose soil firmly over the roots. Replant in permanent places next season.

Transplanting entire established trees or shrubs is riskier than taking grafts, cuttings, or rooted offshoots, because a large root mass suffers more when disturbed. It is usually wiser to buy a new dwarf apple tree, for example, than to transplant one you've had in the ground for four or five years. Sometimes, though, you just can't leave behind special rare varieties or plants with sentimental value—your grandmother's nameless fragrant rose, perhaps, or a black-currant bush you'd have trouble replacing. To move those, cut a circle in the ground around the trunk, making the radius about 18 to 24 inches and the depth of the cut at least 12 inches. That cut should be made several months before you intend to move the tree, to stimulate the production of feeder roots close to the trunk. Then, at moving time, remove as large a root ball as possible, keeping soil packed around the roots. Wrap the root ball in burlap and keep the tree in the shade until it is settled in its new hole. Always move deciduous trees when they're dormant. If necessary, smaller bushes may be moved when in leaf, but you must take extra care with watering, shading, and pruning.

Homeowners who move trees and shrubs from property offered for sale should be careful to make clear to prospective buyers exactly which plants will be removed and when. Reserved plants should be identified in the sales agreement signed by both buyer and seller. When you intend to transplant started cuttings and divisions of perennial clumps to your new place, it's a good idea to group those plants separately in a nursery row—which would be pointed out in showing the house—so the actual garden plantings the new owners are to inherit will not be diminished later by thinning. If you have enough time and the ground is not frozen, you can be certain to avoid misunderstandings by moving your transplants before listing your house for sale. Removing plants not specifically agreed upon would, of course, be unfair.

We've moved six times—often enough to give us some idea of priorities in starting over on new ground. First we plant a vegetable garden, even if it's only a small one. We do that before we start to scrape paint and hang wallpaper, often before we have all the cartons unpacked, and sometimes before we move at all. Then, on one of those trips to town to replace the screws inevitably lost in moving, we treat ourselves to an armload of geraniums, pansies, alyssum, ivy, and such to cram into an old crock by the front door for an instant "welcome" garden—a tremendous boost to morale when we're still hunting through boxes for books, pictures, and everyday dishes. Third on our planting list, before putting in more flowers or enlarging the vegetable garden, is setting out fruit and nut trees so they can start their slow growth to productive size, which may take up to eight years.

One more thing we've learned: Put the garden rake, fork, and spade on the *back* of the moving van, so they're the first things off on unloading day. Planting takes priority!

* For information about ordering rootstocks, send a stamped, self-addressed envelope to Lee Land Nursery, Box 223, North Kingsville, Ohio 44068.

Mistakes of the Well-Intentioned Gardener

The most basic principle of the physician is an ancient one—"first, do no harm." It's a maxim that might well be adopted by the gardener as well, for in our zeal to raise perfect vegetables or flowers, we sometimes unwittingly damage plants.

I'm thinking of the time, several years ago, when a friend gave me a large sack of wood ashes for my garden. I left the sack at the edge of the patch and went on with other tasks, intending to return and spread the ashes when I had time. As it turned out, the sack of ashes stayed there through several rains, growing heavier and harder and more difficult to spread. Eventually I forgot about it, left it there over winter, and allowed the large ash cake to be plowed under in the spring. To my chagrin, the bean plants I raised in that part of the garden the following year produced an unusually poor crop.

Later, when I read the fine print on a Stokes bean-seed packet, I discovered that beans are especially sensitive to an excess of potash in the soil. Too much of a good thing can be worse than none!

An excess of nitrogen can be equally self-defeating in the case of certain plants. Nitrogen promotes leafy growth, and when abundantly supplied to young fruiting plants, it induces leafiness at the expense of blossom formation. When you feel like being generous with the manure tea, head for the corn, lettuce, cabbage, and other

155

leafy green plants but avoid overfeeding peppers, young tomato plants, root crops, and herbs.

Our insistence that "more is better" occasionally tempts us to add *two* tablespoons of fish-emulsion fertilizer to a gallon of water, rather than the recommended *one*. Don't. Fertilizer that is too concentrated can burn plant roots. So can manure that is too fresh. Garden experiments with liquefied kelp have shown that concentrations as low as 1:400 are effective, while high concentrations (1:10, 1:20) can be harmful. To quote that old pesticide caveat, "Read the label and follow directions carefully"—even with the nontoxic stuff.

My guess is that the number of gardeners who use long-lasting chemical pesticides on their vegetables is dwindling. I find more and more gardeners who are raising their own vegetables *because* they want good clean food. If you're new to gardening and you're accustomed to running a pest-free household, you may find yourself instinctively groping for a spray can when you see bugs on the beans. But wait. First, do no harm. How will you feel about eating that food you've sprayed? What will happen to the thousands of helpful insects that spray will hit? And how will you cope with a race of insects that eventually become immune to the pesticide you've depended upon?

Cultivation controls weeds and aerates the soil, but it is easy to damage shallow-rooted plants by chopping too close to their roots with the hoe or rototiller. Corn plants, which form extensive root systems stretching well into the aisles between rows, should be cultivated thoroughly when young to avoid damaging the roots of the mature plant.

I prefer mulching to cultivation in the narrow rows in my garden. Heat-loving crops like tomatoes, cucumbers, peppers, and melons should not be mulched until the soil is thoroughly warm. Mulching too early, especially around melons, will only slow the growth rate of these tropical crops (unless you're using black plastic, a material that absorbs heat).

Plants occasionally get in each other's way. Thinning is painful but necessary, for vegetables will not produce well when crowded. When thinning kohlrabi, cut the extra plants instead of pulling them, to avoid tearing the intertwining roots.

Care in picking vegetables will also help protect your crop. For example, since pea plants have shallow roots that are easily disturbed when pods are pulled off the vine, snap them off with your thumb instead. Cut or twist off summer squash; pulling them will uproot the plant. Beans should also be snapped with the thumb rather than yanked from their moorings.

Staking supports a plant and helps protect it from wind damage, but be careful not to puncture the roots when driving a stake next to a mature plant. The best time to set a stake is when the plant is young, preferably right after planting, before the roots have spread.

Tying plants to fencing or stakes trains vines and helps to support heavy fruits, but rigid ties can chafe and even break a plant. Old stockings or T-short strips make good elastic ties that don't rub unduly.

Careful gardeners tend to see themselves as part of the garden, cooperating rather than dominating. But I suppose I'm not the only gardener who has accidentally pulled up a prize cantaloupe seedling while weeding, run over a promising young cucumber vine with the garden cart while spreading mulch, or stepped on the tomato seedling I'd just transplanted. My grandmother used to say "Haste makes waste." I know now that she was right. The gardener who does no harm at least gives the vegetables a chance. Forgive yourself, though, if you find you have inadvertently hurt a plant. Nature gives us second chances too.

Cover Crops for Natural Fertilizer

Remember that old garden rule, "Put back more than you take out"? The intensive gardens most of us plant, with our succession crops and intercropping, make heavy demands on the soil. And when you consider that most of us start with less-than-perfect garden patches, the trick is to try and improve the soil, to end the season with better ground than we began with.

Consider, then, what a green manure crop could do for your garden. The growing crop holds the soil in place, protecting it from erosion. Legume crops enhance its nitrogen content, especially if they are inoculated. All cover crops, even weeds, build up the humus content of the soil when turned under. The spongier, friable earth that results will soak up rain, preventing erosion. Deep-rooted green manure crops delve far beneath the range of our digging forks and tillers to mine the subsoil for important trace minerals. Their decaying, far-ranging roots leave channels that help to aerate the soil.

It's time now to put back some of what we've taken out, to plant green manure crops by the row and between rows as garden space becomes available, covering as much of the garden as we can with a protective, soil-enriching crop.

Here are some good green manure plants:

As one of our favorite old farmers says, buckwheat puts the soil in good heart. We can vouch for that. The patch of poor soil where we planted our first buckwheat had a thin stand of spindly, pale-leafed plants that first year. The following year, on the same patch —fertilized only by turning under the buckwheat—we had a re-

BUCKWHEAT

157

spectable crop of buckwheat with stronger stems and greener leaves.

Buckwheat grows quickly; in fact, it seems to us that it has no sooner germinated than it begins to bloom. Buckwheat needs only 60 to 70 days from sowing to produce seed. For the best soil-building effect, you should turn it under before maturity, while it is still green and tender enough to break down readily. You may want to set aside a part of your buckwheat planting to raise seed for next year's cover crops, providing a self-perpetuating soil-improvement system. A crop of buckwheat sown now will be ready to turn under by frost.

WINTER RYE Winter rye may be sown now so that it can make some top growth before frost, protect your patch from erosion all winter, and go on to produce humus for you when turned under next spring. The rye plant produces a tremendous mass of root growth, worth even more to your soil than the leafy top growth, since it contributes a large volume of organic matter when turned under.

KALE You can also plant kale now, in time for it to make good top growth before cold weather. Not generally used as a field cover crop (although its cousin, rape, is so used), kale serves the gardener well. Planted thickly in a solid stand, it stays green all winter, even under snow. All this while it is protecting the soil and enabling you to harvest whatever you need for eating. Then, in the spring, turn it all under as green manure. A nurse crop of winter rye sown with the kale will protect it from severe winds and other weather extremes.

OATS Oats, like the other soil-improving crops mentioned here, tolerate a wide variety of growing conditions. They thrive in cool weather. Oats used for green manuring needn't have the special qualities, such as straw strength or lodging resistance that are bred into oats grown for seed. We buy the most ordinary, least expensive oat seed we can find.

In one of our spring plantings of oats, the plants had set seed before we got around to turning them under, and it wasn't long before the field was green again with new oat spears, redeeming our neglect. The best practice, though, as with any green manure, is to turn it under at the peak of succulence, before the plant sets seed.

SOYBEANS Like buckwheat, soybeans must be sown when weather is warm. August is a fine time. Inoculated seed will leave more nitrogen in the soil. The inoculant used must be prepared specifically for soybeans; that sold for garden peas and beans won't do. Some dealers sell pre-inoculated soybean seed. Soybean seed may be broadcast or drilled over your patch, or sown in rows. As with other broadcast seed, raking soil over the seed and firming it help to promote better germination.

HAIRY VETCH Also a legume, hairy vetch tolerates thin, sandy, acid soils where more demanding legumes like alfalfa would fail. Vetch, too, will contribute more to your soil if the seed has been inoculated.

Pre-inoculated seed is commonly sold, but ask to be sure. Where wild vetches grow, the required bacteria are most likely already in the soil. Vetch starts slowly and should be sown with winter rye or wheat in the fall, or with oats in the spring. Once it takes hold, the sprawling, viny plants will hold the soil. There are other good vetches, but hairy vetch is the hardiest and best for northern winters.

White Clover is another winter-hardy legume that is well adapted to northern gardens. This low-growing perennial is an especially good choice for broadcasting between rows. According to the catalogue available from Johnny's Selected Seeds, white clover does well even in the shade of large vegetables like corn and cabbage. It seems especially appropriate to plant this soil-nourishing crop next to vegetables with high nitrogen requirements. Fall sowing is recommended. You can turn the clover under in the spring, or let it continue to grow and try planting hills of robust vegetables like zucchini at intervals in the clover.

Erosion control, soil enrichment, humus building, aeration . . . all from a bag of seed. Plant power, indeed! We plant the seed at the right place and time. Out of earth and air, sun and water, the roots and top growth form. Put them back then, turn them under. Next year's garden will be better.

Other good green manure plants are barley, crotalaria, lespedeza, millet, brome grass, field peas, rape, sorghum, winter wheat.

WHITE CLOVER

SOME SOURCES OF SEED

Johnny's Selected Seeds
Rohrer's Seeds, (wide variety)
Shumway Seeds, (wide variety)
Jung (clover)
Earl May (clover)
Olds Seeds (clover)
For more information and an excellent, informative table, consult *Green Manure*, by Richard Alther and Richard O. Raymond, Garden Way Publishing Company, Charlotte, Vermont 05445 ($2).

How Many Salad Days Are Left?

Your salad garden can remain productive until frost—and beyond —if you renew it now. Most of the crisp, leafy, crunchy vegetables that make good salads grow quickly and thrive in the cool nights of early fall.

A short row of each of the following seeds, planted promptly, will fill the salad bowl for you in September.

For quick results, choose an early loose-leaf lettuce like Oak Leaf, Black-Seeded Simpson, or Salad Bowl, requiring 40–45 days to produce greens of eating size. Plant lettuce thinly—2 or 3 seeds to the inch—and cover lightly with no more than ¼ inch of fine soil.

Summer seedings usually germinate more quickly when you moisten the furrow before planting the seed, especially in a dry season. (Use a sprinkling can with the spray head removed.) Then, after sowing the seed, rake loose dry soil over the furrow.

LETTUCE

Irrigating summer seedings from above often causes a crust to form on the soil surface. To keep the soil surface soft, especially for the slower-germinating seeds, you may want to scatter fine, *dry* glass clippings over the row. (Green lawn cuttings are likely to mat.)

Should you experience difficulty in getting lettuce seed to germinate in hot weather, chill the seeds in the refrigerator for a day before planting. They needn't be soaked—just chilled.

Thin the young lettuce seedlings to stand 6 inches apart and then, when you begin harvesting, pluck every other one, leaving the alternate plants to develop further in the larger remaining space. Lettuce, with its sparse, shallow roots, will develop to its full potential only if not crowded; ideally, the leaves of one plant should not touch those of its neighbor. Cool nights, plenty of moisture, and abundant nitrogen in the soil favor good lettuce production. Side dressings of manure tea will give you a quicker, more succulent crop.

Buttercrunch and Bibb butterhead types (65–75 days) and head lettuces (72–80 days) may be worth trying, too, if you plan on giving them some protection against heavy frost as they reach maturity. You might try planting head lettuce in the open cold frame, shading the seedbed with lath or a piece of old snow fence until seedlings emerge. Then they'll be right where you want them when hard frost threatens.

KOHLRABI Kohlrabi will put some crunch into that leafy green salad mixture. Like lettuce, it grows best in cool, moist weather. Plant the cabbage-like seeds in rows 18 inches apart and thin the seedlings to stand about 8 inches apart. Allow 55 days to maturity. Beware of deep cultivation, especially when seedlings are young, for the plants produce tough, woody bulbs when their roots are disturbed. Kohlrabi is a good vegetable to mulch.

The bulb—in case kohlrabi is new to you—is shaped like a turnip, but grows above the ground. Start picking the crisp, tender globes when they reach 2 inches in diameter. The flavor is cabbage-related but quite mild. Try grating or slicing a kohlrabi into any vegetable salad, just as you would prepare a cucumber.

RADISHES For some reason, most gardeners plant radishes as a rite of spring, and forget about them for the rest of the growing season. They don't do well in hot weather, but radishes planted in August will mature when the summer people have left and nights are turning cool. In addition to cool weather, they need fertile, deeply worked soil and plenty of moisture. Quick growth makes them crisp; slow growth makes them woody. Radishes subjected to heat and lack of water will taste strong or hot.

Thin your radish seedlings to stand about an inch apart (more for large varieties). Although the tap root may grow deep, the feeder roots of most radishes are quite limited. They can't range far for food; it must be right there where they are growing. (Too much nitrogen, though, produces a pithy radish.)

160

Count on 22–29 days for radish production. Here are some dependable, widely available varieties:

French Breakfast (23–25 days) Oblong, red body with white tip
Cherry Belle (22–24 days) Round, red, relatively long standing
White Icicle (30 days) Long, white, crisp
Champion (28 days) Round, red, slow to deteriorate in the row.

With the exception of several special, newly developed spring varieties, Chinese cabbage is best planted in summer for fall harvest, since it bolts to seed if it matures in hot weather. The plants withstand frost but not a heavy freeze. Read the catalogue descriptions carefully; there are many varieties of this delicate, leafy cabbage, ranging from 45–100 days growing time until maturity.

Crispy Choy (45 days), from Burpee, is crisp, with somewhat more pungency than the later varieties.

Michihli (70–78 days), from Burpee and Stokes, heads well and has excellent flavor.

Early Hybrid (50–60 days) from Harris, is shorter and wider than Michihli, with leaves of fine quality.

Takii's Spring, Nozaki Early, and China Queen (hybrid), all from Johnny's Selected Seeds, produce fine fall greens.

Plant the seed right in the row; Chinese cabbage will not form good heads if growth is checked by transplanting. Space seeds about 3 inches apart and gradually harvest and eat the thinnings, beginning when plants reach a height of 4 inches, and working toward an eventual plant spacing of 12–14 inches.

Rich soil and abundant water supply make possible the quick succulent growth that results in a quality leaf cabbage. An inch of compost spread in the furrow at planting time will hold moisture and nourish the plant.

Harvest Chinese cabbage when the loose head has formed and serve it either grated in coleslaw or cut into a tossed salad. (It may be cooked too, of course.)

Bonus Crops

The garden is full of bonuses for people who like to use every available resource. I'm referring to something more than the kind of recycling we practice when we scrape off the cantaloupe seeds for the hens and save gnawed-on corncobs for the goats. Certain vegetables will give you an additional crop besides the root or leaf or fruit for which the plant is primarily grown. In some cases, that dividend is right there ready to use when you gather the primary crop. Other plants must remain in the ground a while longer to produce their secondary harvest. How many of these have you tried?

BEETS AND TURNIPS Next time you make pickled beets or add a turnip to the stew, cook and serve the leafy tops, too. They contain more vitamins and minerals than the roots, which we usually consider the main crop. According to the USDA's *Handbook of the Nutritional Contents of Foods*, one 100-gram portion of cooked beet root supplies 20 units of vitamin A, 6 milligrams of vitamin C, 32 calories, 14 milligrams of calcium, and 23 milligrams of phosphorus. Cooked beet greens are not only richer in nutrients, but also lower in calories, containing 5,100 units of vitamin A, 15 milligrams of vitamin C, 18 calories, 99 milligrams of calcium, and 25 milligrams of phosphorus. Cooked turnip roots provide a trace of vitamin A, 22 milligrams of vitamin C, 23 calories, 35 milligrams of calcium, and 24 milligrams of phosphorus. Cooked turnip greens, on the other hand, have 6,300 units of vitamin A, 69 milligrams of vitamin C, 20 calories, 184 milligrams of calcium, and 37 milligrams of phosphorus. I'm not suggesting that we neglect the root, which is good food too, of course, but it seems poor economy to discard beet and turnip greens and then to purchase vitamin A supplements.

RADISHES Sensible gardeners who plant just enough radishes at carefully spaced intervals might well use all their radishes, but I always seem to have at least a few roots that get ahead of me and go to seed in midsummer. The root toughens, the stalk lengthens, and soon small, white flowers form, followed by seed pods about 1½ inches long. While still young, green, and crisp, these radish pods make excellent eating. They can be chopped into a salad, cooked in soup, or even pickled. The total volume of pods produced in a summer by a single radish plant is usually considerably greater than the amount of food in one radish root. Serve some with a dip and see whether your guests can guess what they are.

SALSIFY Sometimes called the vegetable oyster, salsify has a slender, hardy root that is thinner than a parsnip and longer than a carrot. Like the parsnip, salsify tastes best after frost and is often wintered over in the ground under mulch for early spring harvest. Roots that aren't harvested begin to send out thin, flower-bearing stalks in April. (Salsify is a biennial, setting seed its second year.) You can pick these flower shoots while they're still tender, before they bloom. Steam them as you would asparagus, and serve them in the same way. Here's a whole new vegetable from a forgotten root!

WITLOOF CHICORY Raised for its root, which is customarily dug after frost and replanted in portable containers for forcing indoors [*see* page 190], witloof chicory produces one to three cuttings of crisp, blanched salad heads in midwinter. By the time you've cut a second or third sprouting of leaves from a root, its growing power has been spent, but it's still good for something; roasted chicory root to mix with your coffee or to use alone as a coffee substitute. Scrub the roots clean, roast them slowly until dry and crisp, and then grind them before steeping.

If you also grow okra, you can make your own home-blended "coffee" by combining the by-products of okra and witloof chicory plants. You know how tricky it is to keep up with okra: those fast-growing pods keep coming whether you're ready for them or not, and they are at their best for only a day. If you turn your back for a week, the plants will be festooned with woody pods that are too tough to chew. You can still make use of them, though. In fact, you have two options: You can shell the pods while the seeds are still tender and cook the green seeds as if they were peas, or you can grind up the hard, dry seeds from older pods and use them as a substitute for coffee. OKRA

On a hot, thirsty day, any regret you may feel at getting to the end of a perfect melon can be tempered by the thought of all the rind that can be put away in the winter pantry. In our family, we trim it below the pink zone and peel off the green skin, then cube and pickle the rind. Watermelon pickle elevates simple scraps to special status. Most general cooking and canning books have a recipe. I use the one in Irma Rombauer's *The Joy of Cooking*, substituting honey for sugar. Rombauer's suggested addition of either a star anise or lemon slices to each jar is an inspiration. WATERMELON

This aromatic, anise-flavored vegetable produces celery-like stalks tapering at the top to finely cut, dill-like foliage. Fennel matures about ninety days after planting and may be grown as either a summer or a fall crop. It is one vegetable in which all parts —bulbous base, stem, leaves, and even seeds—are edible. Fennel seeds make good tea and may be ground to flavor cookies and breads. FENNEL

Often grown to lure aphids away from food crops, nasturtiums add a cheerful note of bright color to the vegetable or herb garden. Both blossoms and leaves are edible, either raw or cooked, and the seed pods can be pickled to serve as a substitute for capers. NASTURTIUM

SEPTEMBER

Taking Stock

Although we know the days don't suddenly become shorter in autumn, there does seem to be a certain date when we first notice the light fading sooner. Nights and early mornings turn cool, even cold, and morning dew is heavier on the laden tomato vines. In September—"the corner of the year," as Maine poet Robert P. Tristram Coffin called it—it's time for the garden inventory, when we assess the summer harvest and look ahead, around that figurative corner on the calendar, to determine what the fall garden needs to keep it productive. It's time to take a good hard look at this year's rows, harvest, problems, successes, and to make some notes that will help in planning next year's garden.

Harvest

Your garden calendar can be a big help in planning continuous harvests without hectic overlapping of vegetables ready for freezing. After a few seasons of jotting down planting and harvest dates and amounts of each vegetable put by for winter, you'll discover a pattern than will help you plan future plantings for a continuous supply of such garden staples as cucumbers, lettuce, tomatoes, corn, and greens. If there are gaps in the supply of a vegetable you depend on, make a note to add an early, midseason, or late variety to your next seed order. Many gardeners struggle with a surplus of snap beans, radishes, or lettuce, followed by several weeks of slim pickings. The solution is to make smaller, more frequent plantings, so something good is always ripening. I have trouble, too, with that old compulsion to plant the *whole* row to beans, no matter how long the row, but I've found that varying the vegetables in each row makes it possible to pack more varieties in the same garden space.

Rows

If you found yourself spacing rows too close together to cultivate, or too far apart to mulch effectively, write yourself a reminder for next spring. I like to plant rows of early, quick in-and-out vegetables, such as spinach, rather close together, allowing just room enough for hoeing. For vegetables that stay in the ground all season, such as tomatoes and peppers, I prefer to use a wider spacing and to mulch rather than cultivate. Have you tried planting some vegetables in wide bands? Leaf lettuce, snap beans, turnips, and peas do well in solid rows 8 to 15 inches wide.

Discoveries

If you followed a hunch and it worked, or you found an exceptional new variety you want to plant again, or you improved your yield with a hint from a friend, write it all down in your garden notebook or on the feedstore calendar you keep handy. Gardens really do improve year by year as you accumulate lore and experience.

Some Common Problems

SPOTTY GERMINATION

Causes include stale seed, cold soil at planting time, insufficient moisture, too-deep planting. Cover seed with no more than three times its thickness of soil.

MALFORMED ROOT VEGETABLES

Blame heavy clay soil, rocky soil, coarse clods in the seedbed, or timid thinning for twisted or stunted root vegetables. Carrots and other slender root crops need 1 to 2 inches of space between plants. For well-shaped roots, try raking the soil free of stones and planting the seed in a flat-topped mound made by raking loose soil onto the planting row from both aisles.

LETTUCE

Most lettuce varieties shoot to seed in hot weather. For summer lettuce, try *Kagran* (Johnny's Selected Seeds), which is slower-bolting. Light shade during midsummer helps too.

SQUASH SUCCUMBED TO BUGS

Plant *Butternut* next year; it's more insect-resistant than *Buttercup* or *Mooregold*.

CUCUMBER VINES WILTED

Comb catalogues for resistant varieties such as *Medalist*, *Pacer*, *Liberty*, or *Sweet Slice*.

POTATOES ARE GREEN

Too much sunlight reached the developing tubers. Next time, pile on more mulch or hill the soil higher. New potatoes grow *above*, not below, the seed potatoes you planted.

Around the Corner

There are many things you can do to keep the fall garden productive; here are a few:

PROTECTION FROM FROST

In valleys and in the northern states, the likelihood of frost increases during the coming month. Be ready: Gather scattered pots, cartons, and other plant protectors, and stack old sheets and blankets in the shed. Replace the broken pane in the cold frame, and find a few bales of spoiled hay to make a frost-fending fortress around a choice tomato vine.

WEEDING

Weeds leap ahead during canning season, when one can't be *everywhere*, but a day or two spent whacking and pulling in early fall will give the young hardy vegetables the few weeks' advantage they need to get ahead of the wild growth.

PICKING

Keep cucumbers, zucchini, peppers, and beans picked for a continuous crop. Plants allowed to form mature seed-bearing fruits will stop producing. Fill all available baskets with tomatoes, peppers, and such when frost threatens. Dig up sweet potatoes as needed for early fall meals, but wait until frost to harvest all the plants. When picking escarole and leaf lettuce, leave a one-inch stub and more new leaves will grow within a month.

Pinch off tips of melon and tomato vines so that more energy will go into the developing fruit. As Brussels-sprout knobs develop around the stem, make room for them by snapping off all lower leaves, leaving a tuft of leaves at the crown of the plant.

PRUNING

Go easy on the water and plant food as fall progresses (but do water in case of drought). A dry spell often encourages blossoming and bearing, and plants that aren't too lush with new growth will be better prepared to withstand frost.

WATER AND FERTILIZING

Watch for these end-of-season volunteers in your garden, mulch around them, enjoy and use them: dill, potatoes, tomatoes (keep only if they've begun to set fruit by September), leaf lettuce.

VOLUNTEERS

Improving an Old Garden Patch

When you buy an old house or farm, you often get an old garden spot along with it. If the garden is poorly situated or if you intend to build a new house on the place, you'll probably choose to dig up a new vegetable garden in a different location. But it is surprising how often those old gardens are in exactly the right place: close to the house, on a south slope, in full sun, on well-drained ground. The question then becomes how to make the best of a given situation, how to condition that old, experienced piece of ground so it will produce good crops.

You might want to begin by researching the history of your established vegetable garden. Find out, if you can, what sort of fertilizer the former gardeners used on the place, how much was applied, and how often. Equally important, how were insects controlled—by chemical sprays or by gentler methods? You'd also be wise to ask what crops did poorly on that ground.

When we moved to our farm, we found a 30-foot by 40-foot vegetable garden right next to the old farmhouse. My guess is that people have been raising vegetables on that little patch of land for most of this century. In digging elsewhere on the place, we've found heavy crops of rocks, but virtually all the rocks have been picked out of that small garden over the years. Even the most recent occupants had never had money to spare to buy fertilizer or insect controls, so there was no lingering chemical contamination to worry about. In most of the years recently past, the garden had received an annual application of barnyard manure—probably enough to maintain its fertility, but not enough to boost humus content as high as we wanted it. We learned from neighbors that cabbages, which are heavy feeders, often did poorly in this general area. That suggested that the soil was probably low in nutrients.

167

Corn would have been another good indicator, but our garden was too small to have grown much corn.

In view of the benign history of our little patch, we took a conservative course in renewing it. First, we enlarged the area to 40 feet by 50 feet. Since it was so convenient to the house, we decided to keep it as a kitchen garden and to grow our corn and rambling squash in a new patch a bit farther from the house. We spread a thick layer of manure every spring, so thick that it literally blanketed the ground. And we mulched as much as we could, to add additional humus. We also added rock phosphate, limestone, and wood ashes that first year and again about three years later. During the season, we tried to replace soil nitrogen by watering leafy plants with manure tea. Liming and increasing the humus and nitrogen levels made it possible for us to raise some fine cabbages from that worked-over patch of formerly acidic, ironstone soil.

Should you find that your inherited soil has received applications of persistent pesticides, your best course would be to do everything possible to increase the soil's humus content: mulch, put compost in the planting rows, turn under green manure and barnyard manure. The rich microbial life that flourishes in humus will help to break down the pesticide residues.

Any land that has been used by gardeners for many years probably has good drainage, but sometimes there is a corner of the plot where drainage could be improved. Chisel plowing the area will often improve drainage by breaking up deep hardpan. Growing deep-rooted plants, such as Swiss chard and cowhorn turnips, also helps to establish deeper drainage channels. You might consider building raised beds at the wet end of the garden. If soil is severely water-logged, installing drain tile should help. (Call your local soil conservation service for advice.)

A soil test will reveal the strengths and weaknesses in your soil, showing the availability of major nutrients—nitrogen, phosphorus, and potassium—and the equally vital trace minerals, as well as reporting on humus content. Soil testing is available through the Cooperative Extension Service and often from local feed stores. In some states—Pennsylvania is one—extension agents will provide information that will help you to correct any deficiencies in your soil with natural amendments, if you prefer to use those instead of synthetic fertilizers.

Weeds that flourish in the old garden bed will give you clues to the nature of the soil, too. In good, rich ground, you'll find the following: lamb's quarters (*Chenopodium album*), morning glory (*Ipomoea purpurea*), sweet clover (*Melilotus alba*), smartweed (*Polygonum hydropiper*), jimson weed (*Datura stramonium*), and cocklebur (*Xanthium orientale*). Weeds that grow well in poor soil include bracted plantain (*Plantago aristata*), a sign of acid soil; goose grass (*Eleusine indica*), which grows in poor, hard soil; sedges of several varieties, indicating wet places; sheep sorrel (*Rumex acetosella*), found in highly acid and poor soil; and poverty grass (*Danthonia spicata*), an indicator of dry, acidic soil, low in nutrients.

If the old garden spot is a jumble of weeds, this is a good time to plow or till them back into the soil. And, unless you live in the far North, there's still time—if you act promptly—to sow a soil-building crop of winter wheat or annual rye to be turned under in the spring.

Chances are you can find some interesting local resources to enrich your garden, perhaps even in your own back yard. At our farm, for example, we discovered a moldering pile of old corncobs at the edge of a field, leaf mold in rocky pockets in the woods, rotting stumps, and a few bales of spoiled hay. All of it went on the garden. And when we tore down a wall in the house, we saved all the plaster with horsehair embedded in it. As we sifted the chalky dust over the venerable vegetable plot, we thought it appropriate to be renewing the house and the garden at the same time.

When to Pick Fall Vegetables

Your vegetable garden is probably approaching its productive peak right now, with the tomato harvest well under way, root crops maturing, and beans, cucumbers, corn, and onions filling baskets that gradually line up on the porch. Is there, you wonder, a perfect picking time—a stage of excellence when your crop will be at its best? Perhaps the following hints will help you to fill your picking baskets with vegetables that are not only fresh, but also ripened to perfection.

JERUSALEM ARTICHOKES These delightful, crisp tubers are at their best after frost, when the tops have died back, but many of us start eating them at summer's end, after the plants have bloomed. They have a mild flavor. Dig only what you'll use within two or three weeks for the thin-skinned knobs don't keep well, even when refrigerated. Continue digging until spring, but stop harvesting the roots when new growth starts and they become coarse and tough.

BEANS Nothing looks more impressive in a jar than neatly marshalled pencil-slim snap beans. For the fullest flavor, though, I like to let my beans develop a bit more—until they are well filled out with seed, but before the seeds bulge or the pod toughens and becomes rubbery. The pod of a first-rate green bean should snap readily when bent.

LIMA BEANS Pods should look well-upholstered. Yellow pods are overmature. Save those old limas for soup.

BEETS For pickling, canning, and bunching fresh for the table, you can't beat little 1- to 2-inch-diameter baby beets. Long Season and Lutz Green Leaf are two varieties that remain tender even when large and ungainly looking. Most other beets lose quality after they've grown to a diameter of 3 inches.

BROCCOLI
Cut the flowering stalk while the blossom buds are still tightly closed. Eat the tender leaves that come with the stalk. After you've harvested the main stalk, smaller florets will form in the leaf axils. Keep cutting the flower heads in order to encourage the plant to continue producing, and lop off any blossoms that may have escaped you. If they're too full blown to eat, just discard them.

BRUSSELS SPROUTS
Don't even try sprouts until after frost. Freezing changes their coarse pre-frost flavor to a much more pleasing, delicate taste. If you nip out the growing tip of the plant in September, the sprouts on the upper part of the stem will develop sooner. Sprouts are at their best when firm and green. Yellowing indicates overmaturity. Use a twisting motion to pluck the sprouts and begin picking at the bottom of the stem, where the sprouts are less solid than those that grow higher up.

CARROTS
Pluck the tiny thinnings for use in soups. Your main-crop picking begins when the carrots are ½ inch or more in diameter—up to about 1½ inches, for maximum tenderness. Harvest carrots by digging rather than pulling, unless soil is very moist and loose.

CAULIFLOWER
Pick the heads when they are solid and while they are still compact. "Ricey" heads of cauliflower are past their prime. Watch them closely in hot weather.

CORN
Quality suffers drastically from overmaturity or storage. The sugar content begins to turn to starch as soon as the ear is picked. Check the ears daily; pick when the kernels have filled out and a punctured kernel appears milky. (If watery—too soon; if doughy—too late.) Overmature corn has pale or yellowed husks and dry silks. If you're growing the variety Wonderful, remember that the cobs are deceptively slim. Don't wait for them to plump out before checking them.

CUCUMBER
The freshest cukes make the best pickles. You'd be wise to plan to make your pickles when the cukes are in full production, so you needn't save up a week's supply. Cucumbers start to retire if they're given a chance to produce large fruit with well-developed seeds, so it is important to harvest the crop at least four times a week, and preferably daily.

EGGPLANT
Start picking when the fruits are about 3 inches in diameter. As long as they're glossy, they're good. (Overmature fruit will have a dull skin.) Use a knife to cut the tough stem; pulling may injure the plant.

HORSERADISH
Most of the root growth takes place in the early fall, so newer plantings should be dug from September until the ground freezes. A well-established planting may be harvested at any time.

KALE
Pick after frost for best flavor.

OKRA
Pick all the 2- to 3-inch pods every day, or at least every other day. Pick thoroughly to encourage continuous bearing.

Pull onions when most of the tops have drooped and dried on their own. It's all right to bend over the last few stragglers with your rake, but take care not to bruise the bulb or it may rot. The scullions (thicknecks) don't keep well; store them separately and use them first.

ONIONS

Peppers are good when they're green (highest in Vitamin A) and when they're red (highest Vitamin C content). When picking for storage, leave a short stem on the fruit.

PEPPERS

Let them be until after frost, when their starch begins to turn to sugar. Mulch to extend the digging period.

PARSNIPS

You may steal a few potatoes from the hill for immediate use after the blossoms have formed, but for the main storage crop, let the vines die down before you dig. In prolonged wet weather, if the tops have been down for awhile, you'll probably want to dig the crop before it sprouts anew.

POTATOES

Zucchini is at its best for sautéing and freezing, as well as for pickles and salads, when 4–8 inches long, often still bearing a wilted blossom. Larger specimens are good for stuffing. Pattypan squash is at its tender best when the size of a silver dollar.

SUMMER SQUASH

Only fully mature squash are good for storage. The hard shell should resist thumbnail penetration. Cut them with some stem on.

WINTER SQUASH

Acorn: Hard, dark green skin, often with a yellow spot where the fruit rested on the ground.

Buttercup: Dark green rind, sometimes with yellow or orange marks on the cap.

Butternut: Immature, for immediate eating but not for storage, will be creamy yellow with faint green stripes. Mature butternuts have a hard, buff, or rosy-tan skin.

Hubbard: Warted, dark green, or blue depending on variety; very hard rind.

Leave the fruit on the vine until fully colored, unless frost threatens. Pick only well-developed green tomatoes to ripen inside. Twist the fruit off when picking; pulling may injure the plant.

TOMATOES

Is Your Organic Matter Safe?

Organic matter for the garden soil is generally considered as wholesome as aprons and apples. Most of the once-living plant and animal residues we use to build up our soil are not simply innocuous, but positively beneficial. Once in a while, though, we run across types of organic matter that give us pause. Some of these substances contain actual or potential toxins in addition to their humus-building components. Should we use them or not? Is there any way to make them safe for our gardens? Let's look at some of these tempting but questionable resources.

GRASS CLIPPINGS Lawns in any given suburb produce in the aggregate tons of grass clippings each season. That's a lot of free mulch, and some free fertilizer too. (Analysis of Kentucky Blue Grass reveals a chemical content of 1.2 per cent nitrogen, 0.3 per cent phosphorus, and 2 per cent potassium.) If the grass clippings are your own, you'll know whether they've been sprayed with herbicides, but if they come from other yards, you might want to find out how the lawns have been treated. Many weed killers used on lawns contain 2,4-D to kill broadleaf plants. While the grass isn't harmed by the 2,4-D, it does absorb some of the chemical, and you don't want to put broadleaf plant killers on your garden. It takes soil microbes about a week to break down chemical weed killers. To protect your garden, compost treated clippings first. According to Dr. John Jagschitz of the University of Rhode Island, activated charcoal applied as a dust or slurry helps to absorb and deactivate herbicides.

Lead is another potential hazard in piles of grass clippings or leaves picked up along busy streets. Where traffic is heavy—more than 5,000 vehicles a day—leaves and grass collected within 20 feet of the street are likely to be contaminated with lead. Don't use them; lead accumulates and can't be composted away. Although plants don't always accumulate a lot of lead from lead-contaminated soil, there is danger in eating the products of such soil. Children are more sensitive to lead than adults; they absorb four times as much. Chronic exposure to 500 to 1,000 parts per million (ppm) of lead in soil can seriously damage a child's central nervous system.

COAL ASHES I've talked to elderly gardeners who swear by coal ashes, especially for the onion patch, but I remain unconvinced. Coal ashes will lighten clay soil, it's true, but at the expense of adding potentially toxic amounts of sulfur and iron. Hard-coal ashes contain less sulfur and iron than those from soft coal, but I think the risks still outweigh the benefits.

NEWSPAPER Black-and-white newsprint is generally considered to be a safe mulch, although it has a lead content of 69 ppm, according to a study conducted at the University of Connecticut Agricultural Experiment Station. The study included a simulation of an eight-week rainfall and showed that lead leached from the paper in "negligible amounts." Avoid using colored newsprint or magazine paper on the garden, though; their lead content is much higher. (Incidentally, according to that study, some food wrappers contain as much lead as 7,125 ppm.)

DOG AND CAT MANURE Kennel owners are sometimes tempted to compost dog droppings to enrich their gardens. It's a risky business, however. Humans may be infested by parasites sometimes found in dog manure: tapeworms, roundworm eggs, hookworm larvae, and echinococcus eggs. Cat feces may also contain hookworm larvae and may, in addition, transmit the disease toxoplasmosis, which causes flu-like symptoms in adults who contract it. Pregnant women, especially, should avoid handling cat droppings, because toxoplasmosis can cause birth defects.

Sludge is the effluent from a sewage treatment plant. Undigested sludge should never be used on gardens, because it may contain pathogens. Digested sludge, which has been treated with aerobic bacteria, given time to decompose, and then allowed to settle and dry, is generally considered virtually virus-free. Composting the sludge should kill any remaining pathogens. Most gardeners who have knowingly used sludge on their plantings put it mainly around fruit trees or bushy crops, avoiding areas where root crops or raw foods such as lettuce will be grown.

In recent years, though, the heavy-metal content of sludge has become alarmingly evident in study after study. In 1976 a processed-sewage fertilizer called Nu-Earth was distributed free for use in community garden plots in Chicago. Three years later, soil scientists found that Nu-Earth contained almost twenty times the amount of cadmium considered safe. High cadmium levels are linked to cancer and kidney disease. Plants absorb cadmium readily, but they show no changes until they contain extremely high levels of the metal, and minute amounts are toxic to people: a cadmium content of 75 ppm is high. Cadmium remains in the topsoil for hundreds of years, and if more is added year by year the soil can become hopelessly contaminated.

Three other heavy metals found in sludge also cause serious concern: zinc, copper, and nickel, all toxic to plants at relatively low levels. The amount of toxic metals absorbed by plants depends on soil pH, type of plant, cation exchange capacity of the soil, and other variables. Generally, plants seem to absorb the least amount in soil with a pH of 6.5 to 7. They absorb more toxic heavy metals when the phosphorus content of the soil is low.

In addition to heavy metals, sludge in many areas contains PCBs or PBBs from industrial chemicals. These persistent toxins and suspected carcinogens show up far from their place of origin, and they accumulate in the food chain. You don't want to let them into your garden—not even once.

Of all the sludge produced in the United States, 35 per cent is burned, 25 per cent is buried in landfills, 25 per cent is spread on agricultural land, and 15 per cent is dumped at sea by coastal cities. Some states regulate the distribution of sludge, but many don't. In Pennsylvania, Maryland, and Virginia, for example, all sludges must be analyzed before being distributed. Budget cuts may change that sensible restriction, though. New York State currently has a two-year ban on the agricultural use of sludge, and some soil scientists are recommending that the ban be made permanent.

According to Dr. Donald Lisk, director of the Toxic Chemicals Laboratory at Cornell University, "There is practically no such thing as clean sludge.'' Even sludge from homes can contain cadmium, zinc, copper, nickel, and chromium, and in rural areas sludge often has a high concentration of crankcase oil and toxic chemicals.

It's uncertain exactly how much sludge is produced in the United States annually, but even the lowest estimates indicate that at least 5 million tons of it are spread on agricultural land every year, and not all of it is analyzed first. If we buy food grown or pastured on soil treated with sludge, we're probably already getting more heavy metals than we bargained for. Even though some soil scientists maintain that there is no cause for alarm, it seems to me that it would be poor economy to put sludge on our gardens too.

Fair-Sized Pumpkins and Other Tips

As summer wanes, the bumper crops and the gaps in our gardens become evident. We know now which crops have done well, and which ones didn't work out. We find ourselves thinking about what we should do differently to get a better yield next year. Each week there are new questions in my mailbox from gardeners seeking solutions to problems, or ideas for improvements. Here are some that I found particularly interesting.

Giant Pumpkins

My son wants to raise a giant pumpkin for the fair. Can you give him some tips?

Successful growers of big pumpkins usually use at least some of the following tricks:

(a) Plant the seeds in a hill of your best humus-rich soil that's been further enriched by two or three generous shovelfuls of compost or well-rotted manure.

(b) Space the hills farther apart—5 feet—rather than the usual 3 or 4 feet.

(c) Let the whole plant concentrate its energies on a single fruit. This means that, once a good fruit has formed, you must remove all the succeeding blossoms as they form.

(d) Be careful not to twist the fruit or injure the vine when working around the plant.

(e) Control weedy competition by mulching around the vine.

(f) After the fruit forms, feed the plant weekly with a bucket full of compost tea.

(g) Snip off and discard the tip of a strong runner and poke the cut end of the vine into a jar of milk or sugar solution. (I haven't tried this, but have heard it recommended by so many gardeners that it seems worth listing for those who want to try everything. My most reliable informant used raw goat's milk.)

How long do I need to water the garden to make up for no rain?

In general, vegetable crops need the equivalent of an inch of rain each week. Well-mulched crops can often get by on less. The amount of time you need to leave the sprinkler running on each section of garden depends on the diameter of your hose. A ½-inch hose delivering 10½ gallons of water per minute will apply the equivalent of an inch of rainfall in a little more than an hour. If your hose is ⅝ inch in diameter, delivering 17 gallons per minute, it will take thirty-seven minutes; and, if you have a ¾-inch hose delivering 31 gallons per minute, it will take only twenty-four minutes. Another test of adequate watering is to check how deep into the ground the water has penetrated. The soil should be soaked to a depth of 4 to 6 inches after thorough watering.

How come I have such poor luck with eggplant?

It's not hard to go wrong with eggplant, which is a sensitive crop requiring good soil and plenty of warmth and moisture. One common mistake is planting the seedlings outside too early, at the same time tomatoes are set out. Try giving your young eggplants another week or two of protection before you set them out. Early chilling can drastically reduce later production. Try to prevent wilting, too, from seedling stage to maturity. A plant that suffers from lack of water turns woody and produces less. Choosing one of the smaller early varieties like Early Black Egg (Johnny's Selected Seeds) has made the difference between success and failure with eggplants for many gardeners.

Why is summer lettuce so hard to raise?

Lettuce seeds are programmed to insure the survival of the next generation, which will thrive in cool weather, not hot. So, when the temperature is up, germination of lettuce seed goes down. You can outwit this natural tendency by:

(a) Prechilling the seed in the freezer.

(b) Pressing the seed into the soil but not covering it. (Exposure to light helps to break dormancy.)

(c) Using old seed in which the tendency toward warm-weather dormancy is less pronounced.

Having induced the plants to grow, keep them happy in midsummer heat by providing some shade during midday.

Is it true that zucchini fruits won't develop properly if the plants are set too close to pumpkin vines?

Many people believe that cross-pollination of blossoms between different varieties of plants affects the quality of the fruit those plants will produce. That is sometimes true of corn, but not of other garden vegetables. Your zucchinis make good neighbors for your cucumbers, watermelons, and other cucurbits. Any crossing that occurs this year won't show up until next year, so it would be a problem only if you were to save and plant seed from closely related varieties.

Green Tomatoes

What's the best way to ripen green tomatoes indoors?
There are several good ways. Easiest is to pull up several whole vines and hang them in a dry basement. When picking tomatoes for indoor ripening, choose only mature green ones that are well developed and dark green or beginning to color. Keep the ripest tomatoes at room temperature; those that have started to turn red should ripen in a week. Mature green tomatoes should be spread in a single layer out of direct light. At 60° to 70°F, they'll ripen in about two weeks. Wrapping the fruits individually in newspaper helps to keep them in good condition. Try placing a few apples among the ripening tomatoes; the ethylene gas given off by apples promotes ripening. To hold mature green tomatoes for later ripening, keep them at 55° to 65°F for several weeks, bringing them into a warmer room for faster ripening as you need them.

Winter-Keeping Vegetables

Long before we moved to the country, I was reading to our children stories that—I now realize—influenced me too. One of our favorites was *Old Man Rabbit's Dinner Party*, a Platt and Munk classic written by Carolyn Sherwin Bailey. This tale of a rabbit that collected a burlap sackful of "purple turnips, yellow carrots, russet apples," potatoes, and corn on a frosty fall day somehow captured my imagination and sank into my consciousness. In those pre-*Watership Down* days, it didn't matter to us that his behavior was not authentic Rabbit. The colorful variety of those last vegetables set against a dusting of early fall snow, the glimpse into Old Man Rabbit's tree-hole house, the feeling of preparedness, the spirit of sharing—these were what mattered. Old Man Rabbit had the right idea.

Now as I gather the beets that will help to fuel a six-foot tennis-playing teen-age son over the winter, and the carrots that will provide a taste of what our college-student daughter calls "real food," I remember Old Man Rabbit and all his Beatrix Potter cousins. Planning ahead may be a uniquely human activity, but putting food by is a ritual that confirms our relationship to the animals that live in this world with us. The stores are full of canned and frozen foods, to be sure. Still, the squirreling instinct quickens in us as days shorten and leaves begin to turn.

Storage vegetables—the good keepers that withstand early frosts and retain their eating quality when kept in a cool basement or root cellar—will often last until spring if well prepared and carefully stored. Although storage conditions are crucial, too little attention is often paid to the preparation of vegetables to be put away for winter in root cellars, earth mounds, boxes of sawdust, or buried barrels.

When to Harvest

Timing should be the first consideration. Root vegetables will keep better if they are harvested after a considerable spell of cool—even freezing—weather, just so they are not subjected to a severe killing frost. Low temperatures at digging time promote storage durability in two ways: (1) cold encourages the vegetable cells to fill with stored sugars and starches in place of water, and (2) storage areas are more likely to remain in the desired low-temperature range during a cool spell. If at all possible, dig your root vegetables while weather is dry, again for two reasons: (1) there will be less water, and more stored carbohydrate, in the tissues of the roots. Watery vegetables shrivel and spoil sooner. (2) less soil will cling to the uprooted vegetables. You can't control either of these conditions, of course—only try to work around them. Last fall we had such an overabundance of rain in our area that we counted ourselves lucky to have cool weather for the few relatively dry days on which we could dig.

Which Vegetables to Store

Selection is in your hands. Choose your very best vegetables for storage—mature, well-developed, unbruised. Overripe vegetables spoil readily; so do those that are underripe and watery. Root vegetables grown in soil oversupplied with nitrogen may be on the watery side, low in the stored carbohydrates that make them keep well. Use the nicked, less-than-perfect but basically sound specimens for immediate eating. (You might take a leaf from *Old Man Rabbit* and invite all your neighbors to a great big enormous New England boiled dinner.)

How to Cure Vegetables

Curing promotes the development of a tough skin and helps to reduce water content; both conditions favor long storage life. Root vegetables need only a short period of curing: an afternoon in the sun on a dry day, right after digging, helps to loosen clinging clods of dirt and kill small feeder roots. Pumpkins and squash should bask in the sun out in the open for several weeks until they develop a hard rind. Onions should be spread in the sun for several days.

Cleaning Vegetables for Storage

Cleaning should be minimal. You don't need to wash vegetables for storage. They'll keep better if you wait to wash them until you're ready to eat them. Gently brush dirt from root vegetables. Don't even do that, though, for tomatoes and other soft-skinned short-term-storage vegetables; wiping off dirt is too likely to bruise the flesh. Leave the dirt until you're about to use the food.

Cutting off Greens

Clipping tops off should be done soon after digging. You can remove the whole ferny top from carrots but leave a one-inch stub on the sappier leaves of beets, or they'll bleed. Never snap off the pointed root tips or pull off small feeder roots, though. Such skin breaks will invite spoilage.

Stems of pumpkins and squash should always be left on. Peppers, too. Cut the tops of onions and garlic to a one-inch stub before sun-curing them.

The following extra hints for handling individual vegetables should help make your fall harvest last well into the winter that is just around the next corner.

CABBAGE   Pull stem and all, remove any diseased or unsound outer leaves, store in a root cellar, earth mound, or cold shed. Nancy Thurber and Gretchen Mead, in their book *Keeping the Harvest*, suggest wrapping the heads in newspaper secured with a rubber band.

BEETS   Clip the tops to one inch, store in sawdust, root cellar, buried barrel, or the like. Eat the small beets soon; the large ones keep best.

CARROTS   Wrench off the tops, brush off loose dirt, keep in a cold, damp place as for beets.

PEPPERS   Leave the stems on, pile them lightly in baskets and keep in a cold, damp spot for several weeks. Use the red ones first.

WHITE POTATOES   Leave them in the ground until cool weather comes to stay, but dig them before a hard freeze and rescue them if prolonged rainy weather threatens to cause re-sprouting. Spread them in a shady, well-ventilated spot to dry for a day before storing. Avoid exposing potatoes to the light or they'll develop unwholesome green skin.

SWEET POTATOES   Harvest them right after frost blackens the vines and spread them out in a warm place to cure for about two weeks. Then wrap each one individually in paper. Handle them carefully; they bruise easily.

TURNIPS AND RUTABAGAS   Trim the tops to a one-inch stub and pile them carefully in a slatted crate in a damp, cool storage place.

WINTER SQUASH AND PUMPKINS   Cure them in the sun for several weeks until their rind is so hard that your thumbnail can't pierce it. Use stemless ones first. The scar where the stem was knocked off may be coated with melted beeswax to prolong the keeping period somewhat. Avoid piling them so high that the vegetables on the bottom may be bruised.

TOMATOES   Remove the stems if you are picking individual green tomatoes. Or try pulling the whole vine and hanging it upside down in a cool place. Tomatoes from bushes still in their prime keep best. This is a good reason for retaining a few of those later-starting volunteer plants.

Pull them when most of the tops have fallen over; clip the tops to one inch; cure them in the sun three or four days, then keep them cool and dry.

Frostproofing Your Garden

Late afternoons in September often find northern gardeners scanning the sky, sniffing the breeze, cocking an ear to the radio. A clear sky with no wind is a univeral frost omen, especially if temperatures dip near 40° by early evening. The countryman watches out for frost the week before a full moon.

So often an early freeze is followed by a week or even several weeks of good, frost-free growing weather. But tender tomatoes and peppers are finished for the season if subjected to even a few minutes of killing frost. A little effort spent in protecting vulnerable crops can often extend your growing season, giving you another bushel or two of good fresh vegetables.

When frost seems imminent, we gather all the ripe, tender vegetables and most of the green ones. We cover all the lettuce we can, but in the case of tomatoes and eggplants, we choose several of the best plants to save. If you are selecting your own seed for frost tolerance, this is the time to evaluate and protect those that seem hardiest.

Frost kills plants by turning the water in their leaves to ice crystals, which then puncture cell walls. Plants that do get lightly frosted may often be saved by spraying them with the finest possible mist of water, early in the morning before strong sunlight strikes the plant.

Coverings of boxes, bags, blankets, and bottomless gallon jugs offer the first line of defense, enabling plants to withstand from two to six degrees of frost. Baskets may cover individual large plants. Blankets or feed bags protect rows of lettuce as long as they don't get soaked. Metal coverings shouldn't touch the plant, lest they conduct vital heat away from it. Removing covers each morning and replacing them at night takes time, but then so does a trip to the store for fresh produce.

If you want to go to a little more trouble, you can arrange even more effective, more permanent frost buffers. Row-long tents may be made of clear plastic, draped over wire arches or a tunnel of wire fencing, secured with stones at the sides and ends. Since warm air rises, these tents should be ventilated at the bottom, not the top. The air space between the plant and its covering insulates more effectively than a sheet resting right on the plant.

Sprawling tomato plants are more difficult to protect than tidy heads of lettuce, but keeping your supply of vine-ripened fruit is usually worth the trouble. One of the most effective tomato-savers is an enclosure of hay bales surrounding the plant, topped by an old storm window. If you've grown your tomatoes in cylinders of wire fencing, you can easily bank hay around these and cover them.

Coldframes offer another solution to the frost problem. Vegetables such as early fall lettuce thinnings may be transplanted into the coldframe to carry on past frost.

A thick straw mulch helps to keep soil temperature even and provides emergency insulation that will be drawn up around a low-growing plant. The heat released by the decomposing mulch may have a slight warming effect if the mulch is thick.

Stone mulches absorb heat during the day and release it slowly at night.

Vegetable gardens situated near a body of water often receive extra warmth from heat released by the water, especially if the garden is on the leeward side.

Even small amounts of water can help to protect your vegetables. One pound of water gives off 144 BTUs as it freezes. You can use this principle to advantage by placing pans of water in your coldframe and under your vegetable tents. As the water freezes, it will moderate the air temperature. Shallow water in wide metal containers will freeze more readily than water in deep crockery bowls.

Water can be used to insulate your cold frame, too. Professor Frederick Fry of the University of Toronto found that plastic bags filled with water, set on the glass of the cold frame, kept plants inside the cold frame growing even when average air temperature outside the frame was 20°, as long as a four-inch space was maintained between the plants and the outside air.

Then there is seaweed, free for the gathering in coastal New England, and widely available as a concentrate* at nominal cost. Alaskan gardeners were taught by Eskimos to apply seaweed to their vegetable gardens during World War II, in what is apparently the first recorded use of this native resource for the purpose of inducing frost resistance in crops. Later studies reported by E. Booth in *The Grower* (November 27 and December 4, 1965) suggest that normal plant growth, which ordinarily takes place within a limited temperature range, may be sustained by supplying certain missing metabolic products which the plant is unable to synthesize at low temperatures. The conjecture is that the mineral-rich seaweed must somehow provide vital elements that the plant needs in order to function, thus making growth possible at lower-than-normal temperatures.

Experiments at Clemson College, reported by Aitken, Senn, and Martin of the horticulture department there, showed that plants treated with seaweed survived temperatures of 29° that killed un-

SOURCES OF SEAWEED CONCENTRATE:

R. H. Shumway, Seedsman
Olds Seed Co.
Stokes Seeds
Joseph Harris Co., Inc.

treated plants. A foliar spray of the diluted seaweed concentrate was used.

Although we can't explain it clearly, these reports and others indicate that seaweed seems effective in imparting frost resistance to plants. Why not try it this year? Perhaps you can foil old Jack for an extra week or two.

OCTOBER

Consider the Roots

What's been going on underground in your garden, all summer? Throughout the growing season, we gardeners have been preoccupied with the top growth of our plants—the leaves, seeds, and fruit we've been harvesting. But October is a good time to consider the roots. Just what have they been up to, down there? What can we, putterers and passionate gardeners alike, do to improve conditions for the roots of our vegetable plants and so enjoy a better harvest next year?

Plant roots have long been thought to depend to a considerable extent on the support of top growth, but the latest information coming from plant physiologists indicates that roots are much less dependent than we have considered them to be. Roots, in fact, contribute more to the life of the plant than they receive. They produce many vital hormones that control plant growth. They determine the nature of the plant. In an experiment by Dr. Johannes van Overbeek involving the grafting of tomato tops to tobacco roots and tobacco tops to tomato roots, tomato leaves grown on tobacco roots were found to contain nicotine but not the tobacco tops grown on tomato roots. Such is the power of roots.

The root system of a plant grows continuously. As long as the plant lives, it cannot stop, yet all the while it is growing, parts are dying. Some root hairs, for example, live only a few hours.

The root hairs are the point of exchange between the giving soil and the receiving plant—the place where water and nutrients enter the roots. Each root hair is a single-celled thread, tipped by a tough end-cap that burrows into ever-new areas of soil. An inch of roots may contain as many as 50,000 root hairs.

Within the root, tubes in the core of the root system carry water and mineral solutions absorbed from the soil up to the leaves. Other tubes, located in the inner bark, take carbohydrates that are produced in the leaf by photosynthesis down to the root. Not unlike the human vascular system! According to Charles Morrow Wilson, whose book *Roots: Miracles Below* reports much of the information summarized here, "No man-made system of hydraulic engineering can match the root for efficiency in raising water . . . the process is still, at least in great part, a profound mystery."

Roots are among the most vulnerable parts of the plant. They are affected by the majority of plant diseases. Nematodes, insects, bacteria, and fungi prey on them. (Bacteria and fungi, it should be noted, break down complex organic matter into living soil; most of them, and even most soil-based insects, do more good than harm.)

Of the thousands of kinds of nematodes known, only about 10 percent are harmful to plants. That extremely destructive 10 per cent, however, seriously threatens root health. Most nematodes are smaller than a printed period. They live on moisture that surrounds soil particles and penetrate root tissue with sharp, spear-like mouth parts, debilitating the plant and exposing injured points to secondary fungal and bacterial infestation.

Nematodes live everywhere—even in polar tundra. They almost certainly live in your garden and mine. The damage they cause is widespread but difficult to detect. Infested plants may show signs of gradual decline, stunting, wilting, or yellowing of leaves, but these symptoms may also be the effects of invasion by bacteria and fungi.

When you uproot your spent plants this fall, check the roots for the small knots that indicate nematode damage. (Not to be confused with the larger nodules of nitrogen-fixing bacteria found on legume roots.) If you find evidence of nematode activity, don't despair. Here are four good gardening methods that will help to control your nematode population, foster healthy root growth, and insure better crops next season.

(1) Increase your soil's content of organic matter in every way possible—by mulching, composting, manuring, cover cropping. Numerous studies indicate that abundant organic matter in the soil supports growth of valuable bacteria and predacious fungi that destroy nematodes and other soil pests and pathogens. (And conversely, according to Charles Wilson, heavy applications of commercial fertilizer containing high concentrations of nitrogen have been shown to decrease the population of beneficial pseudomonas and favor the proliferation of bacteria causing plant diseases.) Humus formed by broken-down organic matter holds soil moisture, nourishes roots, and provides an aerated, easily penetrated medium for vigorous root growth.

(2) Plant marigolds in your vegetable garden. The pungent-smelling French or African marigolds give off a root exudate that discourages nematodes. Scatter marigolds in the rows and plant an occasional whole row of them in a different spot each year.

(3) Practice interplanting to avail yourself of the still little-understood power of root exudates—substances peculiar to a certain type of plant, produced by the roots in a probable attempt to define the plant's territory. The roots of some plants attract certain nematodes, while remaining distasteful to others. Nematodes thriving on corn roots, for example, will have nothing to do with rutabagas. A wide variety of intensively planted vegetable crops will help to protect each other.

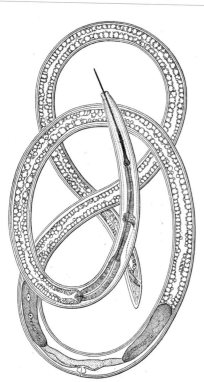

The dagger nematode wraps its serpentine body around a plant's delicate rootlets and plunges its slender spear into the root's fragile inner tissues.

(4) Rotate crops to prevent the harmful build-up of nematodes and damaging fungi, bacteria, and insects that tend to concentrate around plants they favor. Switch things around and keep them guessing!

Alternatives to a Root Cellar

Most serious gardeners end the season with a planned surplus of vegetables, especially the root crops and hard-rinded squash and pumpkins that keep well. Chances are that you have—at the very least—some carrots, beets, and potatoes to put by. It's more than likely, on the other hand, that your country place, like ours, is not among the few that boast a root cellar. Don't despair; you have a choice of alternatives.

Perhaps one of the suggested storage methods listed here will enable you to enjoy your hard-earned produce when the garden is deep in snow and all the transient birds have left.

Leave the vegetables right in the garden This easiest-of-all methods works especially well for parsnips and salsify, which are at their best after a good round of freezing weather. Carrots keep well in the row too, if well protected. Beets are more chancy, but they may last you another month or so. Hill up the rows of vegetables, burying any protruding root shoulder, and mulch the rows lavishly with a foot or two of good solid mulch—hay bales or bags of leaves held down by boards. Your parsnips, carrots, and salsify won't be accessible under four feet of snow, of course, but you can either retrieve them between snows, or enjoy them in early spring. Use a good tall stake to mark the rows.

Dig a hole large enough to accommodate one of the following:
(1) Standing trash can
(2) Barrel set at a 45-degree angle
(3) Large ceramic drain tile
(4) Rectangular wood box with a hinged lid, protected from rodents by an outer layer of hardware cloth.

Choose a shady site with good drainage. Place a few rocks in the bottom of the hole. Stored root vegetables require high moisture (90 to 95 per cent, except for potatoes), but standing water will speed decay.

Put a layer of straw or sawdust in the bottom of the buried container, then a layer of vegetables topped by more straw. The air trapped by the straw helps to insulate the stored food. Build up alternate layers of vegetables and packing material until the

Barrel, Box, and Can Storage

container is almost full. Top it with a thick wad of straw, close the lid tightly, and pack at least a foot of insulating material over the top, held down by a board and several large rocks.

When filling buried barrels, many gardeners like to include a variety of root vegetables—beets, carrots, celeriac, turnips—a provision that makes for more varied winter menus. Cabbage is usually relegated to its own storage box, since the strong aroma it develops in storage permeates other vegetables.

Use of an Unheated Outbuilding

A shed, garage, or barn, or an unheated part of your house—an enclosed porch, basement stairway, or crawl space under a porch. Produce may be kept, covered, in such spots for at least a month after harvest. When the occasional frosts turn to regular freezes and the ground begins to harden, tuck tarps or old blankets around the boxes of produce. For further protection well into the winter, insulate your boxes or cans of fruit or root vegetables with a three-foot batting of hay, straw, or bags of leaves on each side. Or pack root vegetables in boxes of sawdust with a 4-inch layer of sawdust as a base and also as insulation between the vegetables and the side of the box.

Late melons, if well developed, may be kept in hay or straw for further ripening during the early weeks of fall when a temperature near 55 degrees can be maintained.

The Window Well

A good choice for gardeners who need only a small storage space, or for those who don't like to dig. Open a basement window and fit or build a sturdy wooden box into the opening, extending out into the window well. The cold outside air will keep the vegetables cool and the warmer air from the house will prevent freezing.

Storage Boxes

Soil-filled boxes brought into a cool basement will keep celery, Chinese cabbage, leeks, and celeriac in good shape for a month or two. Winter radishes, packed in moist sand, usually keep even longer.

Earth-Covered Surface Mounds

Choose a well-drained spot and spread 6 inches of leaves or straw on the ground for a base. Pile the vegetables in a cone-shaped mound on this base. Cover them with about 10 inches of straw or leaves and top that insulating layer with 6 inches of earth. The earth may be dug from immediately around the pile. The resulting shallow trench will provide a helpful drainage trough to direct rainwater away from your stored bounty. A late bumper crop of cabbage may be stored, head down with root intact, in such a mound.

Attic Storage

As long as you don't forget that you've put them up there, pumpkins, squash, and ripening tomatoes—all vegetables that prefer drier air (60 to 70 per cent humidity) and a warmer temperature (50 to 55 degrees) may fare very well in the attic. Warm air rising from the living quarters below tends to moderate attic temperatures. Air temperature will fluctuate more widely, though, in the attic than in the basement. If your cellar is dry and warm enough, pumpkins and squash will also keep well there on slatted shelves.

Even when you follow all the rules and store only dry, mature, solid, unbruised vegetables, a small amount of spoilage is still to be expected. You can prevent the breakdown of the remaining stored vegetables by promptly removing those that go bad and, when repacking the sound roots, leaving a one-inch space between the individual vegetables.

Squash

Living eleven miles on a beeline from Three Mile Island has made us painfully aware of the hidden costs of all the household power we take for granted. Recently we've been raising more garden vegetables that store well without processing. Squash is high on our list of versatile winter providers because it tastes good, contributes important vitamins, keeps well, and performs well in most gardens. Growing winter squash saves power. You needn't freeze it or can it. When properly cured and stored, squash will remain in good condition well into the winter; some kinds even last until spring.

We've chosen our favorite squash varieties for flavor, disease and insect resistance, yield, and ability to keep. Each of the following strains is worth growing:

BUTTERCUP Tops in flavor, with sweet, dry, fine-grained flesh. Average resistance to pests and disease, and good storage life. (For us, that means they last until January or February.)

BUTTERNUT One of the most dependable. Keeps very well, tastes good, yields well, and stands up to the bugs. *Ponca* is a small early strain worth your attention if your season is short. We prefer the larger, higher-yielding *Waltham* strain.

HUBBARD Large, bumpy, blue-gray squash famous for lasting until spring. Flavor is good, texture dry, yield good to excellent.

HOKKAIDO A Japanese squash (from Johnny's Selected Seeds), has excellent flavor, low yield, fair ability to keep.

SPAGHETTI SQUASH Keeps until midwinter, yields well, and has average disease resistance. To serve spaghetti squash, cook the whole fruit in boiling water for 45 minutes, split it, and fork out the long thin strands of flesh. Excellent with grated cheese or tomato sauce.

ACORN Yields and keeps well, resists squash-bug damage, but rates somewhat lower than others in flavor and texture, although it does not require curing.

GOLD NUGGET A bush squash, yielding less than vines, but with good flavor and storage life.

CUSHAW Keeps well, but can't match the other varieties for flavor.

Buttercup and acorn squash are also available in bush form. These strains take less room, but they yield less too, and in our experience the flavor isn't as good as that of the vining squash.

Plant vining squash one half to one inch deep in hills 5 feet apart, or sow seed every 6 inches in rows about 8 feet apart. Space bush varieties about 4 feet apart. Squash is frost-tender, and the seeds may rot if soil is too cold. Wait to plant until soil temperature reaches 60–65 degrees—about the time the late iris blooms. We often sprout the seeds in damp paper towels, then put a group of six to eight sprouted seeds in each hill and cover with compost. Aim for about three mature plants to the hill, or a row spacing of 12–18 inches. It's best to thin gradually as the season progresses. You may regret drastic early thinning if insects wipe out some of the growing seedlings.

Care during the growing season will ensure a good fall harvest. A tangled patch of bearing vines is difficult to weed, so we always mulch our squash with old hay applied in late June when soil is warm, just before the vines start to ramble.

Predatory insects prevent squash from being a foolproof crop. Squash bugs damage plants by piercing them with sharp mouth parts; cucumber beetles feed on young seedlings and spread bacterial wilt. Planting radishes and marigolds around hills often helps to repel some of these pests, but for more complete control we use rotenone. Hand-picking begun early and practiced regularly is an effective defense in a small patch. To combat the squash borer, which tunnels into the hollow stem and thus causes the whole vine to wilt suddenly, slit the squash stem and destroy the inch-long larva or forestall trouble by covering several vine nodes with loose fine soil to encourage multiple roots that will sustain the plant if one section is damaged. Rotate squash plantings too, from year to year. There are no easy answers here—just consistent, attentive garden husbandry.

Squash you intend to store should be allowed to ripen on the vine until the fruits develop their characteristic color and have skins too tough to puncture with your thumbnail. Leave at least an inch of stem on the fruit when you pick it. Bruised or cut spots spoil in storage. Nicked or stemless squash should be used promptly. To cure the squash for long keeping, expose the fruits to full sun for a week or two after picking. Curing dries the flesh and further hardens the rind. Curing squash can withstand light frost, but should be covered if medium or heavy frost seems likely.

Store cured squash in a dry, well-ventilated place at 50–60°F. Dampness and cold promote spoilage. At temperatures higher than 60° the flesh turns stringy. Spread the squash separately on slatted shelves, if possible, to prevent bruising and allow for good air circulation.

To us, squash is a symbol of abundance. If we've grown enough of it, we know we'll have squash well after the snow flies—without ever heating a blanching kettle or filling a canning jar.

Winter Salads

The crisp, succulent heads of the witloof chicory plant sell in city greengrocers' shops for several dollars a pound. Those you find in your market are often imported from Belgium or France, where they are raised in large quantities. Gardeners who have grown their own chicory can only smile at this costly and cumbersome arrangement. Few vegetables are easier to raise than the chicory root, and the sprouting process is simple, requiring only an hour or less of preparation, a few leaky buckets, and a box of sand. It is another example of the beautiful simplicity of back-yard gardening; any gardener can grow chicory that far surpasses the imported product in flavor and texture, all for an inexpensive packet of seeds and a little—very little—time.

The witloof ("white leaf") chicory that we await so eagerly in midwinter is the blanched, leafy head of *Cichorium intybus*, sometimes called Belgian endive or *barbe de capuchin* (Friar's beard). It is closely related to endive and escarole, but this special strain has been developed for forcing; its large roots are better equipped than those of its relatives to store the energy needed to produce a crisp, leafy sprout in winter.

The salad delicacy that can make a January menu special begins in the most prosaic way, with the sowing of a short row of witloof chicory seeds in May or June. A 10-foot row will produce plenty of roots for your first sprouting venture. Ordinary garden soil is fine. If it is deeply worked and free of rocks, the roots will develop more evenly. I've grown the roots in rather heavy soil, however, with good results. The seeds sprout in a week or two, depending on soil temperature. Young plants should be thinned to a 6-inch spacing. Then just keep them weeded and let them be. The plant does not seem to be attractive to insects, and you won't be tempted to eat the leaves, either; they're rather bitter in summer, and there are many better garden greens around. Once established, a row of witloof chicory demands no summer care other than weeding and occasional watering in a real drought.

By mid- or late fall, when the flood tide of corn and tomatoes is behind you, those chicory roots are ready for your attention. They will sprout more readily if they've been subjected to several freezes before you dig them up, but they should be rescued before the ground has frozen solid. A good root will measure an inch or more in diameter at the shoulder and 10 to 12 inches in length. With a sharp knife, cut the leafy crown from each plant, leaving a stub about an inch long. Set aside the largest roots to be sprouted first. Save the rest by covering them with damp sand, earth, or sawdust, and keep them in a cold place, 32° to 40°F.

To prepare roots for forcing, trim them to a uniform length of about 9 inches and replant them in buckets or boxes of soil. You can use any kind of soil, or even peat moss. It's all right to jam the roots tightly together, just so you pack some soil between them so they aren't exposed to air. The soil serves to support the plant and convey moisture to the root. The power that will produce a crisp, delicate salad head is all in the root.

Traditional directions call for plunging the roots vertically into a 10-inch substratum of earth and topping that off with another 6 to 8 inches of sand or sawdust.* This requires deep containers. I've also tried placing the roots on their sides in a shallow container—an old drawer, for example—with equally good results. Just be sure to top the roots with the requisite 6- to 8-inch layer of sawdust, which blanches the green shoot as it reaches for daylight. (I prefer sawdust to sand because it is easier to wash off.)

Most country households can muster enough old kettles, buckets, and wastebaskets to hold the roots; knock a few holes in the base of them for drainage and, once planted, keep them in a cool, dark place. A temperature of 50°F is necessary to induce sprouting, and a range of 50° to 60°F is ideal. Water the planted roots once a week. It takes two to three weeks for them to sprout. When the leaf tip shows through the thick top layer of sawdust, the head is ready to cut. Push away the sawdust and slice the 3- to 5-inch long, flame-shaped head close to the root. If you don't injure the crown in slicing off the sprout, you can replace the sawdust and harvest a second, smaller witloof chicory head two to three weeks later.

In Europe, where witloof chicory is perhaps taken more for granted, the heads are often cooked. Our witloof chicory never gets past the salad bowl; we couldn't bear to cook something so delicate. We prefer a simple oil-and-vinegar dressing with a few chopped herbs.

If you don't have roots of witloof chicory to dig up this fall, you can substitute dandelion roots. They can be forced in just the same way, and they'll give you some practice for next year.

* A new chicory variety, Normato available from Thompson and Morgan, can be simply packed into flower pots, covered with another pot, and kept in the dark, without an extra layer of sawdust for blanching.

Herbs on the Windowsill

Popular wisdom has it that herbs don't need good soil or special care. That may be true of *some* herbs to a certain extent, but casual treatment has often led to failure in growing herbs indoors. Don't assume that you can simply jam a plant in a pot at season's end and bring it inside to continue growing through the winter.

Some herbs do better than others indoors. Their yield is always considerably lower than that of garden-grown herbs, partly because the plants receive less light indoors, but with care and planning it is possible to provide a steady supply of aromatic snippings for the kitchen from a windowsill herb garden.

It's a good idea to pot any herbs you intend to bring indoors several weeks before cold weather. Then they can get accustomed to the different light, temperature, and air circulation inside the house before they're subjected to hot, dry air when the house-heating season begins. For established plants, use a container large enough to hold the roots without crowding, and cut back at least one third of the top growth. I often obtain new plants for my indoor herb shelf by layering low-growing branches of established plants and then potting the rooted branch. (To propagate by layering, nick the underside of a long shoot, bend it to soil level, cover it with soil, and add a rock to hold it down.) You can also dig up seedlings that have self-sown, or plan ahead and plant seeds for winter herbs earlier in the summer.

Indoor herbs will do best with at least five hours of light a day and temperatures ranging from 50° to 65°F. Dry air can be hard on them. To increase the humidity, you can mist the plants regularly or group pots in a tray lined with moist pebbles. Herbs like good drainage, but some—especially rosemary—need more moisture than we usually give them. The following herbs are among those that generally do well as house plants.

ROSEMARY This shrubby herb with its straight, slender leaves is a perennial in warm climates but must be wintered indoors wherever frost hits. (Mature plants in a sheltered location sometimes withstand light frosts.) Cuttings taken from young shoots can be rooted easily. If your rosemary plant is bushy, you might choose to carry it through the winter by rooting cuttings or by layering a low branch. A whole plant survives the trip indoors gracefully if it has been left in its pot, buried to the rim in the garden, and then unearthed, pot and all, in the fall. (Trim off any roots that have grown out of the pot's drainage hole.) Indoors, rosemary likes a sunny, cool place and regular watering. Plants may die if allowed to dry out or if overfertilized. To compensate for dry indoor air, moisten rosemary with a spray mister several times a week.

BASIL This tender annual should be brought in before the first freeze. I often allow some of my plants to bloom because the bees like the blossoms, but basil plants to be brought indoors should not be allowed to waste strength by forming flowers or seeds, and they should be clipped back to about half their height when dug up. (Dry the clippings for your herb jar.) Basil cuttings also root readily and plants are easy to raise from seed. Give them as much light as possible, either on a windowsill or under lights, and water regularly so they won't wilt. Several pots of basil will produce aromatic leaves which add dash to your salads and tomato dishes during the winter. Plants often become woody toward spring, but you can keep raising seedlings for a continuous supply.

THYME   As many as sixty varieties of this hardy perennial are available, including lemon, English, creeping, and others. Most forms of this tiny-leafed herb are low-growing, and branches often root next to the main plant. Most thyme varieties will live through the winter outdoors, but they tend to get woody after a few years and often need to be thinned or replanted. For a windowsill supply of thyme to perk up soups, stuffings, and such, dig up a whole plant, separate it into rooted clumps, and replant each rooted division in a pot. You might also want to try sowing thyme seed in pots in midsummer for a winter supply. Later in winter, thyme often turns woody and loses leaves, but usually not before it has contributed savor to many winter meals. Thyme needs excellent drainage; avoid letting pots stand in water.

PARSLEY   Potting mature parsley plants for an indoor kitchen garden is almost always a waste of time. Parsley has a deep taproot and seldom does well when dug up. For a decent but by no means overwhelming supply of winter parsley, start young plants in summer and pot them while the roots are still small. In the garden, parsley doesn't mind clay soil, but give it a good, porous potting soil indoors.

CHIVES   The only good chives are fresh chives; neither freezing nor drying can preserve their flavor. Chives make agreeable windowsill plants. They are hardy perennials and often need to be thinned in the fall anyway. Chives don't suffer from frost, so they may be dug up as long as the ground admits a spade. Cut back the tops before potting them. If you purchase potted chives, you can usually break up the clump and divide it among several pots. Chives grow easily from seed, usually taking two seasons to reach cutting size. Like most other herbs, they require good drainage. If your potted chives stop producing new shoots, withhold water and put the plant outside for several weeks. After this dormant period, many plants will resume growth when returned to a warm room and watered.

DILL   Like parsley, this feathery herb has a long taproot. The mature plant is tall and ungainly. It self-sows freely in the garden, though, and often tiny seedlings will be just the right size to be brought indoors in the fall. The delicate foliage adds interest to fish, potato dishes, and salads. Water the seedlings well and cover them with a plastic bag until they recover from transplanting.

192

A few hours spent potting herbs on a bright blue Indian-summer day should reward you with more interesting winter meals, and you might have some live herbs to put back in the garden next spring.

Broom Corn

Cousin Garrison is a botanist who has done extensive research on corn and related plants. In his spare time he builds Shaker furniture. Of course we gave him one of our homegrown brooms. When he wrote thanking us for the gift "to be simple and sweep clean," we knew he had understood our homespun present.

Sweeping is still the best way to clean the floor of a kitchen, workshop, barn, patio, or porch, and the firm but resilient corn broom is beautifully suited to this task. It does a good job on braided rugs too. It is even a self-renewing tool. Seed saved from this year's broom corn may be planted next year to produce another crop of brooms.

Broom corn is a special strain of sorghum related to field and sweet corn by common membership in the grass family. A plume of seed-bearing straws grows at the tip of the stalk, rather than an ear. Each plume is a cluster of individual straws joined at the lower end where they meet the stalk, and brooms are made by fastening dried clusters around a stick.

Plant broom-corn seed in late spring—late May or early June. There's no need to hurry unless your season is unusually short, but the seed should be planted no later than mid-June to take advantage of the long warm growing days of midsummer. Broom corn planted on Memorial Day will be ready for harvest by September or early October. Light frost won't hurt it as long as seed has formed.

We space rows 3 feet apart and sow the small round seeds about one inch deep. When the plants are 6 to 8 inches high, we thin them to stand 3–6 inches apart. Crowded plants tend to be weak-rooted and likely to blow over in summer storms, but those spaced too widely may produce coarse or crooked brush.

Broom-corn plants we've grown have been less vulnerable than sweet corn to attacks by insects and fungus. We've even had a good crop from plants grown in relatively poor soil. (We save our best soil for food crops.) The plants would probably have been even stronger if we had given them a dose of manure tea when they were knee-high. Like its other grassy relatives, broom corn uses nitrogen to fuel the rapid growth of its stalk and leaves. As with sweet corn, cultivate between rows and weed in the rows to keep down the competition.

Toward the end of the summer, seeds begin to form on long stiff tassels at the top of the plants. Veteran broom-corn growers tell us that the best broom material is obtained from plants harvested before the seeds have ripened completely. A neighboring farmer, who grows broom corn regularly, instructed us to bend over the head of each stalk when the seeds have formed, but before they turn red. The length of the bent top should be 20 to 24 inches, and the straws on the tops will hang down naturally—just what you want in a broom. When tassels are left upright too long as they dry on the plant, the straws sometimes splay over into a graceful but not very functional whorl. When they become set in this shape, they don't form a good broom.

Cut each tassel off at the snapped-over joint about two weeks after you've bent them over. Expert broom-corn growers hang bundles of harvested broom straw in a shady, well-ventilated place to cure for three weeks before making them into brooms.

We took the bulk of our broom-corn harvest to an elderly broom maker, who uses a broom press and strong cord to fashion a conventional-looking straw sweeper. I've never had a better broom.

Broom makers are still around, but they seldom advertise. Sometimes you can find them at town fairs and local craft events. Often older farmers know where they are. Sometimes county agricultural agents or the staff at a folk-art museum have a list of these craftsmen. As with all such quests for country resources, we often find that in the course of pursuing our quarry, we pick up an additional store of random information and meet other interesting people along the way.

If you want to make your own peasant-style broom, start by removing the seeds from the straws. Some people comb them out, but Sue Stephenson suggests a better method in her book *Basketry of the Appalachian Mountains:** hold a handsaw against an old table and pull the straws between the saw teeth and the flat surface. The teeth will rake out most of the seeds. To start the broom, gather a bundle of pre-soaked broom-corn straws and with strong cord, make several wraps and bind the straws tightly together. Trim the top and bottom edges so they align evenly. Now find a handle—either an ordinary broom handle or a shapely stick from the woods. Ash, hickory, and oak are traditional handles. Sharpen one end of the stick, poke the sharpened end into the center of the bound straws, and drive two small nails into the stick in the places between the wraps of cord.

Save the seeds from this year's broom corn to plant, and share them with friends. A handful of seed will grow enough broom corn to supply your house and barn with brooms for several years. And short or poorly formed seeded tassels may be tied to posts to feed the winter birds.

* Sue H. Stephenson, *Basketry of the Appalachian Mountains,* New York, Van Nostrand Reinhold Co., 1977.

SOURCES OF BROOM CORN SEED

Grace's Gardens
Gurney Seed and Nursery
   Company
Abundant Life Seed Foundation
   (charge for catalogue)

On Saving Seeds

Good gardeners are always learning, and one of the new/old skills many of them ask about is saving seeds from garden vegetables. We have become so accustomed to buying everything we need that this practice seems new and daring to many. Yet country gardeners have been quietly saving seeds for years and years—for security, economy, and the assurance that Uncle Ben's special strain of early tomatoes won't die out. The new enthusiasm for seed saving seems to have much to do with a desire for involvement in the whole cycle of garden plant life, along with a sporting interest in experimenting with something new and an intention to develop special strains of vegetables especially suited to one's local climate.

When you save seed, you can gradually improve the quality of the vegetables you grow by choosing parent plants according to the characteristics that are important to you—yield, flavor, earliness, size, disease resistance, and so on. Your judgment should be based not on individual fruits, but on the performance of the entire plant. Unless exhibiting is your main reason for wanting large fruits, it makes no sense to save seed from a large tomato on a low-yielding vine; far better to choose a healthy plant with a high yield of larger-than-average fruit, and gradually select for increasingly larger fruit over the course of succeeding generations.

Annual and perennial vegetables are the easiest with which to begin your seed-saving efforts, because they set seed when mature after a single season of growth. Biennials, like the cabbage family and most root crops, do not set seed until their second growing season. Thus they must be kept in good shape during freezing weather if they are to resume growth in the spring. If you want to save seed from carrots, parsnips, or kale you can usually leave a few of the plants right in the garden under mulch, even where winters are severe. The plants will flower and set seed the following spring. In the northern states, beets, cabbage and other less frost-resistant biennial vegetables from which you intend to save seed must be dug in the fall and kept cold (but not frozen) all winter. Store them in the root cellar in sawdust or sand, and re-plant them in the spring. Naturally, not all of the stored roots or rooted cabbage heads will keep well all winter, but by planting out those that do, you are selecting for long storage life—a desirable quality in root vegetables.

It is not worthwhile to save seed from hybrid vegetables, although some curious gardeners may do so just to see what happens. Hybrids are the offspring of highly inbred parent stock and their seed will produce plants that are throwbacks to earlier, less outstanding varieties. Some hybrid seed is even sterile.

Mark the plant from which you intend to save seed. If you are selecting for earliness, better let the rest of the family know what you are doing, or that extra-early ear of corn that you wanted for seed could end up on a dinner plate.

Seeds encased in dry husks or pods should remain on the plant until they are hard and dry. Sometimes it is necessary to tie small mesh or ventilated paper bags over ripening seed heads of such vegetables as carrots, cabbage, and onions in order to catch the seeds, for they shatter readily once they are ripe.

Berries and fruits should be allowed to turn thoroughly ripe before they are harvested for their seeds. Squash and cantaloupe should be fully developed and ripe.

Pick dry seed on a dry day, if possible, and spread it on newspapers in a well-ventilated, but not hot, place for a week before packaging for storage. Crush berries through a sieve to collect the seeds, then wash the seeds in running water and air-dry them for a week.

Proper seed storage is vital. Since heat and moisture impair seed viability, always store dry seeds well sealed in cans or jars in a cool, dry place. Seeds that may have re-absorbed atmospheric moisture are better off in sealed envelopes than in foil or screw-top jars from which excess moisture cannot escape. Be sure to label your seeds with variety, date, and other pertinent information that might help you in your program of selection.

Here are some hints for saving seed of a few popular garden vegetables.

BEANS (Annual)

Although beans are self-pollinating, a very small percentage of a crop will occasionally be cross-pollinated by insects, so space your special rare heirloom varieties 100 feet apart. (This precaution is not necessary for most garden varieties.) Let the pods dry on the plant till they rattle. According to an informant at the Vermont Bean Seed Co., a bean in which you can scarcely make a tooth dent has dried sufficiently to harvest. Hand-shell the beans or thresh them (beat with a stick) if you have a large crop.

BEETS (Biennial)

Beets will cross with Swiss chard and sugar beets. The pollen is very fine and rides easily on the wind for great distances, so wait until next year to save your chard seed if you have beets flowering in the garden this year. Dig the beets before heavy frost, trim the leaves back to a one-inch stub and keep the roots in sand or sawdust in a damp, cold (but not freezing) place. Replant the roots in spring, setting them 18 inches apart in the garden row. Each plant will produce many seed stalks. When the seeds at the base of the stalks turn dry, you can pull up the beets and cure them in an airy shed for a week or so before collecting the seed.

CARROTS (Biennial)

Carrots will cross with other carrot varieties and with wild Queen Anne's Lace within 200 feet. Well-mulched carrots will usually survive the winter, especially under a good snow cover, and may be thinned in spring to 12 to 20 inches apart to allow space for seed stalk formation. They may also be fall-dug and stored like beets. Seeds are ripe within 60 days after flowering and they fall off promptly when ripe. Bag the seedheads or pick stalks when the second group of flowers has ripened seed. Early-ripening heads will shatter before later ones are ripe.

Good and easy. Lettuce is self-pollinated so you don't need to isolate varieties. The thing to remember is to save seed from the last, rather than the first, plant to go to seed. A single plant can produce enough seed for most families. Seeds are ready to gather when wisps of grayish-white down succeed the yellow flowers. **LETTUCE (Annual)**

Although peppers do self-pollinate, different varieties planted less than 50 feet apart are often cross-pollinated by insects. Save seed from red peppers; green pepper seed is immature and will not germinate well. Just shake the seeds out of the pod when you cut the pepper to eat it; no special preparation is necessary. **PEPPERS (Annual)**

The pumpkin family is probably responsible for those tales you hear about the pumpkin and the cantaloupe that crossed. The truth is that crossing occurs only within a species; therefore pumpkins can't cross with cucumbers, cantaloupes, or most winter squash. The species C. *pepo*, though, includes a wide variety of vegetables: zucchini, gourds, small Jack o' lantern pumpkins, acorn squash, patty pan and yellow crookneck squash, and all of these varieties *do* cross within 100 feet or so. Most of the weird crosses you get when you save pumpkin seed are probably from within this species. Pumpkin seed is ripe when the fruit turns orange. Zucchini and other summer squash should be allowed to mature until the rind is hard before seeds are harvested. Rinse off pulp and dry the seeds before storing them. **PUMPKINS (Annual)**

Tomatoes are self-pollinated, so seed of adjacent varieties will come true. Save the best tomato . . . the one you most want to eat . . . and let it remain on the vine until it's overripe but not rotten. Then press the whole tomato into a glass jar, add ¼ cup of water, and let the fruit ferment for several days. Fermentation controls the seed-borne disease, bacterial canker. The pulp and worthless seeds will rise to the top. Good, viable seeds settle lower in the brew and may be strained off, rinsed, and dried after 2 to 4 days. **TOMATOES (Annual)**

NOVEMBER

A Sense of Humus

In November, the vegetable gardener realizes that winter is inevitable after all. The season has turned. The harvest is in. Green tomatoes hang ripening. Rows of jars are packed shoulder to shoulder on the cellar shelves. Thanks to the garden, the freezer is full.

Out in the finished rows, frost has withered crops and weeds alike. Soon snow will fall, and the ground will freeze too hard to admit the digging fork.

November is a fine time to lay the groundwork for an even more productive garden next year. Every garden soil needs humus, and most gardens could be greatly improved by a concerted effort to supply more humus to the soil. If you hope for better things from your patch next year, seize the opportunity now, while days are brisk and before you're snowbound, to gather humus-building materials for your garden. In November, I like to spend some of the time formerly devoted to weeding, mulching, and canning in hunting extra sources of organic matter to enrich my garden patch.

Why the need for a high level of humus? Like the activity of gardening, its value lies as much in the process as in the end product.

In the process of decaying into humus, organic matter produces acids that act as solvents on soil minerals, making them available to growing plants. The decomposing humus also supports the life of many helpful soil microorganisms. Some break down ammonium compounds into nitrites; others convert the nitrites into nitrates, the form of nitrogen that plants are able to absorb.

These processes run in cycles, with a higher level of microbiological and chemical activity occurring while fresh plant matter is decaying. Later, when the most readily decomposed organic matter has been used up, the process smolders along at a slower pace. You can see, then, that periodic additions of even modest amounts of humus-building material tend to keep the soil in a dynamic state, making new nutrients and minerals available to plants at a steady rate.

Humus, then, sustains vital chemical processes and microbial action within the soil. It also improves the physical structure of the soil. If your soil is sandy (less than twenty per cent silt and clay), the addition of humus will increase the water-retaining capacity of the soil. (When soil is too dry, microbial activity slows considerably.) Clay soil, on the other hand, becomes more porous and friable when humus is added. It will warm faster and drain better and may be worked earlier in the spring—a boon to northern gardeners. Humus also has the effect of aerating heavy soils, thus encouraging the life of helpful soil organisms, which live in the spaces between soil particles. (Heavily compacted clay soil has few spaces.)

What humus-building material should you look for? Where can you get it?

Begin at home. As you clear up your garden rows, save what you can. Most of us who grew up with that fine New England maxim "Use it up, wear it out, make it do, or do without" save everything from old pea vines to workshop sawdust to used tea leaves for the garden as a matter of course. But if you're not already doing this, start by looking around you. Don't let a banana peel or a bag of leaves leave your place. (Our children would often bring home their school lunch bags with the banana peel for the garden. I didn't ask them to, honest! They never went so far as to collect banana peels from other students, though.)

Other available residues include vegetable trimmings, coffee grounds, spent plants of all kinds, pulled weeds, grass clippings, and nut shells (except for black and English walnuts, which are toxic to some plants).

Another good way to stockpile humus-building additions to your garden is to collect by-products from the businesses and industries in your community. Every town will offer different local resources, but in most places you will find that much usable potential humus is going to waste. Here are some examples of the kind of thing to look for:

Shoe factories will give or sell leather dust.
Tobacco dealers may have tobacco stems, usually for sale.
Spent compost is commonly available from mushroom growers.
Riding stables and horse farms are often glad to get rid of horse manure.
Quarries have granite or other stone dust as a waste product.
Sawmills, lumber yards and woodcrafting industries, and casket companies are a few sources of free sawdust.
Corncobs may be available from feed mills (usually at a price).
Barbers and barbering schools are good sources of nitrogen-rich hair clippings.
Bagged leaves from lawn raking still go begging in many towns.
Restaurants may be good sources of coffee grounds.
Power companies and tree surgeons often have free wood chips after fall tree trimming.
Farmers may have spoiled hay, but it is often in demand and seldom really cheap.

That's a start. You may be surprised at what else you can find locally.

Seaweed and lakeweed make marvelous, mineral-rich soil improvers. They are free for the gathering—a fine way to warm up on a cold November day. Friends of ours living near Lake Bomoseen in Vermont are building an increasingly productive garden by adding lakeweed to their soil at every opportunity. Big dredges harvest the weed from the lake bottom and fill dump trucks, which then deliver the wet tangle to lucky gardeners nearby.

Good soil-building stuff needn't come by the truckload, though. Every little bit helps. Keep a bushel basket or burlap bag in your car to hold materials you may find while driving. Line your bike baskets with bags to carry back your finds. On a November walk in the woods, fill your knapsack or a duffel bag with pine needles, leaf mulch, moss, or silky, rotted tree-stump wood.

How should you use the soil-building material you've found? Take your choice of the following methods:

Compost it.
Dig it into the ground while you still can.
Save it for mulch.
Tuck it under already-existing mulch.
Spread it on the ground now and as available.
Use it as extra bedding in your barn to soak up more liquid manure.

Material that is dug in and composted will be the most readily available to the soil; that left on the surface will be more gradually absorbed.

The gardener who develops what Bertha Damon has called "a sense of humus" will likely have something good to show for it next harvest season—first-rate vegetables raised in good soil.

Keeping Notes on the Garden

The perennial promise of the gardener is "Next year I'll. . . ." Whatever the mistakes or omissions of this year, next year they'll be corrected. Next season's garden will be better. And it can be, too, if I remember what needs to be changed. That's why I keep a garden notebook.

November is as good a time as any to start keeping a record of your gardening efforts and results, while the rewards and problems of the season just ending are still fresh in your mind.

My own record system consists of a monthly running commentary listing planting times and seed varieties planted, time of first pickings, peak blooming and fruiting times, early and late frost dates, amounts of produce picked, preserved, and stored, dates and amounts of fertilizer spread, descriptions of succession plantings, and more.

In addition, I keep each year's diagram of our garden layout. Even though these pages are usually scribbled up and oddly out of scale by the end of the season, they are a help in planning next year's garden and a reminder of the gardens of other years.

I'll go so far as to say that keeping notes on the garden can lead to a substantial improvement in both the fertility of your garden and the quality of your harvest. Merely amassing the information, of course, won't guarantee better gardening results. The secret is to organize and interpret your findings.

When did the cucumber beetles strike last year? This year we'll start looking, hand picking, and possibly dusting with rotenone about a week in advance of that time. How many beans did we freeze last year? That was plenty. We can relax a little on planting beans this year. When did we start our tomato seedlings? They were a bit leggy when we put them out. We should hold off for another two weeks before sowing the seed.

This kind of solid information, interpreted and applied, can make a difference.

SOIL IMPROVEMENT Noting where we have applied manure, lime, and rock phosphate, and in what amounts, helps us to avoid over-treating one area of the garden and skimping on another. The same goes for cover cropping and crop rotations. We may *think* we'll remember where we planted cabbage last year, but then there were those extra transplants we stuck in.

PLANTING DATES, VARIETIES What varieties did we use last year? Where did we get them? When did we plant them? Was it too early, or could we try sowing even earlier? A glance at my notes reminds me that one year I planted the fall crop of head lettuce too early in the summer, and it bolted to seed. Since then I've waited until at least the last week in July and have had wonderful heads until frost.

YIELDS Yields are easily forgotten too—not that we compulsively want to count each strawberry, but it is good to know when the peak picking days fall over the years, how much we picked and froze, how many bushels of potatoes we stored. True, there is no point in trying to beat the records as long as we are getting enough, but if we don't keep track for a few seasons, how will we know how much *is* enough?

COSTS Gardening expenses can't be guessed at, only computed. Just for fun, we've recorded what we spend for seed and soil improvement, and it looks from here as though home-raised fruit and vegetables are a pretty good bargain. (We don't "charge" for our labor, but then we can't really put a price tag on the extra vitamin content and flavor and abundance of our home-grown vegetables, either.)

202

Still, if you plan to sell some of your produce, you will want to know what it cost you to raise it, and to arrive at that figure you will need records.

The need for maintenance and upkeep begins to catch up with most of us sooner or later. Three years ago we planted those fruit trees. Now they need pruning. We meant to divide the rhubarb last fall. Ah, well . . . next season! That Japanese flowering quince languishing there behind the henhouse—we really should move it out into the sun. The time when we notice that these things need to be done is not always the best season for doing them. When we write ourselves a reminder for the next pruning or transplanting season, we are less likely to let the job ride for another year.

YEAR-TO-YEAR MAINTENANCE

Variety keeps the gardening game flexible and fun. We may want to try a new way of supporting climbing vegetables, experiment with companion planting, improvise ways of protecting our crops from frost. Some of these ideas succeed and some don't, but when some new arrangement does work well, we're glad we took our whim seriously enough to jot it down.

CHANGES AND INSPIRATIONS

As every gardener knows, each season is different. Every year we get some new ideas, make some mistakes, put in some long-term plantings like trees or bushes or bulbs, confirm old favorites and find new ones. Putting the years together—whether in a notebook, on a wall calendar, in a file folder, or in a special garden diary—gives us an idea of what to look for, what to count on, what to change.

Fall Maintenance

End-of-the-season maintenance is an investment in next year's garden. The weekend you spend on fall garden chores might not produce immediately tangible results, but it will save you time and labor in the next growing season, and it could help you to produce earlier and better harvests. There's a fall garden task for every kind of November day from balmy to blustery.

HARVEST

You'll want to rescue the last of the hardy fall vegetables—the beets, carrots, cabbage, cauliflower, turnips, endive, winter radishes, and such—before a hard, killing frost turns top growth to mush or hardens the ground against the digging fork. When you make the rounds of the last green rows, collect even the small vegetables—the tiny turnips, skinny celery, coin-sized onions, and button cauliflower heads. When the basket is full, you'll probably have enough of these small oddments to make a few jars of mixed vegetable pickles. Save the sound, well-developed vegetables for winter storage, and exercise your imagination to find a use for those that were nicked in harvesting but are still good. You can turn them into pumpkin pie, grated carrot salad, cream of cauliflower soup, beet relish, and a host of other delicious autumn dishes.

CLEAN-UP

If the weeds got the upper hand while you were busy canning and pickling and making Halloween costumes for the kids, they probably tower over the last cabbages by now. It's a good idea to scythe them down, leaving a stubble that will help to hold soil and blown leaves without retarding spring warming and drying of the soil. Diseased plants should be killed by burning or by burying them in a hot compost pile, preferably just after turning the pile. If you have time to cut and compost weeds and garden plant residues, or turn them under, you'll be able to interrupt the life cycle of some of the insect pests that live over the winter on dead plant material.

When the November wind drives a sleety rain before it, light a fire in the workshop stove, collect all your hard-used garden tools, repair or replace handles, sharpen hoes, clean and oil blades, and perhaps work out a new system for storing your trusty hand tools.

SOIL IMPROVEMENT

This is a good time to harvest not only food crops, but also an abundance of natural materials that are often considered refuse—hedge clippings, leaves, spoiled hay, sawdust, wood chips, and spent garden plants. Whether turned under in your garden, used as mulch, or composted, those humus-building materials will improve your garden soil.

Since much of the plant stuff available in fall is tough and high in cellulose, and therefore slower to decompose than the green, sappy growth of summer, a winter of weathering in contact with the soil will hasten decomposition. The ethylene gas produced in the soil by decomposing organic matter will help to control soil-borne plant diseases, according to Dr. R. James Cook of Washington State University.

We like to manure and lime at least one of our three vegetable plots in the fall, plowing the area into rough clods that break up over winter, so we have an early-thawing garden in which we can plant peas in March.

WINTER PROTECTION

Turnip greens, collards, Brussels sprouts, kale, and corn salad will stay in good picking condition well into winter if protected by an insulating blanket of mulch. In fact, kale will last *all* winter.

Mulch strawberry beds when the ground is frozen to protect the plants from damage caused by soil's heaving as it alternately freezes and thaws.

Whitewash or wrap the trunks of fruit and nut trees to prevent sunscald on bright, cold winter days. Tree wrapping tape, burlap strips, or plastic spiral tree guards make effective trunk protectors.

Water newly planted trees, especially evergreens, which lose moisture from their needles by transpiration in winter. Soil temperature at root level may be as much as 20 degrees higher than at the surface, so those new trees can form feeder roots late in the fall if given some encouragement.

Are you planning a new garden bed or an addition to your present patch? If you dig up the area now, incorporating manure, compost, lime, or any other soil-improving material you want to add, you'll be well begun (and therefore at least half done) on your spring digging. Leave the patch in rough clods over winter; they'll catch snow and prevent soil runoff. Topping off the plot with a layer of mulch will also prevent erosion.

If you like to take chances that sometimes pay off, try sowing seed of hardy crops in the fall to germinate in the spring. Corn salad, leaf lettuce, peas, spinach, dill, garlic, and parsley are good candidates for fall planting. You can't count on a successful fall planting, but germination will probably average at least 50 per cent —better odds than any lottery.

Spring planting puts a heavy demand on the compost pile. Perhaps it's time to start an extra heap so you can be generous with the compost next spring. The abundance of garden refuse, autumn leaves, and vegetable residues from canning and freezing should provide enough materials to build a good pile. If the ingredients used are not too coarse and tough, and if the pile is turned weekly for several weeks, you should have good compost ready by spring. We've heard of one fitness-conscious gardener who has started turning the compost pile every day in lieu of jogging. He feels great and expects to have enough compost for the first time ever!

Raising Vegetables Indoors

It's a good old gardening game: how long can you keep the fresh food coming? Having your own source of fresh lettuce and herbs is more than a hobby now, when what's available on a store's produce counter is often of indifferent quality, high in price, and drenched with spray.

We experimented with indoor vegetable plantings and found that some widely enjoyed vegetables do surprisingly well indoors if light, soil, and temperature are right. Herbs are even easier; many of them do well on a sunny windowsill.

The winter salad vegetables we've raised have grown under fluorescent lights, which use less power than incandescent bulbs for the amount of light they provide. Nonflowering vegetables grow well under ordinary tubes, ideally one warm white and one cool white tube. (Use pairs of fluorescent tubes—single tubes don't give off enough light—and position plants 3 to 7 inches below them.) Flowering plants such as tomatoes perform best under one of the full-spectrum, plant growth lights. Often such plant lighting arrangements can be installed in a spot where some illumination is needed anyway. Since we live without a TV, clothes dryer, or dishwasher, we've felt comfortable with our lights so far, but we look forward to the day when we grow these and other vegetables without using any electricity in a sun-heated growing pit we're planning to build. We're convinced that, no matter how modest our use of electricity, each of us is responsible for paring his and her power use even further.

Cool weather vegetables—those you'd grow in your spring or fall garden—produce best indoors. I've kept my indoor vegetables in a cool room where the daytime temperature was around 60 degrees, dropping to 50 degrees at night. Seeds need warmth—70 to 80 degrees on the average—for germination, but growing plants do well at cool temperatures, in the 50–60 degree range. Vegetables growing under lights require 16 to 18 hours of light each day, although tomatoes need more intense light.

LETTUCE

Butterhead types like Bibb and Boston do well under lights. Bibb grows more slowly, but its leaves are darker green. Sow seeds thinly in 5- to 6-inch-deep containers filled with a mixture of garden or potting soil, compost, and vermiculite. I like to put a layer of moss in the bottom of each container. If you don't line containers with moss, poke holes in them (or use leaky ones) to provide good drainage. Standing water rots roots. Thin seedlings to stand 5 inches apart. We begin to harvest leaves 52 days after planting seed. Repeated sowings will give you a winter-long supply. Feed the young plants weekly with diluted fish emulsion fertilizer, increasing to twice weekly as heading begins. Keep them well watered.

CHINESE CABBAGE

A pleasant surprise. We've grown small heads of this crisp, tender delicacy under lights in 5- to 6-inch-deep dishpans lined with moss and filled with the soil mixture mentioned above. Space seedlings 6 inches apart and fertilize weekly. The plants make delicious salads—if you can bear to cut them. We thought ours were attractive enough to qualify as houseplants.

SPINACH

Spinach will grow well under lights in a cool corner or in a cool sunny window with some extra light in the evening. Sixteen hours of light is about right, and a temperature in the fifties—no higher than 65 degrees. Eat the thinnings until your plants stand 3 to 4 inches apart.

RADISHES

These may surprise you too; they're often milder in flavor when grown indoors. You can even plant them in a large flowerpot. Good porous soil, frequent watering, and at least 4 inches of growing depth are your secrets to success with radishes. Thin seedlings to 1½ inches apart. Young leaves are good in soup.

CARROTS

Carrots don't develop well if the roots hit bottom, so plant a short variety like Baby Finger or Gold Nugget. Containers should be no less than 4 inches deep, and 5 to 6 inches is much better. As you thin, aim for 1½ inches between plants. Carrots take at least 49 days to form roots.

Grown 2 to 3 inches apart, beets produce dainty rosy roots and nourishing leafy tops. Give them a 5-inch-deep pot or pan. You can crowd them more if you're just counting on using the leafy tops.

BEETS

Tomatoes take some doing. In order to set fruit, they need warmth (70 to 75 degrees) and a lot of light (2,500 foot candles, compared to 1,000 foot candles for lettuce). Four to six 40-watt fluorescent tubes should provide enough. Reflectors positioned around the lighting set-up will help too. Small-fruited tomatoes are easier to raise indoors. Give them 6- to 8-inch pots. The blossoms are self-pollinating, but you might want to bump the plant from time to time to stimulate the kind of pollen-releasing vibrations a plant would experience outdoors. If it's too cool—under 60 degrees—fruit won't set. Feed the maturing plants with diluted fish emulsion every 5 days.

TOMATOES

Thyme, chives, marjoram, rosemary, and basil may be potted up from the garden and kept on a sunny windowsill—or under lights—all winter. Mature parsley plants have a deep tap root, which makes successful transplanting difficult. I've had better luck with parsley as a winter plant when I've planted seeds in late summer or fall and then transplanted the seedlings to pots or deep flats for winter snipping.

HERBS

If you have some often-used fluorescent lights in your home—under a kitchen cabinet, in a study or workshop—put them to work for you. Let them help grow some winter greenery for your table.

Drying the Garden's Year-End Surplus

If you've already canned enough garden produce to fill the pantry shelves, and have the freezer loaded with the full range of the year's bounty, from peas to pumpkin-pie filling, perhaps you'd like to try preserving some vegetables by traditional methods that pre-date the more technical, energy-intensive processes. Freezing, the most power-costly way to preserve food, has only been in general home use for the past thirty-five to forty years, while home canning has been commonly practiced since around the turn of the century.

For centuries before the advent of home freezers and glass jars, people used other means to keep the best of the fall bounty. Accustomed as we are to the rapid transportation and high-technology packaging that put tasteless greenhouse tomatoes within reach, we have forgotten that for most people, in years gone by, careful preparations at harvest time were vital to winter survival.

Root vegetables were traditionally kept in cold, moist cellars or buried in barrels or left in the ground. In addition, methods of processing vegetables so as to reduce bacterial action, and therefore spoilage, had been worked out over the centuries. These processes require some work, but little equipment. They were developed long before anything was known about microbiology, but —devised as they were by trial and error, along with some luck and astute observation—they work. It is only in the last moment of time—since Pasteur's discovery, in 1857, that microorganisms cause spoilage—that we have understood *why* they work.

Drying, the oldest and simplest food-processing technique, makes food unattractive to destructive microorganisms by removing 80 to 90 percent of its moisture. Unlike canning, drying does not kill the microorganisms on the surface of the food; it just makes conditions inhospitable for their growth.

Moisture content below 20 per cent prevents yeast growth; below 18 per cent, bacterial growth, and below 13 to 16 per cent, most mold growth.

The time-honored method of drying has been exposure to the sun or to a hot, well-ventilated shady spot like a hot attic. When flies became recognized as disease carriers, protective cheesecloth or screening was employed to keep the dehydrating food clean. Twentieth-century technology has introduced the options of gas, electric, or wood-heated food driers, or small-batch makeshifts such as a screened tray in a foil-lined box warmed by a 60-watt light bulb. The top or oven of a cookstove, especially one that is heated with wood, will provide the slow, even heat needed to remove moisture without cooking the food. Drying temperatures should be kept between 95° and 140°F. Higher temperatures may either cook the food or cause the formation of a hard, outer skin that can prevent thorough drying of the interior of the piece of food.

What can you dry? Just about any garden produce, including tomatoes and zucchini. You can even dry greens. Old favorites from early American days include leather-britches beans and dried pumpkin rings.

To make the pumpkin rings, string slices of pumpkin ⅛-inch thick on clean white string and hang in a hot attic or chimney corner until they're shriveled and tough. Leather-britches beans are even easier: simply string the green beans on heavy thread, piercing each bean with a needle. Hang the garlands in a hot, well-ventilated place. When dry enough, they'll be brittle.

Corn dries well, too. Blanch the cobs for two minutes in water, or five minutes in steam, to stop enzyme action. Cut the kernels from the cob and oven-dry them for two to three hours at 140°F, or in a steady sun for six to eight hours. Kernels that are ready for storage will be brittle.

Eggplant, okra, tomatoes, celery, onions, and carrots can be dried best when sliced ⅛-inch to ¼-inch thick and spread on trays. Cut peppers in rings or ½-inch squares. Slice florets of cauliflower or broccoli in quarters. Small plum tomatoes may be halved, but larger ones should be sliced.

Pieces of food in any one batch should be as uniform in size as possible to promote even drying. Spread the food on whatever drying surface you're using in such a way that pieces do not touch. Put no more than two pounds of vegetables on each square foot of tray space, or four to six pounds in an average oven.

When drying greens, whack each leafy sprig against a firm surface to dislodge any resident insects, and spread the greens on a clean surface in a hot, well-ventilated place. I dry comfrey on cloth-covered screens and large pieces of corrugated cardboard in our hot attic. When the leaves crumble readily, they're dry enough.

If you want to make drying trays, use cheesecloth, slatted wood, plain wicker, or stainless steel hardware cloth to support the food and admit air. Avoid aluminum, galvanized metal, fiber glass, copper, or vinyl screening; for various reasons, these materials react with foods to form unwholesome substances.

Whether you're drying vegetables in the oven, chimney corner, warming closet, attic, solar drier, or directly in the sun, good air circulation is as necessary as warmth. When using an oven, leave the door ajar—just a crack, no more than an inch. If you build a drying rack to use in the sun, over a hot-air register, or near a warm stove, allow an air space of several inches at the bottom, under the lowest tray. You'll find directions for building food driers, as well as more elaborate instructions for treating individual vegetables, in the books listed below.

Most vegetables dry in two or three days when exposed to the summer sun, but since they often lose color when sun-dried, many people prefer to dry them in the oven, over a hot-air register, or in a hot attic. Oven drying takes two to four hours at 140°F for most vegetables. Vegetables that are properly dehydrated are usually brittle. Fruits tend to be leathery and tough. Depending on their original moisture content, foods lose from one sixth to one third of their bulk when dried.

It's important to remember that the drying process is reversible if the foods are exposed to normal atmospheric moisture. Well-dried vegetables, though, will stay in good condition in glass jars or tightly sealed cans, which should be kept in a cool, dry, dark place.

When preparing dried vegetables for the table, soak them for several hours before cooking and then stew them gently—on a wood range or box stove it possible—for two to four hours. Leather-britches beans require overnight soaking and four to eight

BOOKS ABOUT FOOD DRYING

Dry It—You'll Like it! by Gen MacManiman, Living Foods Dehydrators

How to Dry Fruits and Vegetables at Home by the Food Editors of *Farm Journal*, Countryside Press

Home Drying Vegetables, Fruits and Herbs by Phyllis Hobson, Garden Way Publishing Company

Each of the following general storage books has a good section on food drying:

Keeping the Harvest: Home Storage of Vegetables and Fruits by Nancy Thurber and Gretchen Mead, Garden Way Publishing Company

Stocking Up: How to Preserve the Foods You Grow Naturally by the Editors of *Organic Gardening and Farming*, Rodale Press

Putting Food By by Ruth Hertzberg, Beatrice Vaughan and Janet Greene, The Stephen Greene Press

hours of cooking. You'll want to avoid prolonged (twenty-four hours or so) soaking, because plenty of bacteria, yeasts, and molds are still alive and well on the surface of your dried food, and that long period of moist warmth may initiate spoilage.

As prices of oil and electricity rise to more nearly reflect their true cost, those jars of wrinkled carrot wafers and wizened zucchini slices, those garlands of beans and pumpkins and dried red peppers will be as much a source of satisfaction, security, and good eating as the neighboring jars of juicy pickled beets and crisp dilled cucumbers.

Salt Your Vegetables Away

Low-technology methods of keeping garden vegetables become increasingly attractive as fuel prices rise. In addition to drying, another time-honored procedure—fermentation in brine—uses simple equipment to produce a long-lasting, special-flavored product.

The use of salt to preserve food can be traced back at least as far as the third millenia B.C. in Egypt's Nile civilization. Once traded for an equal weight in gold, salt was an expensive necessity in ancient times; consequently it was more often used to preserve meat than vegetables. Somewhere along the way, though, it was discovered that vegetables preserved in brine kept well and tasted good. Quite recently we have begun to realize what earlier peoples knew only empirically: the lactic acid developed during fermentation promotes health.

Salt preserves food by discouraging the growth of bacteria. As the vegetables steep in their own juices, which have been extracted by the salt packed with them, they ferment and lactic acid is formed. This acid also helps to preserve the food. Brined vegetables will last over the winter if kept in a cold shed or porch where the temperature remains below 40°F. At 45°–50°, the vegetables will keep for a month or so, but warmer temperatures induce more rapid spoilage.

These products may, of course, be refrigerated, frozen, or canned (sauerkraut should be processed for 30 minutes) in a boiling water bath. From the Mason-Dixon line south, and in the warmer parts of the West, it is more difficult to keep kraut and other fermented vegetables for any length of time without canning or chilling them to discourage further bacterial action. (Brining, like drying, preserves food by making conditions inhospitable for bacteria, not by killing them.)

The best time to make sauerkraut and other fermented vegetable products is in late fall so that the crock may be kept cool by natural refrigeration when the brining process is complete.

Salted, fermented cabbage has, of course, traditionally been known by the German term "sauerkraut," except for a few years during World War I when some nice-Nelly cookbooks described it as "liberty cabbage." Although cabbage is probably the vegetable most often shredded and brined, the process works equally well with turnips, rutabagas, and beans. Whole green tomatoes and cucumbers also keep well in brine.

To begin with, the vegetables must be shredded in order to expose as much of their surface as possible to the brine. Snap beans may simply be sliced the long way, as for French-style beans. In addition to the shredder or slaw cutter, you will need a crock or jar, a kitchen scale, measuring spoons, stones or a jar for weights, and a wooden tamper or a clean, short two-by-four.

Use only sound, firm vegetables, as fresh as possible. Shred the vegetables into a pile on a clean table. Weigh the food as you pack it into the crock and sprinkle about two tablespoons of salt over each three pounds of shredded vegetables. Use plain salt; iodized salt makes the vegetables turn dark. We vary the salt concentrations from one tablespoon to each two pounds of vegetables, to two tablespoons to each three pounds. The produce may spoil if too little salt is used, unless fermentation proceeds rapidly enough to produce sufficient lactic acid to take over preservation. Too much salt, on the other hand, inhibits the fermentation process and produces food without much zing.

Tamp the salted vegetable shreds with your wooden weapon until the juice rises. This takes some patience at first, but once the juice starts to flow, the tamping becomes progressively easier. Snap beans release less water than cabbage, turnips, and rutabagas. If, after tamping, the liquid level isn't high enough to cover the beans, add a brine made of eight parts of water, by weight, to one part of salt.

When the crock is full to within an inch or two of the top, spread clean cabbage or grape leaves over the surface. Never pack food all the way up to the rim of the container, or you'll lose too much juice when it bubbles over during fermentation. A two-gallon crock will hold about fifteen pounds of vegetables. Crocks are traditional, but not obligatory. If cracked or badly checked, they may in fact harbor unwholesome molds. Wide-mouth gallon glass jars are quite satisfactory and easier to lug around.

Choose a spot where your vegetables can ferment undisturbed for a month or more. On a pad of newspapers, set out enough shallow pans to hold your crocks or jars. Juice overflow during fermentation will be much easier to clean up if you've made these preparations. When you've settled your vegetable-filled crocks in place, top each one with a clean plate and a weight to keep the food submerged. Vegetables exposed to the air will spoil. The traditional weight is a scrubbed-clean stone. We find that a clean canning jar filled with water (a two-quart jar for a large crock) works quite well.

Most sauerkraut directions advocate the periodic removal of the mold that forms on top of the brew. We've found, though, that mold spores tend to scatter into the brine when the top scum is lifted off, and so it is our practice to clean the top surface of the kraut only when fermentation is complete. The warning often given—that microorganisms in the mold may consume the lactic acid, thus causing spoilage—makes sense, but we've never had an unskimmed batch spoil.

Curing time for brined vegetables depends on the temperature, which is not always easy to control. Our best batches result when fermentation begins promptly at temperatures of 75°–80°, held for the first two to four days, followed by several weeks at 60° to promote slower, sustained action in the brew. Most batches we've made have taken a month to cure, but anywhere from two to six weeks is normal. Fermentation is complete when bubbles no longer rise in the liquid. Tap the side of the container to be sure that no more bubbles will come to the top.

Now remove all the old leaves from the top surface and carefully skim off any mold and mushy vegetable shreds. Then either store the covered crock in a cool place or process the kraut in quart jars for thirty minutes in a boiling-water bath. To keep the brine level up to the top of the vegetables, you may need to add some extra brine, which you can make by dissolving two tablespoons of salt in one quart of water.

Peppers, green tomatoes, and cucumbers develop a delicious pickled flavor when fermented in brine and vinegar. Simply pack the clean, quartered vegetables in a crock or jar. Add a few peeled garlic cloves, a bay leaf, several heads of dill, and a hot red pepper or two (optional) to each crock. Pour over the vegetables a brine made of a cup and a half of salt dissolved in a mixture of two gallons of hot water and two cups of vinegar. Cover the crock with a clean plate or disk of wood (not pine, which imparts a resinous flavor) and weight it with a water-filled jar. Keep the crock in a cool place—not above 70°—for several weeks. When fermentation is complete, store the covered crock in a cold place or can the pickles for ten minutes in a boiling-water bath, adding enough brine (made in the same proportions as the original) to cover the food.

Properly cured vegetables and pickles are firm and sometimes crisp, but never mushy. They should be free of white spots. Kraut may be rinsed in a colander just before serving to remove excess salt, but it should not be soaked in water.

The Seed Traders

When we moved to our farm, a neighbor—who had lived on our place and loved it—stopped by to welcome us. She brought with her a brown paper bag of bean seeds she had saved from her last garden. The seeds were nameless, but the beans they grew were delicious. And the gesture established a common ground between us, leading to an informal seed and plant exchange that keeps the best of our gardens in circulation throughout the neighborhood. Like neighbors everywhere, we share our surplus and trade good new varieties.

Little pockets of informal exchange like ours exist all across the country. There are many backyard gardeners who have kept alive forgotten strains of limas or tomatoes or corn by saving seed through the years. Some of these seed varieties are no longer offered in catalogues. They continue to exist only through faithful replanting and saving of seed. Once a variety dies out, it cannot be recaptured.

Concern for the conservation of irreplaceable vegetable varieties led to the development of the Seed Savers Exchange. Founded in 1975 by Missouri homesteader Kent Whealy, the Seed Savers Exchange is, in his words, "an organization of serious gardeners dedicated to spreading heirloom vegetable varieties before they are lost. . . . We are garden experimenters testing vegetable varieties and cultural techniques and reporting results through our newsletter. We want to introduce foreign vegetable varieties and bring to light little-known food crops. We are looking for members who are presently keeping the following seeds: vegetable varieties that have been in their families for generations; vegetable varieties that their families brought over from the old country; vegetable varieties that they have selectively improved over the years; vegetable varieties that are no longer available from any seed catalogue; unusual vegetable varieties (not just novelties, but genetic mutations or sports that seem of value); or any vegetable variety that is extremely disease-resistant, very hardy, of exceptional quality, or has any other outstanding characteristics. We welcome persons who are trying to find vegetable varieties that they have lost. If they do find them because of us, we hope that they will become a source for them in the Seed Savers Exchange."

Now the Exchange has made it possible for gardeners in different states and even in different countries to enjoy the sort of neighborly sharing of special seeds that until recently has been highly localized and unstructured. An obscure vegetable variety is naturally less likely to become extinct if several gardeners in different locations are planting and replanting that kind of seed, and trading it with other distant gardeners for special varieties they want. If you're searching for an old soup bean remembered from your father's garden, or a white mulberry like your Uncle Charlie used to grow, or perhaps a certain kind of long-keeping squash, you might find that you and the Seed Exchange have something to offer each other.

In 1981 the Association had more than 300 members and received non-profit status. For yearly Seed Savers Exchange dues of $6.00 (as of 1982), subscribers receive both the Fall Harvest Edition and the Winter Year book, and the privilege of requesting seed from other members. Only those who offer vegetable seed to other gardeners through the Exchange are considered members. Those who subscribe to the directory but do not offer seeds must pay $1.00 for each seed sample requested. The Exchange deals primarily in vegetables; flower listings are accepted only as a part of a vegetable listing. When requesting seeds from another member, a person encloses a self-addressed envelope and stamps to cover postage. Requests for plants and bulbs should be accompanied by $1. Non-members may order seed from members for $1 and a self-addressed stamped envelope. In order to give the proferred seeds the widest possible dissemination, only small amounts are sent to each requesting member—just enough for a start, from which members can then save seeds to increase their own stock.

Seed listings are different every year, of course, but the latest directory includes all the common vegetables and many unusual ones, ranging from sugarcane, Hopi Blue corn, bitter melon, sorrel, soybeans, and mangel beets to multiplier onions, banana muskmelon, money plant, lemon balm, Spanish peanuts, heirloom beans, and Old English pumpkins. Through the seed exchange I've found several kinds of plant seed for which I had long been searching, including nettles and white mulberries. The contact with other gardeners is a delightful bonus.

The Seed Savers Exchange has recently taken over the care and maintenance of the Wanigan Associates bean seed collection, founded by New England bean fancier John Withee. Withee's phenomenal collection—more than 1200 samples—could never be replaced. To keep the seed sources alive, they must be grown and allowed to produce new seed every fourth year. Seed loses vitality in storage. You can't file it away indefinitely and expect to grow food from it at some remote future time. Only by replanting and saving seed can such collections—and other valuable isolated strains—be saved for our children and grandchildren to plant, and for future plant breeders who may find the genetic strengths of these old varieties invaluable in breeding disease resistance or other desirable characteristics into new cultivars. These and other endangered seeds will be multiplied—or at least kept in existence —by a growers network—volunteers who grow one or more varieties from seed supplied by the Seed Savers Exchange, and return seed to the Exchange at the end of the season.

Kent Whealy has also compiled a vegetable variety directory to aid gardeners in locating hard-to-find seeds, and to help to save good tasty vegetable varieties before they are lost. Commercial seed catalogues drop many perfectly good vegetable varieties every year if orders for these strains have fallen below a certain level, often because seed growers need a certain minimum guaranteed order before setting aside acreage for individual varieties, which must often be isolated from other varieties in order to ensure seed purity. As Kent explains, "During the first half of this century, most deleted varieties had been superseded by superior ones. But most often that hasn't been the case during the last twenty years. Far from being obsolete or inferior, the varieties being dropped today are literally the cream of our vegetable crops. Each is the result of millions of years of natural selection, thousands of years of human selection and usually almost a decade of intensive and costly plant breeding and testing. Only the very best make it to the catalogues and each is unique and irreplaceable. But they are being allowed to die out, due to the economics of the situation, with no systematic effort being made by government agencies or lay organizations to keep them alive or store them. We must stop this shortsighted destruction. . . . The Inventory's most important value is that it will clearly show which varieties are the rarest and in the most danger *before* they are dropped. I believe that we should place in frozen storage all varieties that are available from only one or two sources."

Address: Seed Savers Exchange
c/o Kent Whealy
RFD 2, Princeton, Missouri 64673

215

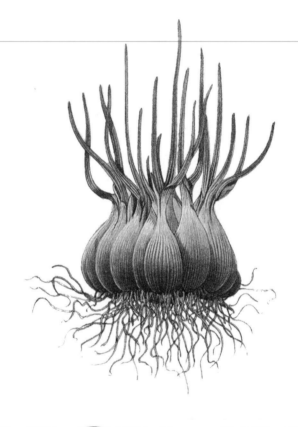

DECEMBER

Gifts from Your Garden

And the gardener his produce, dried, strung, preserved, and arranged by his own hand. The following suggestions are offered in the hope that you may find among them a gift you can make from your garden bounty to please someone special.

It has become a matter of tradition in our garden to grow more hot-pepper plants than we use so that we can string and dry some of the bright pods for gifts. Hot peppers require full sun, but are otherwise undemanding in their culture; they thrive even in fairly lean soil, perhaps because they are close to the original wild form. Long Red Cayenne, with pods averaging four to five inches long and a half inch thick, is the variety we favor for drying. We string the glossy red pods on a doubled length of heavy-duty thread, leaving a loop of thread at the top of each twelve- to fifteen-inch pepper string to hang it for drying. Using a large needle, we pierce the green calyx at the tip of the pepper, rather than the red flesh, to insure a long-lasting garland. The strings are hung in a hot, dry, dark place for drying. Peppers that are still green when strung will gradually turn reddish, but they will not be as bright as those that ripened on the plant.

A string of dried peppers adds a festive air to any kitchen—a bright decoration from which your friends can snip off pieces or whole peppers to season their meals throughout the year. You may want to try tying the dried pods in evergreen wreaths or on the Christmas tree. As an added inducement to practical gift givers, consider: dried red peppers weigh very little, resist breakage, and last for years.

More gourmet friends on your gift list? Consider making a garlic braid. We plant the garlic cloves in our best soil and give them plenty of moisture. Garlic must be well weeded, as we found out by neglecting ours one year. Dig the plants when the tops have dried, cure in the sun for two days, and store in a cool, dry place. To make a garlic braid, select plump garlic knobs with strong but dry tops of varying lengths. Place three garlic bulbs and a three-foot length of strong white string on a table. Tie the four strands together at the top with a short length of string, allowing an extra five inches of string at the top of the braid to form a hanging loop. Then braid the garlic tops, always twining the string with one

The only gift is a portion of thyself. . . . Therefore the poet brings his poem; the shepherd, his lamb; the farmer, corn; the miner, a gem; the sailor, coral and shells; the painter, his picture; the girl, a handkerchief of her own sewing.
Ralph Waldo Emerson

FOUR-ALARM KETCHUP

48 medium tomatoes
4 bell peppers
4 hot peppers
4 onions
3 cups vinegar
1¾ cups honey or 3 cups sugar
3 tbsp. salt
1½ tsp. allspice
1½ tsp. cloves
1½ tsp. cinnamon

Wash and quarter tomatoes. Seed peppers and cut into strips. Peel and quarter onions. Blend all vegetables in blender. Add remaining ingredients and simmer in oven or on top of stove until thick, stirring more often as it thickens. Pour, boiling hot, into clean pint jars and seal. Makes about five pints.

TOMATO CHUTNEY

About 20 ripe tomatoes, medium size
5 chopped peeled apples
1 large cucumber, chopped
4 bell peppers, chopped
2 hot peppers
2 cups chopped onions
1 cup seedless raisins
3 cups sugar or 1½ cups honey
3 cups vinegar
3 cloves garlic, crushed
1 tbsp. powdered ginger
1½ tsp. salt
1 tsp. ground cinnamon

Peel, core, and chop tomatoes. Cook all ingredients together over low heat until thickened. Stir almost constantly as mixture approaches proper thickness. Ladle, boiling hot, into clean hot jars. Seal. Makes 3 pints plus.

Give some, keep some. Happy Christmas!

strand and adding in new strands as necessary. When the braid is as long as you want it to be, tie it off at the bottom with a piece of thin string, snip off any pieces of the garlic tops that protrude too much, and hang the braid to dry in a cool, dry, airy place for another week.

To me, a garlic braid hanging in the kitchen seems to give promise of good things to come. A young friend of ours whose reading runs heavily to ghoul and vampire lore assures us that garlic at the doorway turns away evil spirits! Be that as it may, giving your friends a garlic braid is a fine way to convey your good wishes for the year to come.

Perhaps your Great Aunt Sarah relishes a good cup of tea. You could well be the only family member in a position to give her a gift of home-grown, hand-picked and dried mint leaves, lovingly packaged, perhaps with one of those perforated-metal tea balls you can find in most hardware stores. We pick our mint at noon on a dry, sunny day and put it in the attic on paper-covered screens. When it's dry enough to crumble, we strip the leaves from the stems and store them in jars.

Herbs are treated in the same way. Basil, thyme, and rosemary are especially good choices. A little jar of perfectly dried basil leaves sent by friends at Christmas last year has followed us through the year in our tomato soups and stews, reminding us of the givers. We've dried our own basil for gifts to other friends this year.

Potted herb plants make welcome gifts too. Start with rooted cuttings from your established perennial herbs or raise annual herbs from seed at summer's end. Grow them on a sunny windowsill or under lights until time to arrange them in a pretty basket or bowl. Rooted cuttings should be planted at least a month before giving time so that you can make sure the plant has begun growing on its own. We use Thalassa Cruso's recommended mixture of equal parts of bagged potting soil or leaf mold; wet sphagnum or peat moss; and sharp sand or perlite.

We've sometimes given dried arrangements of weeds, herbs, and other wild findings to friends who live in more-manicured neighborhoods. Using a base of florist's clay, you can arrange an assortment of grape tendrils, tansy, yarrow, Queen Anne's lace, pampas grass, milkweed, teasel, and any other pleasing dried forms you can find on your property.

Bird lovers among your friends and family will appreciate a supply of sunflower seed you've raised yourself—a good way to wish them "birds at the feeder" through the rest of the long winter. We raise a big patch of sunflowers each year, letting the heads dry on the plant and cutting them down gradually after frost. When thoroughly dry, we rub the seeds off and sift them through hardware cloth to winnow out trash. The seeds can be stored in cans or covered bins.

Most households can use a supply of home-canned condiments.

No doubt you have your own specialties, but here are two favorites from our farm kitchen, in case you've had good luck ripening your last tomatoes indoors.

The Well-Furnished Garden

I've never been tempted to paint a cut-open tire for a planter, put a windmill on the lawn, march a convoy of plastic ducks along the garden path, or install a statue of Pan among the perennials. No good garden needs to be adorned; rich soil and flourishing crops are beautiful in themselves. That's not to say that I don't have my own wish list of garden furnishings, but the things I'd choose are ordinary, practical, everyday gadgets—things to be used. Most of them would blend unobtrusively with the garden scenery, making the garden a more productive, convenient, and interesting place to be.

First, I'd have a neat little outdoor tool closet built on the north side of the house for my trusty hoe, spade, and fork. I use them regularly for a good ten months of the year, and too often I leave them by the front door, where they'll be handy. A shallow closet just 14 to 20 inches deep and about 4 or 5 feet long would be large enough for the tools, but not roomy enough to encourage me to accumulate an inefficient jumble of potting flats and string bundles.

While I had a carpenter on hand, I'd ask for an overhead grape arbor, one of those canopy frameworks you can sit under (when you're not dodging bees and wasps on their way to the grapes). We could make the posts out of some of the 4- to 6-inch cedars growing here on the farm, and we could have a large cedar tree milled into 2-by-6s and 2-by-4s for the top.

Next, I'd ask for two more cold frames. One would actually be a double cold frame, a back-to-back arrangement with two glass panels sloping from a central support. Handles on the ends would make it easy to lift and move. The other cold frame would be like the one I use now, with an automatic vent that prevents overheating.

I could always use some new supports for my vegetable plants. A lattice A-frame for the cucumbers would be nice, and so would a brand-new supply of sturdy bean poles—preferably locust, 8 feet long and 1½ inches thick. At the store, I'd splurge on 100 yards of concrete reinforcing wire, enough to make cylinders for all of my tomato plants and then some. And if price were no object, I'd buy yards and yards of string-pea or trellis netting, which is inconspicuous, easy to stretch, and easier to store than chicken wire.

My fantasy list of garden furnishings includes a few things for the birds, too. I'd have several hummingbird feeders and some rustic wren houses for the orchard. Perhaps I'd even put up a simple birdbath. And I'd definitely provide a house for Toad, who winters in the greenhouse. He'd like an upside-down clay flower-pot with a neat doorway chipped in one side, set in a moist, shady spot.

To keep order in the garden, I should have not one but two row markers—each made of sharp sticks and 100 feet of untangled string—and a carton full of newly sharpened stakes for identifying row ends. And to help me guard against a surprise frost, I need a top-grade maximum-minimum thermometer posted on the house. Of course, I also want a rain gauge so I can be sure my plants have received the inch of rain they need every week.

For tending plants, I'd add to my wish list a soil-soaker—no, make that several: one of canvas, slowly oozing water into the rows, and another made of punctured plastic tubes that trickle at low water pressure and spray when pressure is higher. Both kinds deliver water close to the roots, where it's needed, and with less waste than conventional sprinklers. Add a water spigot close by the garden, with four long hoses to reach everywhere, a watering can with a handle that's easy on the hands, and garden gloves in every closet, always there when I need them. The trombone sprayer, which I prefer to the backpack sprayer, is an elegantly simple tool for distributing nontoxic insecticides, and the red metal duster can poof sifted wood ashes and diatomaceous earth on bug-infested plants. Throw in about a thousand hot-caps—enough so that I'd feel free to use as many as I need.

Both the appearance and the effectiveness of my sprawling compost pile would be improved if I had a sturdy bin with two easy-access enclosures. Would I want a garden shredder? Yes, I'd love to have one, if someone else would do all the shredding for me; I don't get along too well with machines.

At harvest time, my list would expand even further to include a long-handled fruit picker, a lot of bushel and half-bushel baskets, more woven willow and oak picking baskets for my collection, and an accurate scale. Come to think of it, a solar food dryer would be nice, too.

If we wouldn't have to mow or till around it, I'd like a big flat-topped rock at the edge of the garden to serve as desk, table, and chair. My friends Harriet and Howell have a lovely garden bench inscribed with Bronson Alcott's well-chosen words: Who Loves a Garden Still His Eden Keeps. They don't get to sit on it very often, because they are so busy tending their beautiful and productive garden, but at least they can see the inscription clearly as they work. I think I might wish for a sturdy wooden bench too, but I'd probably put it on the porch where I could enjoy it while shelling peas and stripping elderberries.

As long as I'm fantasizing, I might as well wish for two more things I need every season of the year: an ever-sharp hoe, and an endless supply of mulch. If, of all the items on my list, I were granted only those two things, I'd be satisfied.

Houseplants in the Soup

When winter draws us all indoors, we notice—all at once—the bare shelves and windowsills we had ignored in the bustle of summer and fall activity. A few houseplants would soften and enliven the indoor scene. Why not try a few edible houseplants, especially for the kitchen?

The following plants will thrive indoors, preferably on your sunniest windowsill. Snip from them now and again as you need the tonic of fresh greenery during the dark days of winter and put them out in the garden again next spring if you wish. (They may also be kept indoors year round or summered on a porch.)

Christmas Pepper

This delightful ornamental bears tiny, fiery-red peppers. The fruit is hot, not sweet, but it *is* edible.

All peppers need good drainage, plenty of magnesium in the soil, and a light helping of nitrogen, and these decorative peppers are no exception. Meeting these needs is not difficult. Mix in a handful of sharp sand or perlite with each quart of potting soil to provide extra good drainage. Add dolomite lime, which contains magnesium, to your potting soil: one tablespoon to each quart of soil will be plenty. Give the plants a good supply of humus, but avoid strong doses of high-nitrogen plant food. If overfed, peppers will be leafy but fruitless.

Choose a warm, relatively humid spot in your house for your pot of ornamental peppers. In dry air, the plants will sometimes lose their blossoms. When that happens you will, of course, get no fruit. Atmospheric dryness may be partly counteracted by: (1) placing the plant pot on a bed of pebbles in a pan containing a half inch of water; or (2) misting the plants at least once a day with warm water; or (3) better yet, finding a spot for your plant near a warm kitchen range that is used often to brew tea, make soup, and prepare other steamy cold-weather delights.

Christmas pepper plants are often sold by commercial growers. You can also grow your own from seed—a satisfying project requiring a little patience but yielding a lot of plants.

Keep the seeds moist and warm until they germinate and then give the young seedlings full light, either fluorescent or window light, transplanting them into individual small pots when they develop their true leaves.

When harvesting the pods of your Christmas pepper, cut the stem instead of pulling the pepper off. The tug necessary to free the pepper may also loosen the roots of the plant.

Finally, avoid handling tobacco when working with your pepper plants. Most peppers are susceptible to mosaic and other tobacco-borne virus diseases.

Comfrey

While not usually considered a houseplant, comfrey fares very well indoors. It is eminently edible and very nutritious. The fuzzy leaves, with their bland flavor, blend readily with soups, stews, casseroles, and herb teas. They may also be steamed and served like spinach. The plant contains allantoin, a recognized healing agent, and is often used medicinally.

Indoors or out, comfrey is a hearty grower, forming an attractive bushy plant in a few weeks. You can start your comfrey house-plant either by (1) planting a root cutting obtained from another comfrey grower or from a mail-order firm; or (2) potting up a division from an established plant. According to most reliable reports, comfrey does not set viable seed.

To start a plant from a root cutting, fill a six- to eight-inch flower pot about half full of your best potting soil, to which you have added an extra handful of compost to each quart of soil. Place the fragment of comfrey root on the soil surface and cover it firmly with two more inches of soil. Water the pot thoroughly and keep the soil moist but not soaking. Watch the soil surface closely for a folded, downy rabbit-ear of growth—the first comfrey leaf—which should appear within a month, but which may surprise you sooner or exasperate you by taking longer. Feed your comfrey plant with diluted fish emulsion fertilizer every two weeks when it is in active growth, every month or so when the shortest days of winter slow it down.

Chives

This perennial member of the onion family sends up many thin, tubular, 10-inch-long green quills, softened later by a lavender flower. It readily recovers after cutting and may be repeatedly harvested all winter long.

Start chives from seed if you haven't already potted up a likely young specimen from your garden, or if you can't beg a division from a friend. Sow the seed thinly and give the grass-like young seedlings all the light you can. Avoid overwatering indoor chives. They do well in a cool place; a sunny kitchen windowsill is ideal, making it easy to add their fresh green piquant touch to winter soups and omelets.

These indoor edibles and any other houseplants you keep on a windowsill should be moved or protected when severe subzero temperatures persist outdoors.

Houseplants from Seed

Creative gardening can continue indoors long after the ground outside has frozen. For a satisfying winter adventure, you might consider growing houseplants from seed. It's a special accomplishment to be able to display potted indoor plants you've raised yourself. The process is absorbing, rewarding, and not at all difficult.

For your first efforts, try one of the easier varieties. If you've already done a fair amount of seed starting, you're probably ready to tackle one of the trickier plants. Don't hesitate, though, to take a chance on a special kind of plant if it appeals to you, whether you're experienced or not. Your desire to succeed will give you a growing edge. If something goes wrong, try to figure out what happened and try again.

Plant seeds in a flat of damp vermiculite, shredded moss, or potting soil. Keep them warm and moist—but not soggy—until the seeds germinate. As soon as seedlings appear, expose them to light. Thin the seedlings to a 2-inch spacing. When they're 2 inches high, transplant them to 2-inch pots. Use quarter- or half-strength fertilizer solution such as fish emulsion to feed young seedlings.

ACHIMENES

With its spreading pendant branches, achimenes is a perfect hanging-basket plant for a partly shady place. Its waxy, tubular blossoms come in a range of soft, pleasing colors. The very fine seeds should not be covered when planted. Germination takes two to three weeks. A temperature of 70–80°F is best for germination and also for mature growth, with nighttime temperatures of 60–65° for the growing plants. During their period of active growth, achimines plants need plenty of moisture, but the pots should not be left in standing water. An east window with some morning sun suits them well. When mature, they form a small, scaly rhizome that may be stored over the dormant period and replanted after a four- to five-month rest.

WAX BEGONIA

This plant grows readily from seed, which is superfine. Settle the dustlike seeds on a bed of damp vermiculite. Don't cover the seeds with soil; light promotes germination. Stretch a layer of plastic wrap over the flat to admit light and retain moisture. In a warm place with plenty of light, the tiny seedlings will begin to appear in two to four weeks. With less light and warmth, it may take six weeks or more. Wax begonias grow well in a loose, well-drained soil mixture that is moist but not soaked. They like morning sun.

CACTUS

Cacti grow slowly but easily from seed. A packet of mixed cactus seeds could be the start of a whole new windowsill collection. The seeds need moisture for germination, just as other seeds do, and the seedlings must have a steady supply of moisture, too. When transplanting the seedlings, keep soil moderately damp but don't overwater. Roots bruised from handling rot quickly. Mature plants

223

are able to store water, so they can survive underwatering better than many other plants. They *do* require water, though—weekly, biweekly, or monthly, depending on the size and site of the plant. Equally important, they need good drainage, so add a cup of sand and a handful of perlite to your regular potting-soil mixture. Keep your cactus plantation on a sunny windowsill.

COLEUS   The foliage plant with magic-carpet colors, coleus is easy to raise from seed. Germination takes a week to ten days at 65–75° and the little plants soon show their true colors, which are especially vibrant when the plants are grown under fluorescent lights. A packet of mixed colors and varieties is great fun to grow. Colors include burgundy, copper, fuschia, dusty pink, apple green, and an elegant green and ivory mixture. Dwarf coleus plants are a good choice for indoors. You'll still want to pinch off the growing tips periodically to encourage the plant to grow bushy rather than leggy. Give the plants bright light—but not necessarily full sun—all day. Don't let them dry out. They tolerate a variety of conditions.

GERANIUMS   Geraniums flower 90 to 120 days after seeds are sown. They germinate in two to four weeks at 65–75°. To hasten germination, nick or file the seeds to they'll absorb water more readily. Geranium plants need good drainage. Add half a cup of perlite to your regular potting soil. Let the soil dry between waterings. It should never be allowed to become soggy, but a steady supply of moisture is essential during flowering. Geraniums need plenty of light; put them on your sunniest windowsill.

GLOXINIAS   These are showy plants with large, richly colored flowers and handsome, velvety leaves. They are not as genially adaptable as, say, coleus, but when given the conditions they require they can be truly impressive house plants. Start by sowing the fine seeds on a bed of damp, milled sphagnum moss or potting soil. A temperature of 70–75° promotes germination. Don't cover the seeds with soil, but protect the flat with glass or plastic wrap to prevent drying. Germination takes two to three weeks. Plants raised from seed can flower in five to six months, but some take as long as eight months. Keep the soil moist but not soggy. Many growers keep their gloxinias in trays of moist pebbles to maintain a 50–60 percent humidity, which can be hard to achieve in heated houses. A temperature of around 70°, dropping to 65° at night, is just right. A bright east window is a good spot for gloxinias in spring and summer, changing to a southern exposure for winter. Gloxinias need lots of light. They also do very well under fluorescent lights.

How to Make a Terrarium

If you need an excuse for a walk in the woods, make a terrarium. Gathering terrarium ingredients sharpens one's appreciation of the rich variety of life at boot level. Terrarium makers see the world in fine. No detail escapes their attention. A confirmed devotee could probably wander in a redwood grove with gaze fixed on the ground—looking for moss of just the right texture, tiny seedling trees, interesting bark chips. After I made my first terrarium, I found myself gathering tiny plants, lichens, and pebbles on every walk—and mentally collecting when I was not walking our own land.

Woodland plants are perfect for the terrarium. Most things that grow on the forest floor thrive in cool, moist, partly shady situations, which are easy to provide under glass. Many house plants adapt equally well to life in a terrarium. You can even grow exotics like the Venus flytrap, which requires warmth and moisture and gets along on soil nutrients when no flies happen by.

Whether you gather the makings of your miniature landscape on the trail, in a greenhouse, or from among your houseplants, the procedure for assembling the terrarium is the same. First, you need a container. Any kind of transparent, waterproof, easily covered container may be used to house a terrarium. Some of the more popular enclosures for these self-contained gardens include brandy snifters, apothecary jars, fish bowls, rectangular aquarium cases, and large glass carboys. Wine jugs, large test tubes, butter jars, mason jars, gallon mayonnaise jars (from restaurants), and even baby-food jars may also be used. Jean Hersey, the authority on wildflowers, once constructed a terrarium in the globe of a 150-watt light bulb with the threaded end broken off.

Wide-mouthed containers are easiest to plant by hand; those with narrow necks are tricky but by no means impossible. You need a few tools—a planter made of a length of wire coat hanger straightened out, with a loop on one end to hold the plant; a tamper, which could be a dowel stuck into a cork, or whatever you can improvise from materials at hand; a digger, a long-handled spoon, or any kind of long, thin poker capable of making a hole in loose soil. A long-handled tweezers is also useful. Use a rolled-up newspaper as a funnel to direct the soil to the bottom of the jug.

Begin by putting down a base composed of several layers, as follows, remembering that each layer serves a purpose. First, put down a mat of moss to absorb moisture and form an attractive lining. Then pour a layer of sand or fine gravel over the moss to promote drainage and prevent waterlogging. Next scatter a handful of charcoal pieces over the gravel to prevent souring of the soil.

Now add the final layer—soil. Bagged potting soil is fine, but if you want to mix your own, aim for the following proportions:

2 parts topsoil

1 part sand

1 part leafmold or compost.

Put in a thin layer, just covering the charcoal. Then set the plants in place and firm the remainder of the soil around their roots. Much of this soil will later settle lower around the roots.

Arranging the topography of the terrarium is a matter of taste. You might keep in mind that a variety of leaf textures is usually pleasing, and that plants of different heights and shapes—pyramidal, tall and spiky, short and shrubby, trailing—make the scenery interesting. If your container is large enough you can even make a small hill or a path within its bounded wildness. Color may be provided by including partridge berries, mushrooms, lichens, and stones. No well-made terrarium needs a plastic deer or a china bird, but the woods are full of props that can add local color to your small scene: mossy twigs, weathered pieces of wood, scraps of textured bark, squirrel-gnawed nutshells. A weird craggy stone may be just the boulder you need for a classic gothic scene—a _romantische Landschaft_ in miniature.

The pleasure of terrarium building, though, has more to do with the freedom to improvise, collect, see, play with your materials, arrange a world as _you_ would have it, than with conformity to a form. Do with it what you wish. Arrange and rearrange the plants until you are happy with the way they look.

When all the plants are in place, water the soil lightly, using less water than you think you'll need. You can always add more but you can't remove it. Overwatering encourages rot, mold, and fungus.

Covering the terrarium makes it a self-contained system, with its own weather: water vapor condenses on the walls and returns to the soil. Use the cover provided with the vessel or simply place a circle of glass over the top. (Plastic wrap is a more temporary but nonetheless practical cover.) Since each terrarium is a different ecosystem with its own water balance, it is impossible to formulate definite schedules for watering. Observation is the key. If the glass is misty, or if you notice mold anywhere within it, or water pooling on the bottom, the terrarium needs to be ventilated. Uncover it for about a day. Some people ventilate their terrariums routinely once a week.

When should you add water? Seldom, if at all. If the terrarium is too dry, the soil will be lighter in color and the whole thing will feel lighter than normal when you pick it up. Use an eye dropper to add water—you'll be less likely to overwater.

Terrarium plants need some light, but direct sun will cook them. Indirect light on a table or light from a north window should suit most plant populations. If leaves turn brown, the terrarium is probably too hot. Try putting it in a cooler place.

Those of us accustomed to fertilizing houseplants may tend to

Here are some examples of wild and woodland plants that will do well in a terrarium. When digging the plant, take some of the soil surrounding the roots.

ferns
tree seedlings
wintergreen
pipsissewa
partridgeberry
violets
wild ginger
mosses
surprise—bring home a clump of soil and see what will grow from it.

Appropriate houseplants include:
strawberry begonia
ferns
prayer plant
begonias
Venus flytrap
coleus
grape ivy
baby's tears

The following firms offer a good variety of rooted plants by mail:
George W. Park Seed Co. Inc.
Mellinger's
Wilson Bros.

include the terrarium in that routine, but it is best to keep terrarium soil on the lean side, lest the plants outgrow the container. Choice of plants influences the length of their stay too, of course. Our first house—a mid-nineteenth-century Philadelphia weaver's cottage—is now guarded by a pine that spent its first two years in a terrarium. When its top hit the cover we planted it in front of the loom shed. Now, twenty years later, it towers over the house. The loom shed is gone, but pine needles fall around its foundation. Everything lasts, we think as we drive by—just in a different form, sometimes.

Your Christmas Tree

On a country place, the choice of a Christmas tree is often determined by what the land has to offer or what it needs. If cedar trees have started to reclaim an old pasture, then cedar might well be the best choice. When we moved to our farm, we decided to use what was abundant here instead of purchasing a tree, so we trudged to one of our cedar-dotted fields and chose a shapely evergreen to grace our home. We later learned that our neighbors cut cedar Christmas trees too, and that cedar has been a traditional countryman's choice since the custom of decorating an evergreen took hold in America in the early nineteenth century. We often select a tall cedar, cut off the bushy top for our Christmas tree, and save the thick trunk for later use as a fencepost.

Not all country places need to be cleared. Some need more trees—perhaps for a windbreak for the garden, orchard, or house. In that case, a live evergreen is a good choice, as we discovered at our first country home. The house there was swept by strong west winds that blew across what seemed like miles of neighboring cornfields. We bought live spruce trees for Christmas, planted them, and now, ten years later, those short little trees are tall and thick, and they help to break the force of the wind hitting the tall, old house.

If you have decided to augment your landscaping with a beautiful live Christmas tree, your first consideration will be to select a good, healthy plant. The evergreen should be one that was recently dug, kept in a protected spot, and given good care. Its needles should feel springy and should be firmly attached to the tree. Avoid trees with yellowing or falling needles. A small tree will suffer less from transplanting shock than a large one. If you want a lot of indoor greenery, consider buying two small trees rather than one large one.

227

Sometimes it is possible to buy a live tree from a cut-your-own operation if you are able to ball it yourself. Here's how: First, tie up the branches around the trunk so they won't snap off when you're handling the tree. Next, measure and mark out a circle around the tree. A tree with a trunk 3 inches in diameter needs a ball of soil 24 to 27 inches in diameter; 16 to 18 inches should be sufficient for a 2-inch trunk. Clear weeds and rocks from the surface of the ground; then dig in a circle around the tree, making deep cuts to get a generous ball of earth around the roots. Use your spade to raise the tree with its ball from the ground. Clip off excess roots. Now, wrap a long strip of burlap around the ball of soil to keep it together. Next, ease a burlap bag under the ball and wrap another one around the top. Fasten the bags with nails driven into the soil. Wrap and tie with binder twine for good measure.

Dig the hole where you want to plant the tree before the ground freezes hard, even if it will be several weeks before you need it. Make the excavation a foot wider and at least 6 inches deeper than the ball of soil. Save the soil from the hole in a place where it won't freeze solid, and line the hole with bags of leaves or hay and mark it with a stake in case Christmas is *really* white.

Your live Christmas evergreen will be more likely to thrive if it doesn't stay in the warm, dry house too long. If possible, keep the tree in a cool, humid room, away from the fireplace or stove. Plan to plant it outside after about a week indoors. While inside, the tree should be kept in a large tub, crock, iron kettle, or other planter that does not crowd its roots. Keep the soil damp but not soggy. It's a good idea to cover the soil's surface with damp moss.

When planting your Christmas tree outdoors, remove the bags of leaves from the hole and toss in a shovelful of the loose soil you've saved. Gently lower the tree into the hole, using ropes if it's heavy. Clip any strings that tie the burlap bags together and untwist any burlap that has been wrapped around the trunk. The burlap may be left on the bottom of the ball; it will rot and the roots will grow through it. Fill in around the tree with soil. Water the tree just before the hole is entirely filled; then top off the hole with loose, dry soil to prevent crusting.

Evergreens lose moisture from their needles in all seasons of the year. Just as dry air and high temperatures are hard on them, dry winters and high winds can be damaging as well. In a nearly snowless, dry winter, newly planted evergreens will suffer unless watered regularly—every week for a month after planting, then monthly if the season continues dry.

Finally, before you forget, jot down in your farm and garden log the position of the tree and the year you planted it. Chances are you'll be glad you did.

Security Is Having a Garden

There are more of us than ever before—gardeners, that is. According to a survey reported by GARDENS FOR ALL, 43 percent of American households grew some of their own vegetables last year, a 4 per cent increase over the previous year. Why do so many of us garden? The Gallup National Gardening Survey reports that the three main reasons we grow our own food are for better flavor, for the pleasure of the task, and for the resulting savings. But as I see it, there's something even more basic going on here: call it self-reliance, or independence, or even self-sufficiency, so long as it's understood that none of us is wholly self-sufficient. In my search for better flavor, I'm developing a discriminating palate and the will to satisfy it on my own. In deriving pleasure from the growing process, I'm entertaining myself without depending on TV or summer's many trumped-up "gala" events. And whenever I can save money by expending some pleasurable effort and get a better product to boot, then I'm that much less vulnerable to the effects of food shortages, price boosts, strikes, and shipping delays.

In an early issue of *The Whole Earth Catalog*, Norman Gurney wrote that the organic gardening movement is "exquisitely subversive." What did he mean? I think he was describing what Thomas Jefferson envisioned as his ideal: a nation of small landholders, each a responsible participant in the life of his community. People who can do things for themselves are less easily shoved around, are less dependent on the marketplace and the federal government to deliver their goods and solve their problems, and are more likely to band together with neighbors to solve local problems.

Yet for most of our food we still rely on distant sources and a complex distribution network that could be snagged at any point by strikes or energy shortages. Even a prime farm state like Pennsylvania imports more than 70 per cent of its food (99 per cent of its lettuce, 96 per cent of its broccoli, and 88 per cent of its carrots). A 10 per cent increase in energy costs could raise the price of fruits and vegetables sold in Pennsylvania by 55 per cent. And farm production, much of it in California, is vulnerable to disruption by insect damage (remember the recent Medfly scare?), and to the increasing demand of California's burgeoning population for food and limited water supplies essential to agriculture.

It's a good time to be a gardener, and it's getting better. If you have even a small plot of tomatoes and lettuce, you're doing something good for yourself. If you decide to grow more vegetables, you'll be less dependent on the market, better fed, and more satisfied with your achievement. You'll even save money. The next step is to grow enough vegetables to supply your family year-round. But whether you're preparing for a deep cold winter or for

229

some less predictable interruption in the food supply, here are some steps you can take to make your garden produce more for you.

Build at least one raised, intensively cultivated garden bed that you can work with hand tools. You'll learn how to grow more vegetables in less space, and all the soil improvements you add will benefit the vegetables and not the weeds in the border.

Buy some well-made hand tools—a spade, a fork, a hoe, a trowel—and take good care of them.

Save your own seeds from open-pollinated vegetables. Once started, you will always have something to plant next season, and you will gradually select strains well adapted to your local growing conditions.

Try new vegetables, and learn to like a variety of foods. Even more important, encourage in your children a spirit of open-mindedness toward new foods.

Experiment in the kitchen, and develop simple, tasty dishes using vegetables you can grow.

Store winter vegetables and fruits, such as root crops, squashes, celery, onions, cabbages, and the like. Experiment with different varieties to see which keep best.

Increase your food-growing and -storing capacity by building simple structures like cold frames and a root cellar. Then consider a solar food dryer or even a solar greenhouse.

To make use of surpluses and provide foods you don't grow, join forces with other gardeners in an informal barter system, or organize a food co-op.

This winter, as you begin your planting, think of your garden as more than a pleasurable source of fresh vegetables. It's also a reliable source of food you control—a measure of independence and security.

Burgess Seed and Plant Co., 905 Four Seasons Rd., Bloomington, IL 61701

W. Atlee Burpee Co., Warminster, PA 18974; Clinton, IA 52732; Riverside, CA 92502

D. V. Burrell Seed Growers Co., P.O. Box 150, Rocky Ford, CO 81067

Butterbrooke Farm, 78 Barry Rd., Oxford, CT 06483

Comstock, Ferre and Co., Box 125, Wethersfield, CT 06109

William Dam Seeds Ltd., P.O. Box 8400, Dundas, Ontario, Canada L9H 6M1

DeGiorgi Co., Inc., P.O. Box 413, Council Bluffs, IA 51502

J. A. Demonchaux Co., 827 N. Kansas Ave., Topeka, KS 66608 (catalogue 50¢) Seeds for herbs and French vegetables

Farmer Seed and Nursery Co., Faribault, MN 55021

Henry Field Seed and Nursery Co., 407 Sycamore St., Shenandoah, IA 51602

Grace's Gardens, 520 Westport Ave., Norwalk, CT 06851

Gurney Seed and Nursery Co., Yankton, SD 57079

Joseph Harris Co., Inc., Moreton Farm, Rochester, NY 14624

The Charles Hart Seed Co., Main and Hart Sts., Wethersfield, CT 06109

Herbst Brothers Seedsmen, Inc., Brewster, NY 10509

J. L. Hudson, Seedsman, P.O. Box 1058, Redwood City, CA 94064 Veg./herb seed catalogue free; complete catalogue $1.00

Le Jardin Du Gourmet, Box 51, West Danville, VT 05873 (catalogue 50¢)

Johnny's Selected Seeds, Albion, ME 04910

J W. Jung Seed Co., 335 S. High St., Randolph, WI 53956

Kitazawa Seed Co., 365 Taylor St., San Jose, CA 95110 (Oriental vegetables)

Liberty Seed Co., P.O. Box 806, New Philadelphia, Ohio, 44663

May Seed and Nursery Co., Shenandoah, IA 51603

Midwest Seed Growers, Inc. 505 Walnut St., Kansas City, MO 64106

L. L. Olds Seed Co., P.O. Box 7790, Madison, WI 53707

George W. Park Seed Co., 909 Cokesbury Rd., Greenwood, SC 29647

Plants of the Southwest, Bldg E15, Plaza de Comercio, 1507 Pacheco St., Santa Fe, NM (catalogue $1.00)

Redwood City Seed Co., P.O. Box 361, Redwood City, CA 94064 (regular catalogue 50¢ herb/wholesale catalogue free)

R. H. Shumway, Seedsman, Box 777—628 Cedar St., Rockford, IL 61105

Stokes Seeds Inc., Box 548, Buffalo, NY 14240

Thompson and Morgan Inc., P.O. Box 100, Farmingdale, NJ 07727

Tsang and Ma International, 1306 Old County Road, Belmont CA 94002 (Oriental Vegetables.)

Otis S. Twilley Seed Co., Inc., P.O. Box 65, Trevose, PA 19047

Vermont Bean Seed Co., Inc., Garden Lane, Bomoseen, VT 05732

Vesey's Seeds LTD, York, Prince Edward Island, Canada C0A 1P0

Willhite Seed Co., P.O. Box 23, Poolville, TX 76076

Wyatt-Quarles Seed Co., P.O. Box 2131, Raleigh NC 27602

Unless otherwise indicated, all catalogues are free and offer a general line of vegetable seed. Most also carry flowers.

Index

The Country Journal Book of Vegetable Gardening
was designed by Thomas Morley.
The text was composed on the Linotron 202 in Palatino
by Dix Type Inc., Syracuse, New York.
The book was printed and bound by The Alpine Press, Inc.,
Stoughton, Massachusetts.
The paper is 60-pound Mohawk Vellum Satin.
Production was supervised by William Farnham.
Copy editing was done by Barbara Hewes.
Ann Kearton was the art assistant.